COACHING STRIKERS

Wayne Harrison

**Library of Congress
Cataloging - in - Publication Data**

Coaching Strikers
by Wayne Harrison

ISBN-13: 978-1-59164-246-6
Library of Congress Control Number: 2015941416
© 2015

All rights reserved. Except for use in a review. The reproduction or utilization of this book in any form or by any electronic, mechanical or other means, now known or hereafter invented, including xerography, photocopying and recording, and in any information storage and retrieval system, is forbidden without written permission of the publisher.

Diagrams created using Soccer Specific Session Planner
www.soccerspecific.com

Front cover photograph © PA / Martin Rickett

Art Direction, Layout and Proofing
Bryan R. Beaver

Reedswain Publishing
88 Wells Road
Spring City, PA 19475
www.reedswain.com
orders@reedswain.com

CONTENTS

INTRODUCTION-1

SIMPLE, FUN AND EFFECTIVE SHOOTING AND FINISHING EXERCISES-3
- VARIOUS STRIKER MOVEMENTS (WARM UP)-3
- DEVELOPING GOOD TECHNIQUE FOR SHOOTING AT GOAL-5
- ONE TOUCH FINISHING-7
- FUN PRACTICES WITH ONE OR TWO TOUCH FINISHING-8
- FINISHING WHEN CLEAR OF THE DEFENSE-9
- ATTACKING ON THE BREAK-10
- A DRILL ORIENTED FINISHING SESSION FOR STRIKERS-16
- MOVEMENT AND FINISHING UP FRONT-18
- CROSSOVER AND OPPOSITE RUNS, BALL PASSED DOWN THE SIDE-19
- OUTSIDE RUNS, BALL PLAYED THROUGH THE MIDDLE-19
- FIRST STRIKER SHORT, 1 – 2 OFF SECOND STRIKER-20
- STRIKERS MAKE OPPOSITE SPLIT RUNS TO GET MIDFIELDER IN -20
- SHOOTING AND FINISHING DRILLS -21
- INDIVIDUAL STRIKER MOVEMENT-24
- MOVEMENT OFF THE BALL FROM A CROSS-26
- STARTING THE RUN FROM A DEEPER POSITION-31

SMALL SIDED GAMES FOR STRIKERS-35
- THE NUMBERS SHOOTING GAME-35
- PASSING; SUPPORT PLAY AND SHOOTING IN A 2 v 2 -37
- PASSING AND SUPPORT PLAY IN A 2 v 2 -38
- A 3 v 2 SITUATION-39
- A SHOOTING GAME FROM DISTANCE-41
- ONE TOUCH FINISHING IN THE BOX-44
- POSITIONING FROM CROSSING #1-45
- POSITIONING FROM CROSSING #2-45
- FINISHING IN AND AROUND THE BOX WITH THE 4-2-3-1 DIAMOND SET UP-46
- ATTACKING FROM CROSSES-53
- MAKING TRANSITIONS AND SWITCHING POSITIONS-56
- A 3 v 3 ATTACKING AND DEFENDING TRANSITION GAME-57
- CHANGING THE POINT OF ATTACK THROUGH THE -58
- DIRECTIONAL FOUR GOAL SWITCHING PLAY SMALL SIDED GAME-58
- AN AWARENESS THREE TEAM PASSING AND FINISHING GAME-60
- A CROSSING AND FINISHING SMALL SIDED GAME-65
- EXAMPLES OF TYPES OF PLAYS-67
- SIDEWAYS ON / FACING UP STRIKER POSITIONING IN A SMALL SIDED GAME-69
- DEL PIERO MOVE: -70
- VIALLI MOVE:-71
- FOUR GOALS-73
- USING FULL SIZE GOALS-75
- DEFENDER DROPS OFF TO PROTECT THE SPACE BEHIND-76
- STRIKERS CAN NOW INTERCHANGE AREAS -77
- SIDEWAYS ON TRAINING IN A GAME SITUATION-80

FUNCTIONAL AND PHASE OF PLAY STRIKER WORK-81
    A CROSSING AND FINISHING FUNCTION-81
    ANOTHER FUNCTIONAL CROSSING AND FINISHING SESSION-89
    COMBINATION PLAYS CREATING MOVEMENT AND SCORING OPPORTUNITIES-93
    COMBINATION PLAY LINKING WITH THE FIRST STRIKER-94
    COMBINATION PLAY LINKING WITH THE SECOND STRIKER-95
    LINKING PLAY BETWEEN THE FIRST AND SECOND STRIKERS-96
    A CENTRAL MIDFIELDER LINKING WITH A WIDE MIDFIELDER -97
    A MIDFIELDER LINKING OFF THE FIRST STRIKER'S PASS-98
    A MIDFIELDER LINKING OFF THE SECOND STRIKER'S PASS-99
    A SMALL SIZED FUNCTION AND PHASE OF PLAY: -100
    STRIKERS RECEIVING / TURNING AND LINKING UP PLAY-100
    FUNCTION: CENTRAL MIDFIELD PLAYERS RECEIVING AND TURNING-101
    CENTRAL MIDFIELD AND STRIKERS RECEIVING AND TURNING -102
    MOVEMENT OF THE STRIKERS AND MIDFIELDERS IN A SHADOW PLAY-103
    STRIKER MOVEMENT STARTING FROM BEHIND DEFENDERS-104
    SPLIT RUNS OF STRIKERS TO GET CENTRAL ATTACKING MIDFIELDER IN-105
    L – SHAPED SPLIT RUNS OF STRIKERS TO GET CENTRAL ATTACKING MIDFIELDER IN-106
    IDEAL TEAM SHAPE DURING CROSSING PHASE OF A GAME-107
    PLAYING TWO UP AND ONE IN BEHIND (ATTACKING MIDFIELDER)-108
    PLAYING ONE UP WITH TWO IN BEHIND-111
    PHASE PLAY: QUICK PLAY AROUND THE PENALTY AREA-115
    COMBINATION MOVEMENTS IN A PHASE OF PLAY-118
    PLAYING THREE UP WITH A STRIKER AND TWO WINGERS AGAINST A MAN MARKING BACK THREE-121
    SPREADING THE ATTACK -128
    GETTING MIDFIELDERS AND STRIKERS / WINGERS "IN"-128
    GETTING FULL-BACKS "IN" -129
    COMBINATION MOVEMENTS OF THE FRONT THREE -130

TRAINING SPECIFIC MOVEMENTS AND FORMATIONS-135
    WORKING OPPOSITES WITH MOVEMENT OF STRIKERS-135
    WORKING WITH THE CENTRAL STRIKER ONLY-136
    OPPOSITE RUN SHORT TO GO LONG -138
    OPPOSITE RUN LONG TO COME SHORT-139
    OPPOSITE RUN INSIDE TO GO OUTSIDE-140
    INTRODUCE A DEFENDER-141
    INTRODUCE A BACK FOUR AND MIDFIELD TWO-142
    NOW DEVELOP THE WIDE STRIKERS (OR WINGERS / OUTSIDE MIDFIELD PLAYERS)-144
    PHASE OF PLAY-150
    SMALL SIDED GAME-152
    THE MOVEMENTS OF THE WIDE ATTACKERS TO GET FREE-153
    MESSI OF BARCELONA-157
    USUAL POSITIONING OF STRIKERS WITH THEIR BACKS TO THE DEFENDER AND TO THE GOAL-158
    INDIVIDUAL STRIKER MOVEMENT OFF THE SHOULDER-160
    STRIKERS RECEIVING THE BALL TO FEET WITH THEIR BACKS TO GOAL AND INTRODUCING QUICK PLAY IN AND AROUND THE BOX-162
    RECEIVING TO FEET WITH YOUR BACK TO GOAL-164

VARIOUS "START POSITIONS" FOR THE STRIKER IN THE BUILD UP -166
SOME STRIKER MOVEMENTS TO GET FREE OF AND POSSIBLY FACED UP AGAINST THE DEFENDER-172
PHASE PLAY: (A 3 v 1 IN MIDFIELD)-173
DEVELOP: A 4 v 2 OVERLOAD IN MIDFIELD-175
DEVELOP: ADD A BACK FOUR-176
A 3RD MAN RUN FROM A REBOUND PASS FROM THE STRIKER IN THE BUILD UP-176
AN 11 v 11 GAME SITUATION-177
PASSING AND RUNNING ANGLES OF SUPPORT-180
INDIVIDUAL STRIKER MOVEMENTS-183
OFF THE SHOULDER : THREE FURTHER MOVEMENTS TO CONSIDER-184
THE THREE MOVEMENTS-185
MOVEMENT ONE-187
MOVEMENT TWO-189
MOVEMENT THREE (PROTECTING THE SPACE BEHIND)-193
SIDEWAYS ON SOCCER USING CORRIDORS-196
THREE CORRIDORS TO PLAY IN-199
FRONT PLAYERS CAN CHANGE CORRIDORS-200
DEFENDERS MUST FOLLOW THEIR STRIKERS-201
INTRODUCE KEEPERS AND FULL SIZE GOALS TO THE GAME-202
INTRODUCING MIDFIELD PLAYERS USING THREE UNITS OF PLAYERS-203
FOUR CORRIDORS TO PLAY IN-205
A VARIETY OF INDIVIDUAL STRIKER RUNS DEVELOPING MOVEMENT AND FINISHING TECHNIQUES-206
FINISHING-215
STRIKERS ATTACKING IN PAIRS-218
A 3 v 3 GAME CREATING TURNING OPTIONS-221
OBJECTIVE: AN AWARENESS OF WHERE THE SPACE IS TO EXPLOIT USING THE SHADOW STRIKER-223
POINT STRIKER / SHADOW STRIKER-225
INTRODUCE DEFENDERS-227
INTRODUCE DEFENDERS AND THE POINT STRIKER-228
SUPPORT STRIKER PRACTICE-232
COMPETITIVE PRACTICE-233
SUPPORT STRIKER AND MIDFIELD-234
A PHASE PLAY FOR THE SHADOW STRIKER POSITION IN THE 4-2-3-1-236
PHASE PLAY FOR THE SHADOW STRIKER POSITION WITHOUT THE FREE ZONE 14-244

THE 3-ZONE AWARENESS GAME-247
DROPPING OFF TO RECEIVE AND TURN IN POSSESSION-247

ABOUT WAYNE HARRISON-265

INTRODUCTION

Striker movement is one of the greatest and most difficult ARTS to master. The situation is constantly changing and the striker is constantly moving to create space for himself but also for teammates.

At the same time on some occasions the answer is not to move at all; and the when and where to do this comes from experience and playing.

Often the answer is to move AWAY from the ball and take the marker away from where you ultimately want to go.

Many strikers get caught up in always moving towards the ball, thus taking their marker with them and closing their OWN spaces down and making it more difficult to receive and keep the ball.

This can be addressed by making an OPPOSITE RUN to get free. So even if a striker closes his own space down too quickly he can always rectify it by moving away from the ball and into the space he left behind. If a striker moves a defender AWAY from the ball then the defender is at an immediate disadvantage in that he cannot see the ball and the striker at the same time. When the striker moves towards the ball the defender can see both at the same time, making his job much easier.

Movements of strikers are usually quite anaerobic (without oxygen), and short and sharp; unlike midfield players longer runs (very aerobic, with oxygen) so training should be performed with this in mind to build their anaerobic capacity. In this book I will show many checking movements that cover short distances and at the same time are usually "late and fast" to fool the defender.

Striker movement is REALLY a THINKING game, trying to out-fox a marker by clever and intelligent movement OFF the ball and learning to move off the ball is just as important as learning to shoot and score goals. The two go hand in hand.

I have tried to cover individual striker work as well as combined striker work. From a 1 on 1 technical finish with the keeper to building the ideas using more players and moving to small sided game situations, small sided Functions, to more player involved Phases of Play; to 11 v 11s.

Included also are sessions that are not so obvious as striker sessions but are equally important; such as the dropping off and receiving and turning 3 zone session in Zone 14.

I have enjoyed putting this book together, I use effectively all the sessions in the book and I hope you have as much pleasure and success from these ideas as I have with my teams and my current and previous clubs.

Best wishes, Wayne Harrison

SIMPLE, FUN AND EFFECTIVE SHOOTING AND FINISHING EXERCISES

VARIOUS STRIKER MOVEMENTS (WARM UP)

Players jog inside a 15 by 15 yard area. They must suddenly change direction and speed. Moves should be specific to the types of short and sharp movements strikers often have to make. Players must move as fast as possible over five yards.

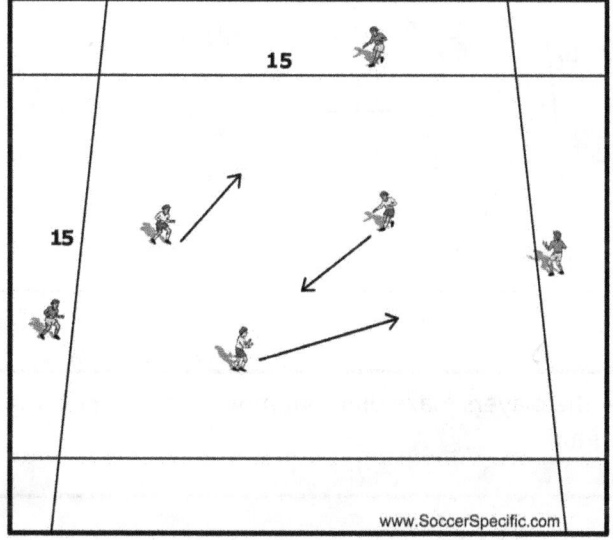

In the diagram below, players are making two movements because it is easy for defenders to read only the one run.

Progression 1: Now players make three directional changes, each run about 5 yards long and as fast as possible. Rest between each sequence and inside players switch with the outside players. Players should be aware of where the other players are as well as the boundaries. When changing direction players must PLANT their foot firmly and explode away.

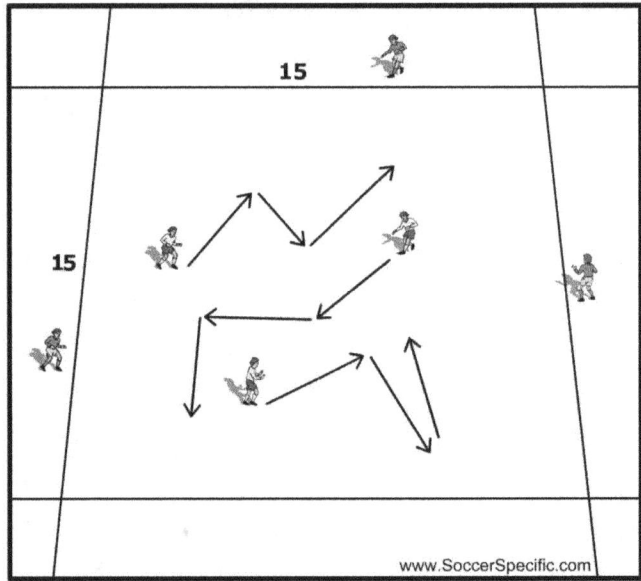

Progression 2: Have the players make different movements, for example the "Del Piero Spin" in the next diagram.

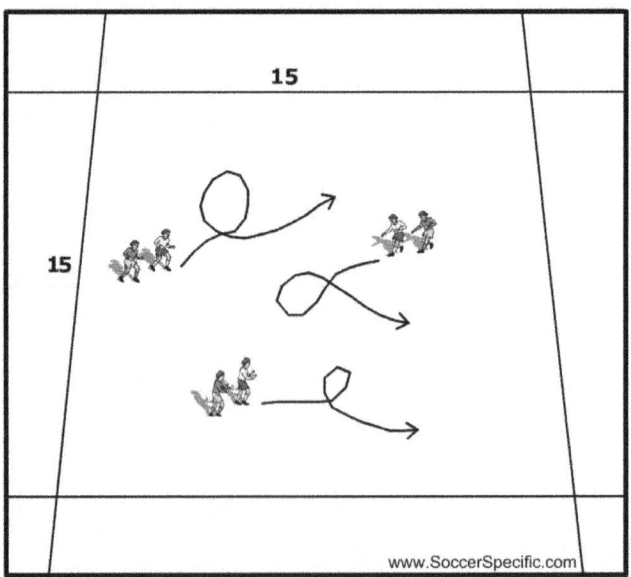

Progression 3: Now practice in two's with an attacker and a defender. The defender does not know when or where the striker will move or what moves he will do. This is a good practice for defenders too. The coach can dictate one, two or three movements.

Players must follow their pass and the passing must be sharp and accurate.

DEVELOPING GOOD TECHNIQUE FOR SHOOTING AT GOAL

WARM UP: As always with a ball each and stretching.

In two's, shooting through the empty cone goals to each other. We are looking for accuracy and good technique. Have the players count the number of goals they score. Have a few rounds, adding up scores each time.

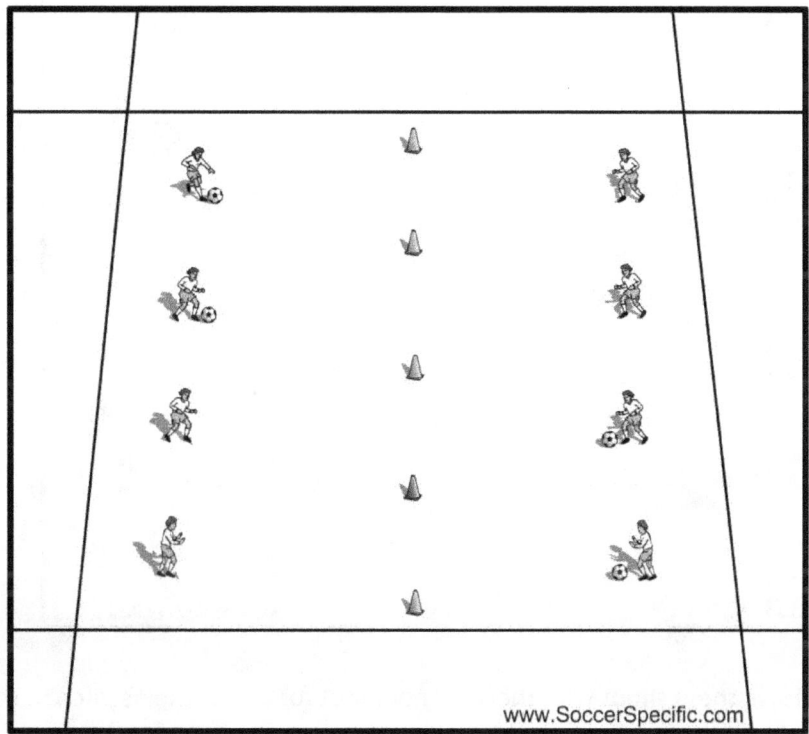

If working with tall pylon cones, have the players shooting to knock over the cones. Do it alternately per player each side and count which team knocks the most cones over (competitive). Ensure players are all organized properly behind an end line so they all shoot from the same distance.

COACHING STRIKERS

Simple shooting practice. Players are in two's 10 to 20 yards apart, distance depending on the age group. Each has a goal to defend and they have to score past each other. Keep it to two or three touches per shot.

Focus on the technique of striking the ball and explain and demonstrate this to the players.

Develop 1: Have them shoot with their stronger foot for a time then switch to their weaker foot.

Conditions: Work on side foot shooting, instep shooting, swerving the ball with the inside and outside of the foot etc.

Competitive: After two minutes of shooting have the winners play each other and the losers play each other.

COACHING STRIKERS

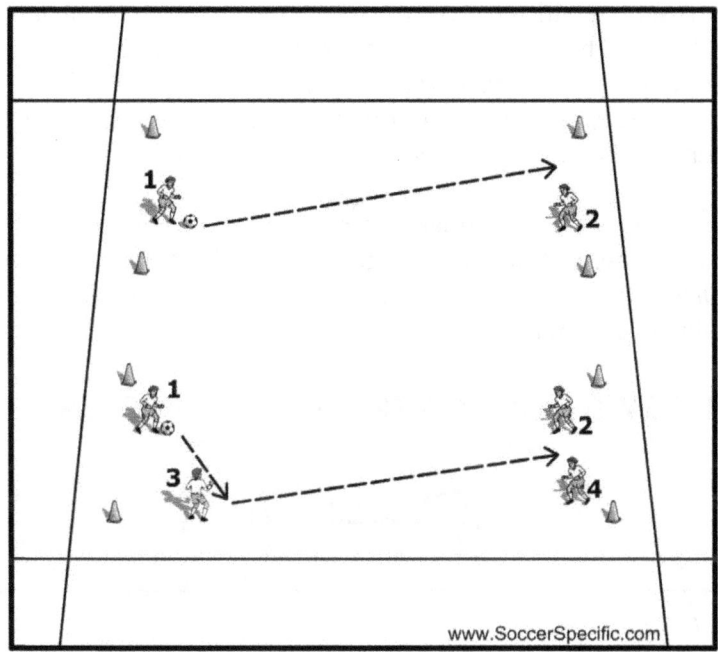

Develop 2: Have two v two games so some passing and shooting is developed; encourage a one touch shot from a well weighted pass

ONE TOUCH FINISHING

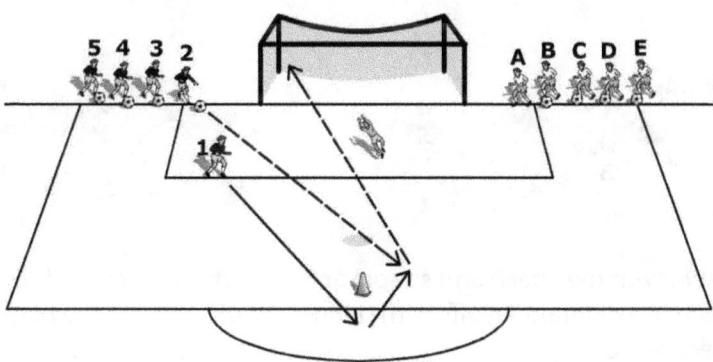

70% of all goals are scored with one touch so it is important to practice this technique regularly. (1) runs around the cone at pace to receive the pass from (2). Go left then right, varying the call to keep the players concentrating. Each player except the one running has a ball to serve. Shooter switches sides each time. One touch finishing.

This is a continuous practice with lots of work for the keeper also. As soon as a pass has gone in, call the next player to start his run.

Develop: Vary the service with easy passes to begin so you get a lot of goals, then chip it in for volleys, half volleys, headers, diving headers, and so on (players can throw the ball in to maintain accurate service if needed to ensure strikes on goal). Working on a positive attitude to score, accuracy and/or power, correct shot selection, awareness of rebounds. Have players counting the number of goals they score (competitive).

First team to score 10 goals is the winner. Alternatively the coach can stand behind the cone and receive the pass and vary the service for the end product, creating opportunities to volley and half volley the ball, or even head it on goal. Vary the distance from the goal depending on what you want to achieve.

FUN PRACTICES WITH ONE OR TWO TOUCH FINISHING

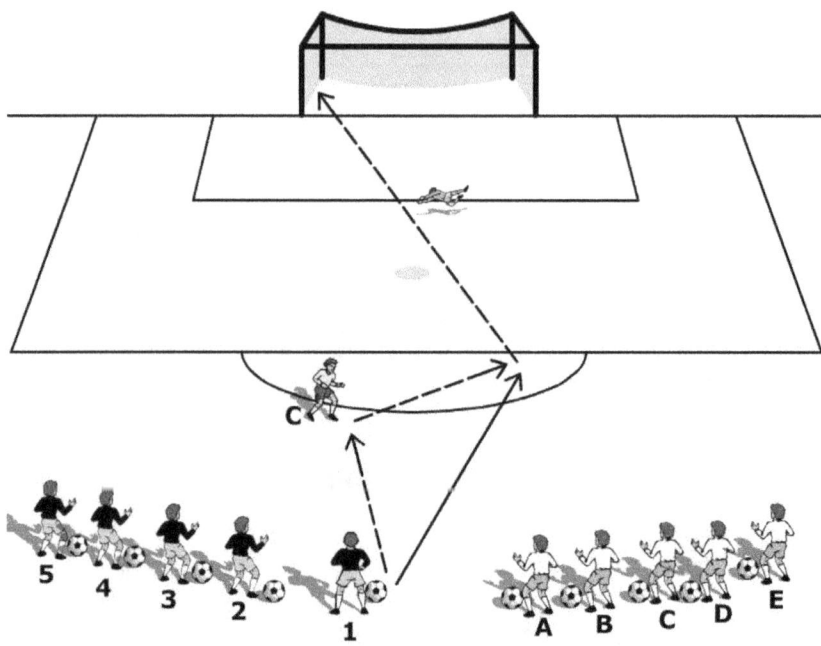

(1) plays a one-two with the coach and shoots at goal with a one touch finish. Go right and left. The coach can use different layoffs with degrees of difficulty as the players improve their finishing technique.

Develop 1: The coach changes position with the server who faces the goal
a) Throw the ball over the player's shoulder for volleys and half volleys
b) Throw from the side for side volleys and half volleys
c) Throw off at an angle so the player chases down the ball and shoots.

Player turns around (now back to goal). The coach passes to the player's feet and the player must receive and turn and shoot quickly. Serve to feet, control and turn, chest control and turn, thigh control and turn.

Develop 2: In two's (1 v 1's), make it competitive, the first to the ball has the shot.
Variations of service:
a) Down the side of each player,
b) Between the players,
c) In the air,
d) Players in various stances, sitting, lying down so they have to get up off the ground and get the shot in first.

Do the same with all players facing the goal so they can't see the ball coming and must react to it, there are lots of variations you can use for this and it helps their sharpness and composure in finishing.

Do all these quickly so the players are not standing around waiting too long. Have plenty of balls ready to go.

FINISHING WHEN CLEAR OF THE DEFENSE

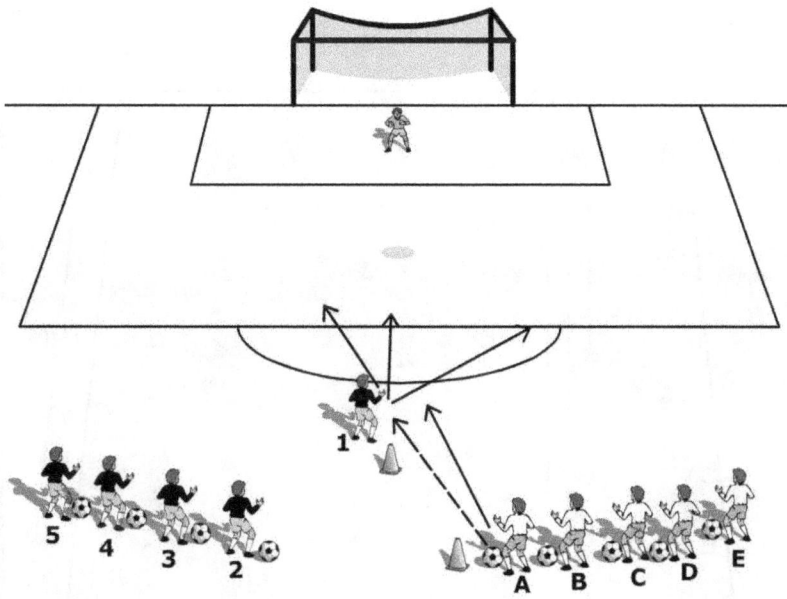

(A) passes to (1) and chases to put him under pressure to prevent a goal being scored. (1) has a start on (A) and has the advantage.

Choices to score are:
a) Shoot past the keeper.
b) Dribble around the keeper.
c) Chip the keeper.
d) Use the toe end for power.

Attackers must make a good first touch out of their feet, keep their head up, observe the keeper's position, be composed, and use the correct decision and technique to score.

If a defender is quick and catches up the attacker has three options:
1. Shoot quickly, though this may rush the shot
2. Move away from the defender to open up the angle to shoot (may push too wide)
3. Cut across the defender to stop his run (defender has to pull up, so giving more time to shoot, or bring the attacker down; probably in the box for a penalty).

MANY GOAL SCORING SITUATIONS OCCUR IN GAMES IN A 1v1 WITH THE KEEPER, SO PRACTICING THIS IS IMPORTANT.

Encourage a one touch shot from a well weighted pass

ATTACKING ON THE BREAK

Pass and follow warm up - Players are split into 3 teams and set up as shown in the diagram:

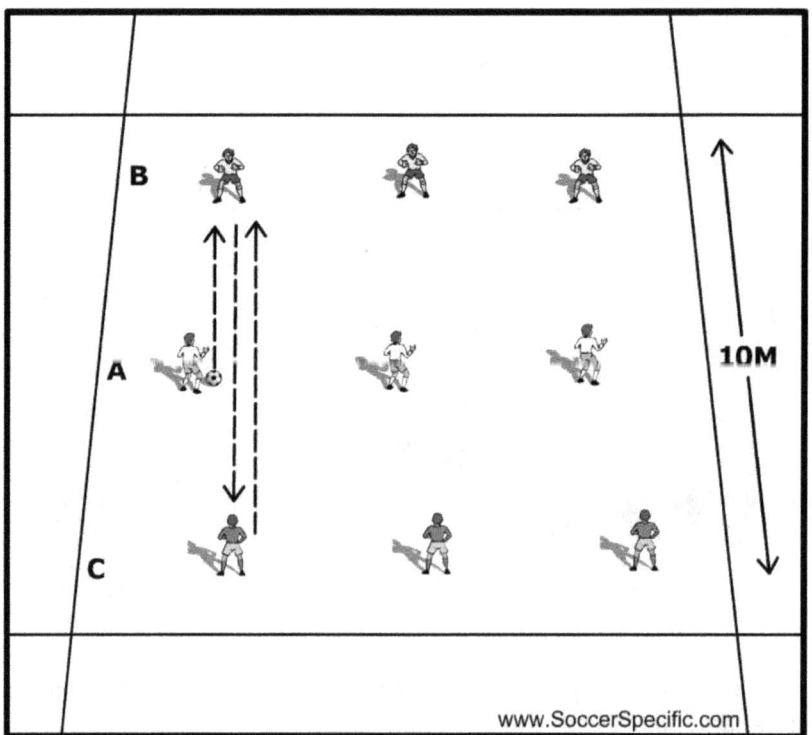

Players in team A start with the ball, pass the ball to B and follow the pass.

Player B passes to player C and follows the pass, then player C passes back to Player B and follows the pass.

Continuous practice for 3 minutes.

Players complete 2 sets, 1 minute active rest in between sets (players must do keep up's).

Coaching Points:
- Players on 2 touches during first set, emphasis on control and passing with inside, outside, instep etc.
- Players must follow their pass with a quick burst of speed specific to closing down and supporting play during a match.

Development 1:
Progression from previous practice. The distance is now doubled to 20m.

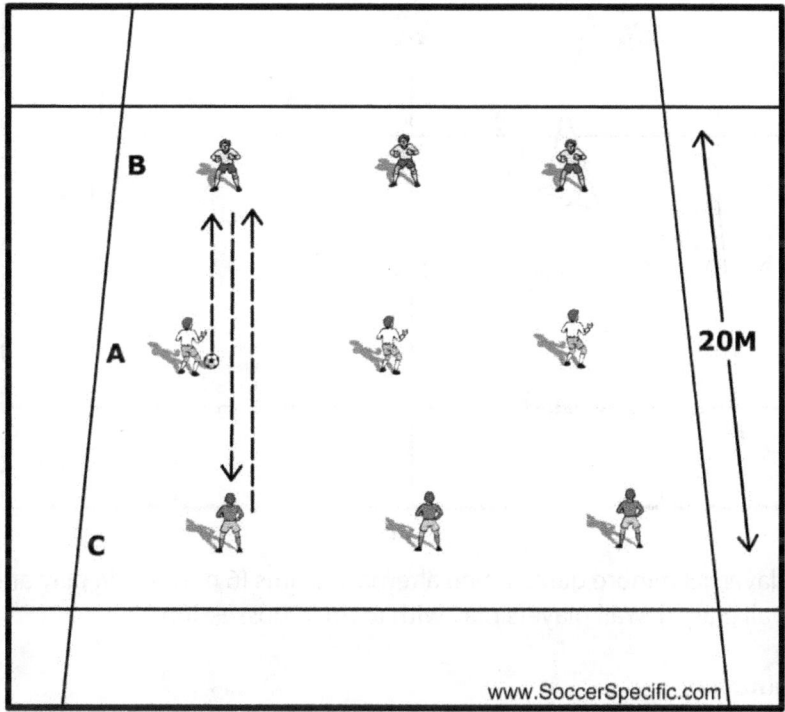

Players to complete 2 more sets, 1 minute active rest in between sets.

Coaching Points:
- Players on 2 touches during first set, emphasis on control and passing with inside, outside, instep etc.
- Players must follow their pass with a quick burst of speed. Liken it to closing down and supporting play during a match.

Development 2:

Players set up as in diagram. 3 teams of 6 + 4 GK's (GK's are optional, use smaller goals)

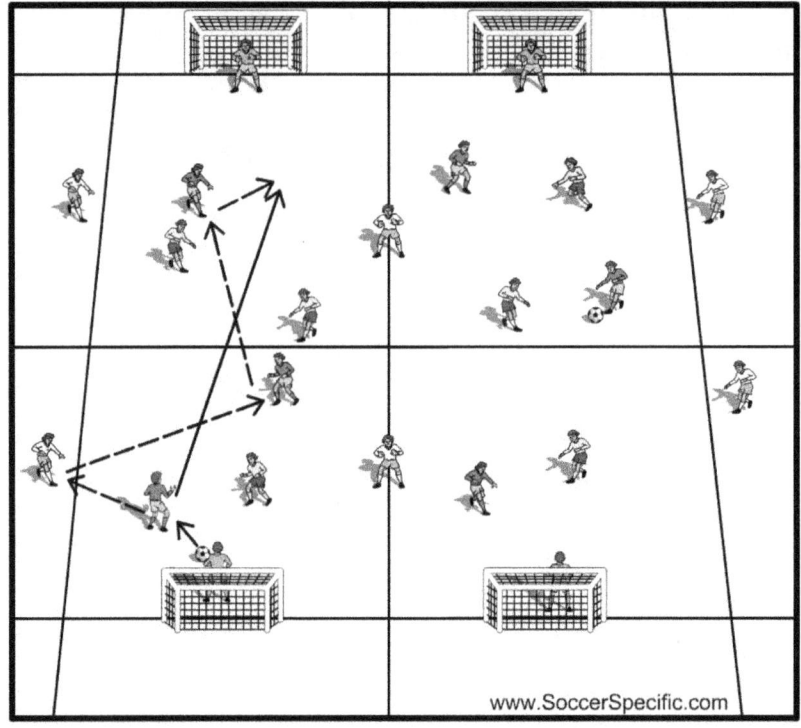

3 v 3 + wall players; 3 minute games then alternate teams (6 minutes in play and 3 minutes resting as a wall player). Wall players play with team in possession.

Coaching Point:

Emphasis is on high tempo, closing down, angles and weight of pass.

Development 3:
Progression from last activity

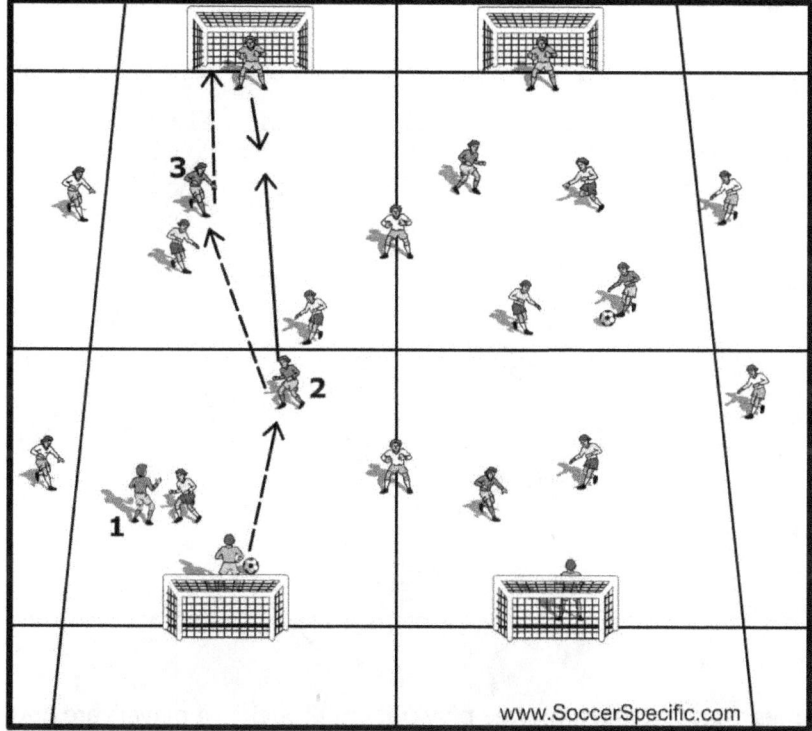

Play is now end to end. If a team scores they keep possession and play to score at the other end of the area.

In the diagram the attacking team has moved the ball up the pitch quickly. When player 2 passed the ball to player 3, he followed the pass to support 3 but also to anticipate a goal, now being in a position to pick up possession from the GK.

Coaching Points:
- The emphasis is on high tempo, supporting play and communication.
- The team who are not in possession of the ball are looking to close down, intercept passes and counter attack at pace.

Development 4:
Progression from last activity. 3 teams of 6 + 2 GK´s. Large area to encourage fast break attack

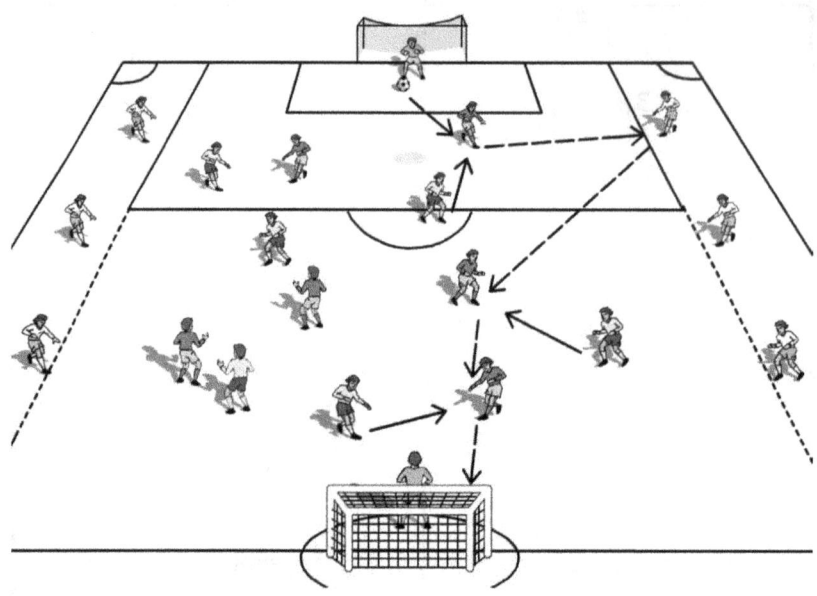

5 minute games then rotate teams, free play but limit touches if players are getting caught in possession.

Coaching Points:
- Emphasis is on high tempo, supporting play and communication, keeping touches down to a minimum.
- The team not in possession of the ball is looking to close down, intercept passes and counter attack at pace.

Development 5 - Final Game:
Progression from last activity. Split players into 2 teams. Adjust the size of the pitch to accommodate the number of players in the practice. Use full pitch for 11 v 11.

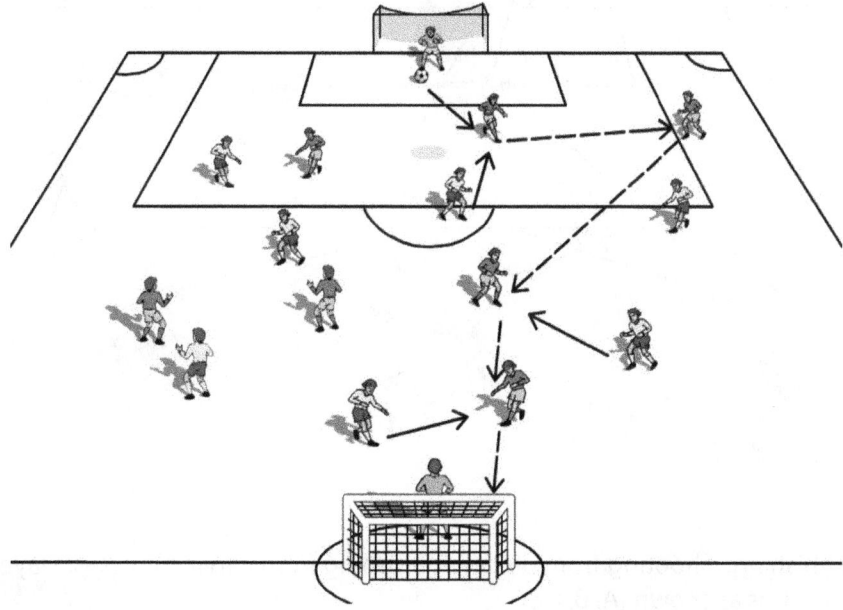

15 minute free play

Coaching Points:
- Fast interceptions and quick counter-attack when possible, immediate pressing of the ball when possession is lost.
- Work on combination play and angles to receive the ball.
- Cool down and stretches to end session.

A DRILL ORIENTED FINISHING SESSION FOR STRIKERS

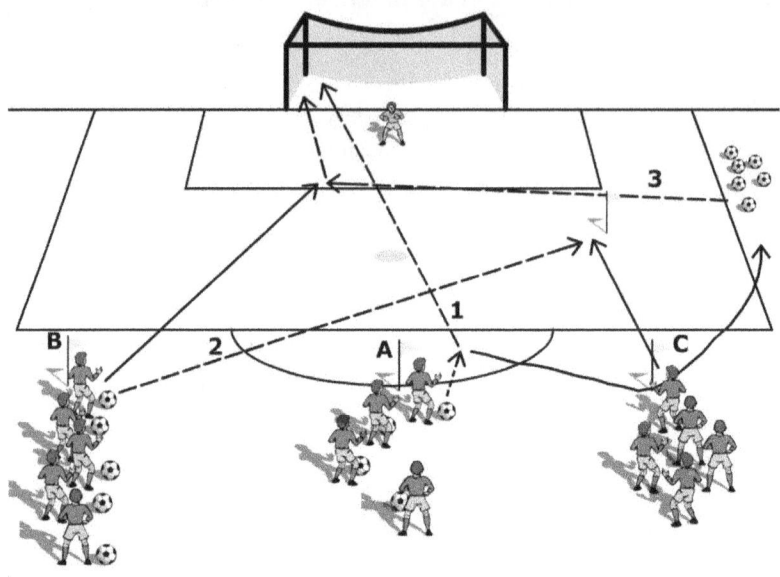

Game-like finishing: Shooting from distance, finishing from varying crosses. Players are split into 3 groups as shown (A, B, C).

Three flags mark the starting points for each group.

Another flag is placed approximately 8-10 yards out at an angle to one of the goal posts. Balls are located with groups (A) and (B) as well as outside one side of the 18-yard box. All players start at one of the three flags.

One goalkeeper in goal with extra goalkeeper waiting off to the side of the goal.

The exercise is initiated by player (A). Player (A) takes a touch to the side of the flag and then strikes a shot at goal.

He then immediately starts sprinting around the flag at group (C). Player (B) passes a ball in the direction of the flag located approximately 8-10 yards from goal.

Player (C) must time his run from his starting point to get to the ball for a shot on goal. Player (A) then crosses one of the wide balls into the box for both player (B) and (C) to attack.

After approximately 4 minutes, change direction to ensure crosses and shots from both sides of the field.

COACHING STRIKERS

Coaching Points:
- Attempt to do everything at game speed.
- Player (B) must drive the ball across the face of the goal towards the flag for player (C) to attack at the back post. (C) must time his run to slide in before the ball reaches the flag.
- Player (B) must NOT get into the box too early when attacking the cross from player (A)
- Player (C) must "stay alive" in the box by making a second run to receive a cross from player (A)

Progression:
Three players are positioned approximately 35 yards away from goal to act as servers as shown in the diagram.

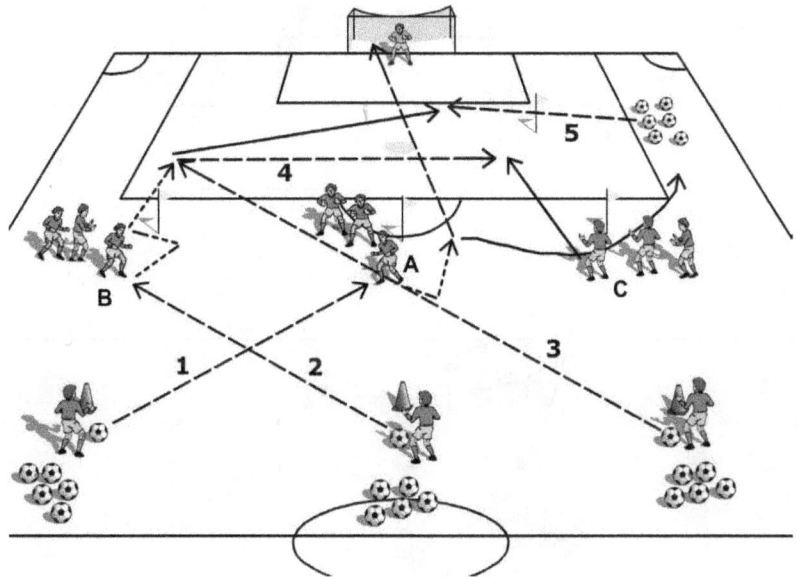

Supply of balls at each passing station. The exercise is initiated with a pass (1) to player (A) who is checking to the ball.

Player (A) must spin and strike a shot at goal before immediately sprinting around the flag at group (C). Pass (2) is played to player (B) who spins inside the flag to create an angle for a quick shot on goal.

Player (B) immediately spins back out around the flag to receive a diagonal driven ball (3) from server.

Player (B) must control this ball quickly before driving a ball (4) along the ground towards the back post space for player (C). Players (B) and (C) must stay active in the box to time their runs for a cross (5) from player (A).

Coaching Points:
- Attempt to do everything at game speed.
- Firm and driven passes from servers.
- Player (B) must drive the ball across the face of the goal towards the flag for player (C) to attack at the back post.
- (C) must time his run to slide in before the ball reaches the flag.
- Player (B) must NOT get into the box too early when attacking the cross from player (A)
- Player (C) must "stay alive" in the box by making a second run to receive a cross from player (A).

MOVEMENT AND FINISHING UP FRONT
WORKING WITH THE STRIKERS, RUNS DOWN THE SIDE

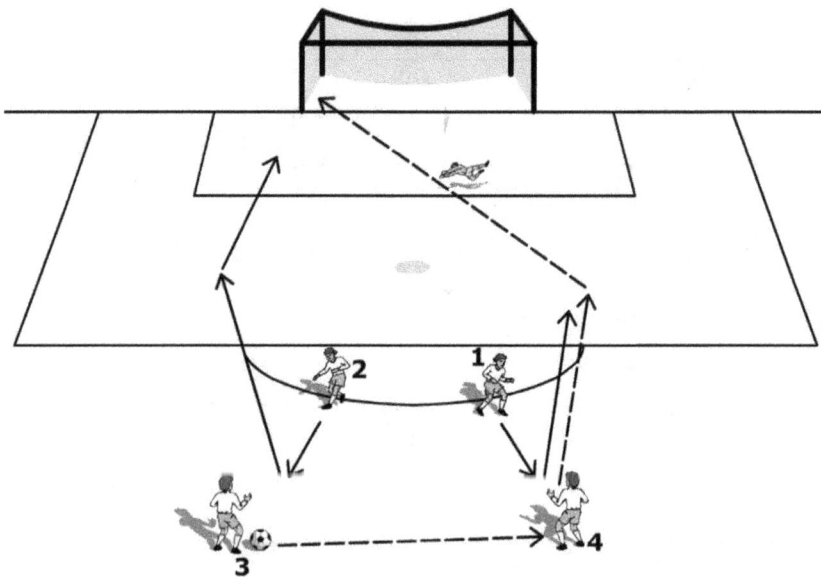

WITH THIS BEING SPECIFIC TO STRIKERS, USE THE TIME TO DO 2 SESSIONS, THIS ONE FOR STRIKERS AND ATTACKING MIDFIELDERS AND ANOTHER FOR GETTING THE BALL TO THE FRONT.

Passes made as if from central midfield. Work both sides. First player (3) moves the ball away then checks back and passes to other central midfield player (4).

This helps prepare the strikers (1) and (2) in the timing of their runs. Ensure they don't go too early (which is normally the case) or too late.

Other striker follows in for rebounds. Turns / spins should be short and sharp.

CROSSOVER AND OPPOSITE RUNS, BALL PASSED DOWN THE SIDE

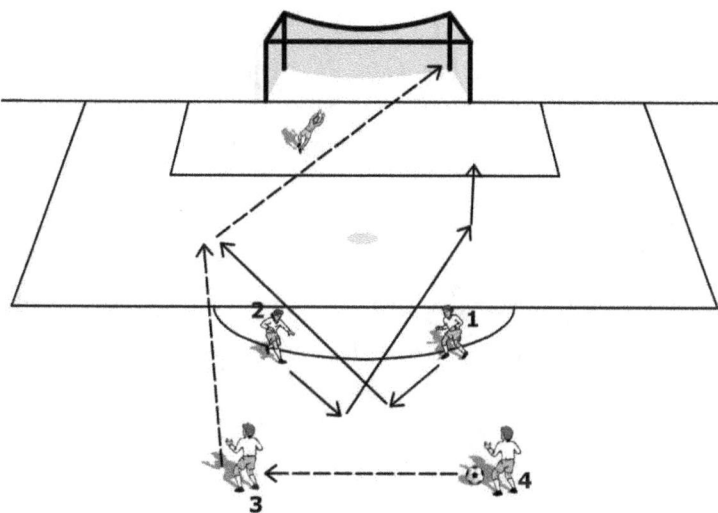

Crossover runs to move defenders and create space for attackers.

First run towards the ball is to draw defenders to them. Turn / spin must be short and sharp across the defender's shoulder so his turn to track the run is more difficult.

Avoid an arc run which is easier for a defender to recover against.

OUTSIDE RUNS, BALL PLAYED THROUGH THE MIDDLE

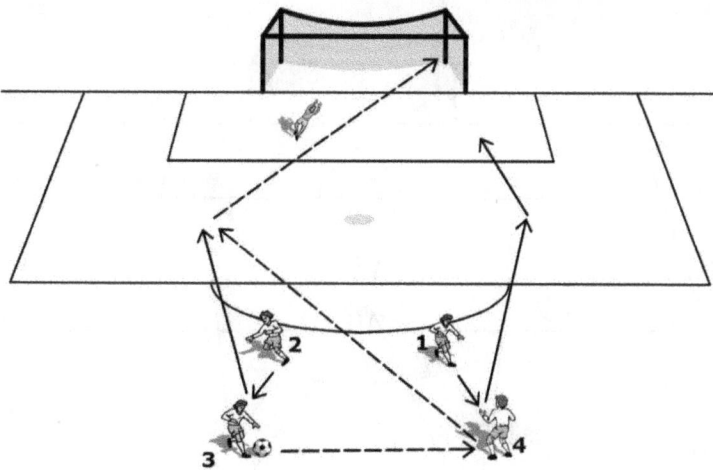

Split runs to create space centrally for the pass. Same split runs by strikers but the ball is played through the middle instead of down the side.

Think about the turn / spin movement of the striker. Does he turn inside (and see the ball all the time) or outside (and momentarily lose sight of the ball).

Which is more difficult for the defender to deal with? (Depends on from which side the ball is delivered).

FIRST STRIKER SHORT, 1 – 2 OFF SECOND STRIKER

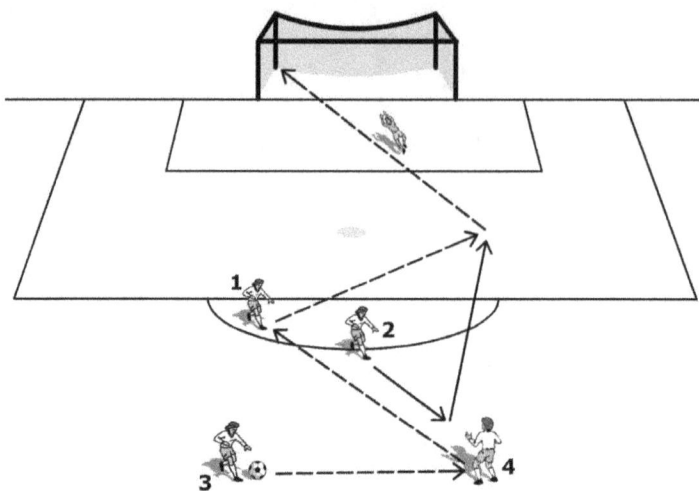

Striker (2) goes short and pulls the defender forward, creating space in behind.

(4) plays the ball to striker (1) who plays the ball into the space created by striker (2)'s run.

Striker (2) spins sharply and enters that space to receive the pass and shoot. (1) follows in for potential rebounds.

STRIKERS MAKE OPPOSITE SPLIT RUNS TO GET MIDFIELDER IN

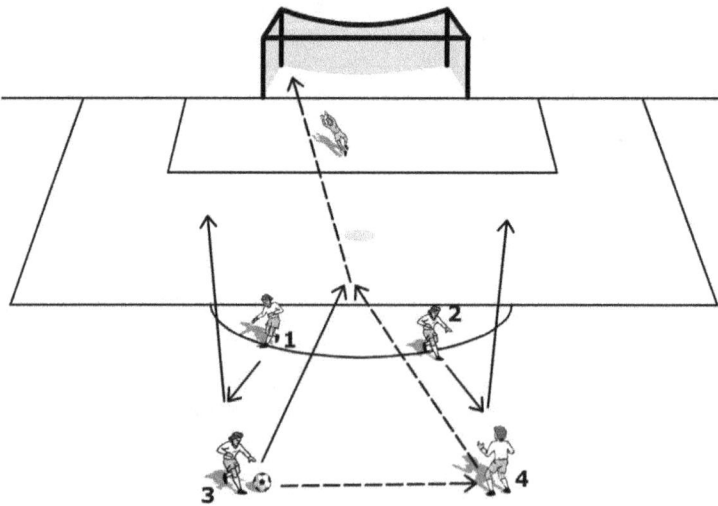

(3) passes to (4), (1) and (2) make runs to split and create space through the center for midfielder (3) to receive the pass from (4). Timing of all runs must be coordinated.

SHOOTING AND FINISHING DRILLS

Phase I: The squad is split into 2 groups as shown in the diagram below. Players move freely around the pitch for several minutes, without a ball, before stopping to perform various individual static stretching exercises.

Phase II: Players pair off. One partner serves the ball from his hands while the other returns the ball with volleys etc.

Players perform static stretches as a group. After several minutes of stretching the players move around the pitch passing with their partner.

COACHING STRIKERS

Development 1:
Players are split into 2 groups and positioned as shown in diagram below. A target player (center forward) is positioned just outside the penalty area. A supply of balls is placed next to each line of players.

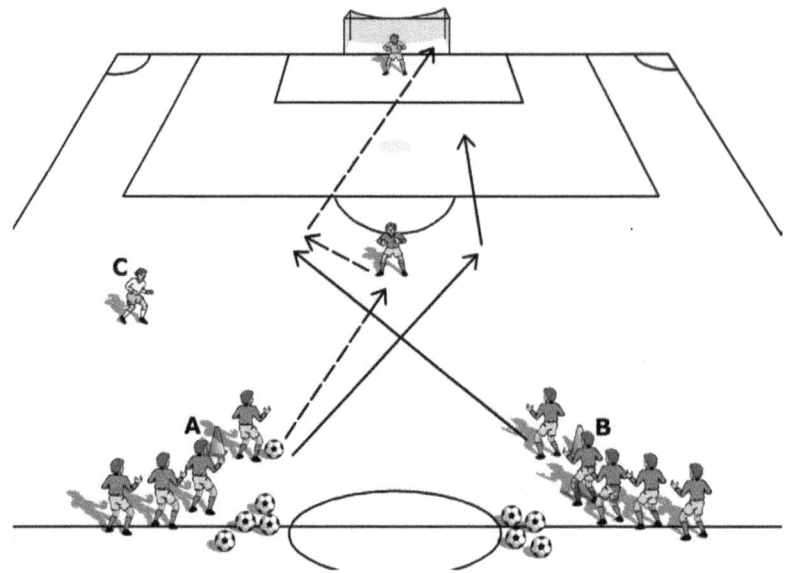

A pass is made from either line to the center forward as shown above.

The center forward controls the ball while both players make a cross-over run.

The center forward turns quickly and "plays in" one of the players for a shot.

The other player follows in for any rebounds.

The center forward is switched every minute while the other players switch lines after each repetition.

Coaching Points:
- Good weighted pass into the forward.
- Good runs off the ball.
- Quality control and pass from the center forward.
- Quality finishing.
- Everything must be done at realistic game-like speeds.

Development 2:
Two groups are positioned as shown in the diagram below. A supply of balls is placed next to each group.

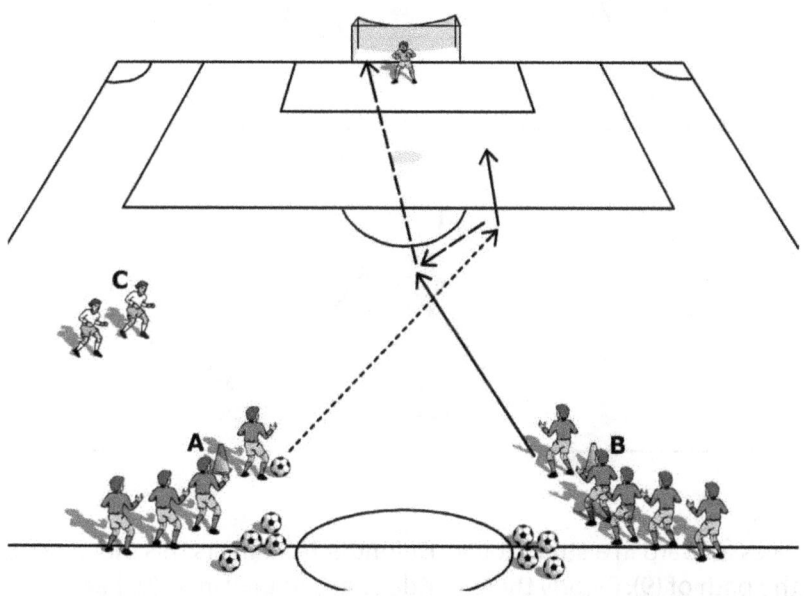

Either player (A or B) dribbles at pace to goal. Just outside the box, he fakes the shot and stops the ball or back-heels it for his partner. The partner attempts to finish with one touch. The next ball begins from the opposite line.

Coaching points:
- Be direct – go for goal.
- Good communication.
- Quality lay-off
- Timing of runs and release of pass.

Observations:
- Very basic activity that all players seemed to really enjoy.
- Players usually perform this activity with a high level of enthusiasm

INDIVIDUAL STRIKER MOVEMENT

Striker (9) moves forward in a straight line. Defender (A) mirrors this movement. The ball is played into the path of (9). Clearly there is little space to play in as (9) has not created space for himself due to the straight run he made.

The EXACT same pass into the SAME PLACE. But look at the difference in space due to the run. (9)'s run is AWAY from the ball and if (A) mirrors the run, which is likely, then he will run with him and AWAY from the inside space. It is clear here that the exact same pass in the exact same space will be more EFFECTIVE NOW.

In making this run away from the ball the striker (9) may even be able to affect (A) such that he is facing away from the ball in order to stay on track with the striker.

As the striker runs he can look over his shoulder at the ball so he knows where it is. For the defender this is more difficult as he can't see both the striker and the ball at the same time when running away from the ball unless he is faced up. If he is faced up and recovering back he will not be able to run as quickly. So either way the striker should have the advantage.

As (A) checks away with the run of (9), (9) will then check back into the space he has created for himself. If he can do it as the defender plants his right foot down then even better. This may only create one yard or even less of space but it may be all that the striker needs to get away and get a shot in on goal.

MOVEMENT OFF THE BALL FROM A CROSS

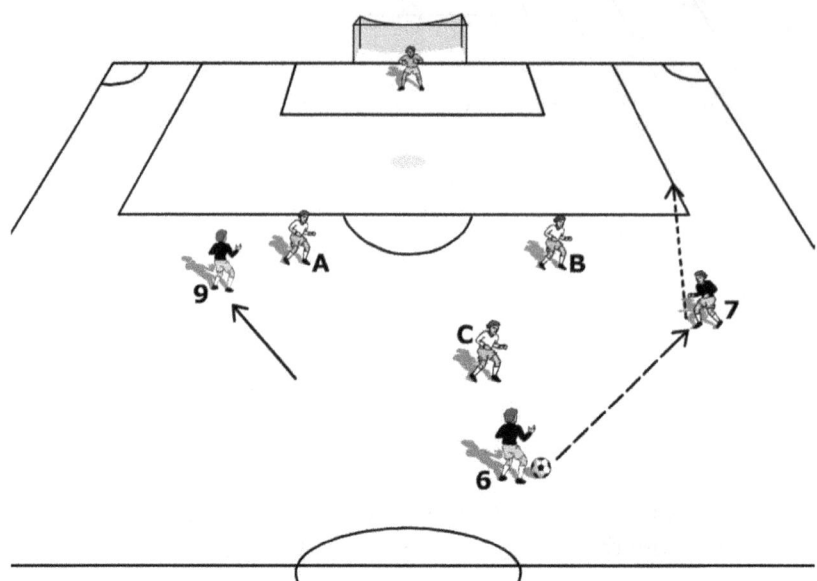

Initially have defenders play passive so we get success. This is about the quality of the delivery and the movement of (9).

Here (9) moves behind (A) so the defender cannot see the ball and the striker at the same time.

Coaching Points:
- Wide player (7) getting free of his marker to receive
- Creating space to cross
- Verbal or eye contact between (9) and (7) as the phase of play progresses
- Movement of the striker (not in a straight line)
- Timing of the run by (9) late and fast
- Angles of each run by (9) to get free of defender (A)
- Timing and quality of the cross by (7)
- Quality of the finish

Too many strikers run at goal in a straight line, making it easy for their markers. The time to go in a straight line (the shortest route to goal) is when the cross is coming early and there is no time to do otherwise.

Strikers run AWAY from the goal to draw defenders away from the target area and into areas they do not want to go into. They take up a position "off the shoulder" of the defender.

A striker, moving away from the goal and taking the defender with him, puts the defender in a disadvantaged position. If the defender looks at the striker he can't see the ball, or when and where it is delivered. If he looks at the ball, he can't see where the striker is or when he makes his move. Thus, the defender's head is effectively on a swivel, trying to watch both the ball and the striker he is trying to mark.

From the striker's perspective these runs are the best ones to make in terms of moving defenders into unfavorable positions and away from the danger area.

Strikers need to learn how to move defenders around to create even a yard of space for themselves, which could be the difference between scoring or not scoring.

In the diagram below, players (C) and (6) are part of the set up to get the session moving but it is really all about the timing and quality OF THE CROSS BY (7) AND THE TIMING AND ANGLE OF THE RUNS BY (9).

Defender (A)'s first movement is back towards his own goal. We hope he will go tighter to (9) who has moved away from where the ball is coming from, and follow his run and leave more space inside for (9) to attack; but likely he will give himself space and time by just dropping off.

Here (9) still runs inside and across (A) to attack the ball. Timing is the key here; if he gets free and in space in front of the defender and the cross is coming early then this may work.

If the cross were to come in now it is possible (9) has gotten in front of (A) to get a free header or shot. But if it still has not been delivered then this is the moment for (9) to draw (A) towards the ball then check back and behind.

COACHING STRIKERS

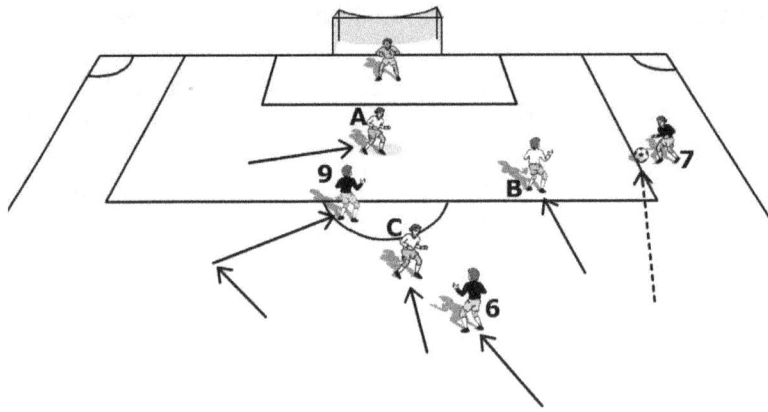

The defender (A) reacts to (9)'s outside to inside run and looks to get goal side of (9) to be first to the header from the cross from (7). Here he is positioned in front of (9) so any cross in front should be his to win.

Again it is about the timing of the runs of (7) and (9) and the position of the defender as to when the cross comes.

All these individual moments by each player happen in less than a second, so the timing of both the movements and the cross has to be good.

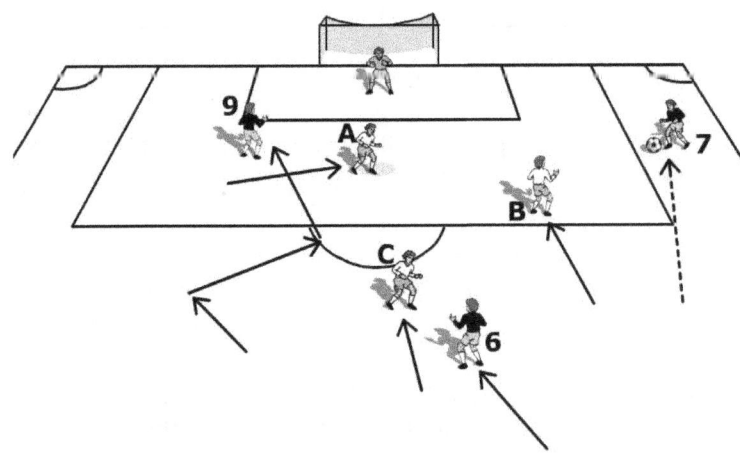

(7) should be running with the ball but looking at the movements of (9) to know exactly where to cross the ball to.

Likewise (9) is making movements looking at the run of (7) trying to anticipate when he may cross the ball.

My belief is that (9) makes the runs and (7) times his cross based on those runs if at all possible. More likely, though, is that (7) just has to get the cross in when the best opportunity to do so arrives (unless he is has gotten free and has time to watch and analyze the movements of (9) and (A)). They may have a plan worked out before the game where if (9) goes near with his first run it means he will check far, and if he goes far, it means he will check near.

So, (9) has run towards the ball and taken (A) with him. In a split second (A) gets back in front of him and goal side but as (A) plants his front foot down to get in position, (9) checks back outside and off the shoulder of (A) into the space that is now available again due to the positioning of (A). (A), when planting his foot down, has his body rotating forward and he will be slightly off balance if he tries to check back, which gives (9) the advantage.

So, perhaps in practice you have the plan that if (9) makes the run to the near post just as the ball is about to be delivered, (7) knows to play it beyond the near post for (9) checking off to receive, and vice versa. But do not tell your defenders what the plan is, and see how long it takes for them to work out what is happening. By then hopefully we have had success and scored some goals. It needs to become an instinct between the strikers, an almost telepathic understanding, and this will only come with continued repetition in training.

This is like a pre planned set play, only it takes place in open dynamic play. If done right, it is a nightmare for the defenders to play against. Whilst the game itself is dynamic, imaginative and mainly "off the cuff", in some areas of the game we can have pre planned ideas which we need to work on again and again in training. So when a particular situation arises in a game, the players recognize it, have a set idea what to do at that moment and repeat their practiced training movements and understanding.

(9) can also work off the body language of (7) as to the timing of the delivery and the timing of his run.

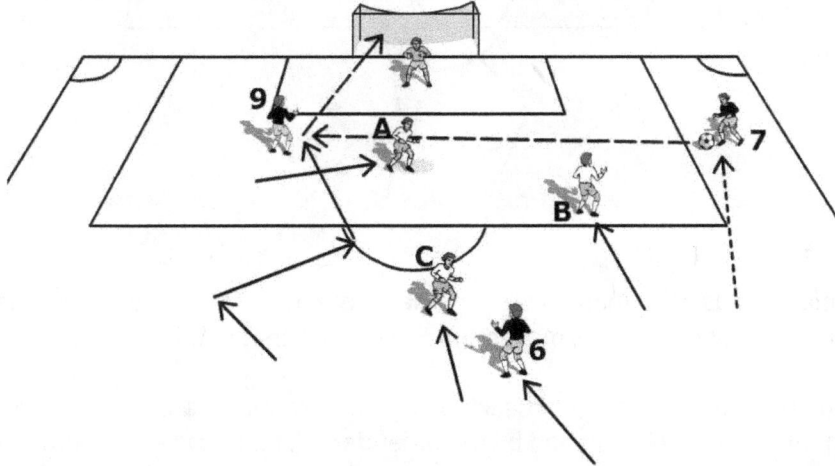

Here they get the timing perfect and (A) is caught flat footed and ball watching as the ball goes over his head from the cross after (9)'s movement has drawn him with his outside to inside run towards the ball and (9), now in space having checked back off and behind (A), scores a goal.

All this happens in a matter of a few seconds and the more these two players practice this in training, the better the timing (of runs and crosses) and understanding between them will be.

COACHING STRIKERS

This session can be very simplistic to begin and then developed with more players and more pressure, building it up as we go along to make it more and more game realistic. For longer runs further away from goal there is time before the ball is delivered. In this case, as the striker attacks the defender and the goal with a sharp solid run, he can do a zigzag to try to escape and / or confuse the defender.

Running behind the defender, then running in front of him, then behind again, then in front again and so on, the defender may be thinking "Is he going to attack the far post behind me, or the near post in front of me"?

All this movement helps the striker get away from the marking of the defender and may result in a chance to score a goal by getting space he otherwise may not have had if he had simply run forward in a straight line attack on goal.

The final move must be made as late and as quickly as possible to get away from the defender. The cardinal sin is to get in too early. Better to be slightly behind the play and able to make up for it with a burst of speed than be in front of the play and therefore much more easily marked out of the game and arriving before the cross.

You may play with two strikers then get their combined movements or one striker and show how his movement may free up space for another player (perhaps a deeper lying player coming in late).

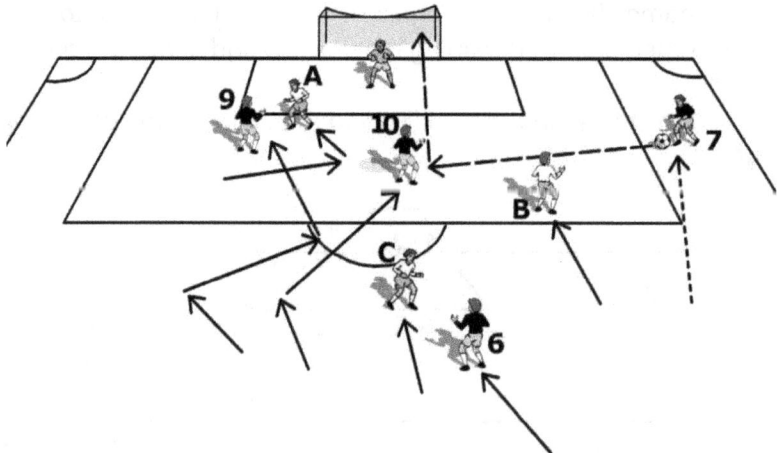

Let's imagine (10) has been marked by the other center back (not shown here due to a lack of space on the diagram) and his movement is based on that of (9).

(9) is moving (A) around with tight checking angled movements are he runs to goal and his movement may be well matched by the defender (A). BUT, at the same time this is creating space for (10) who is watching and waiting and getting ready for the moment the ball is crossed.

If (10) can time his run late and fast he may lose his marker and be first to the ball, as he is at the near post when (9) has taken (A) to the far post.

Having players attack both posts is better for the crosser now so wherever he plays it someone will be there. With one attacker only in this situation he has to be more precise; knowing he has to put it in a certain place which is a more difficult technique to perform (and based on the lone striker's movement).

STARTING THE RUN FROM A DEEPER POSITION

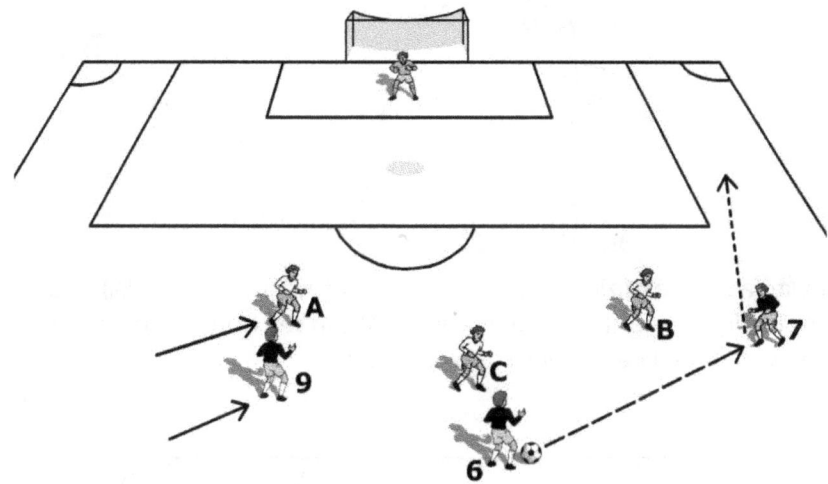

Here the striker (9) is further away from goal in the buildup. The crosser (7) has a way to go to get into the crossing position so (9) can move defender (A) around to try to create some space for himself as he gets closer to the goal.

Initially (9) runs away from the ball and (A) tracks him. Unless (A) can track him at pace running backwards it is likely he will track HIM WITH HIS BACK TO THE BALL so he is already at a disadvantage as he can't see when or where the ball is being delivered.

(9) is running forward to the goal, but at an angle away. (A) is running back towards his own goal. He cannot in this position look at the player and the ball at the same time.

Striker (9) makes a couple of zigzag runs to try to confuse and disrupt (A)'s tracking and marking (running in a straight line would mean (A) can see both the player and the ball at the same time so it would be easier to defend against).

Striker (9) finally moves towards the ball drawing (A) towards the ball too.

Defender (A) needs to get in front of (9) to be first to the crossed ball and be able to clear the cross.

Defender (A) gets goal side and in front of the ball and at that moment (9) checks back behind him into the space they left.

Timing is the key and as (9) takes (A) towards the ball that is the time to deliver the cross aimed beyond (A); as by the time it arrives (9) has checked away and behind (A) to get free hoping (A) is ball watching for that split second to give him an extra yard of space.

PRACTICE, PRACTICE AND MORE PRACTICE !

SMALL SIDED GAMES FOR STRIKERS

THE NUMBERS SHOOTING GAME

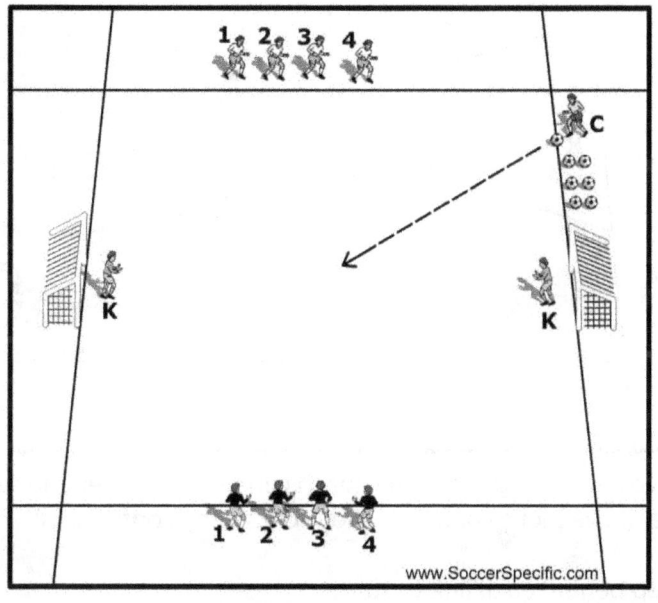

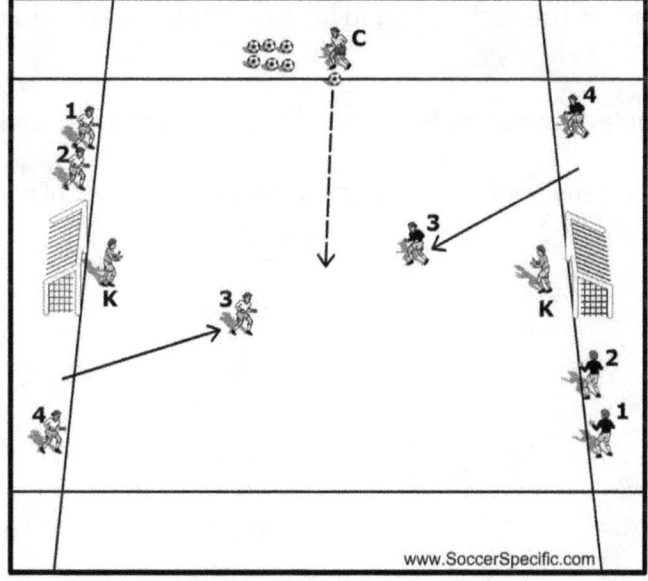

Number players off and have a competitive game with two teams. Call numbers out to create 1 v 1's, 2 v 2's, 3 v 3's etc.

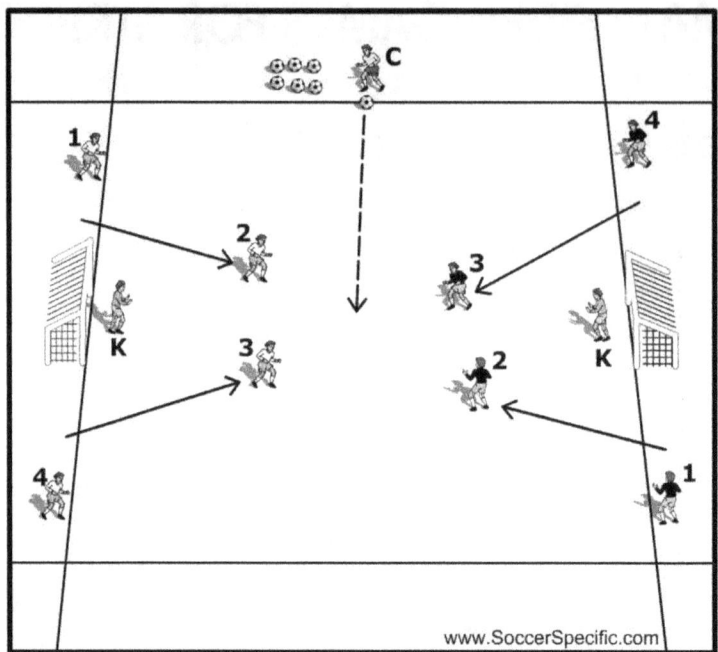

Make it competitive by keeping score, the coach can be the keeper and serve the ball calling the number (have plenty of balls handy so it's fairly continuous).

Ensure players keep behind each line to start.

If you have two coaches, use both goals and have each team attacking a different goal as in a game.

You can have a couple of games such as the first team to score five goals is the winner.

Build the exercise eventually into a 4 v 4 game if that is the number of players you are working with.

PASSING; SUPPORT PLAY AND SHOOTING IN A 2 v 2

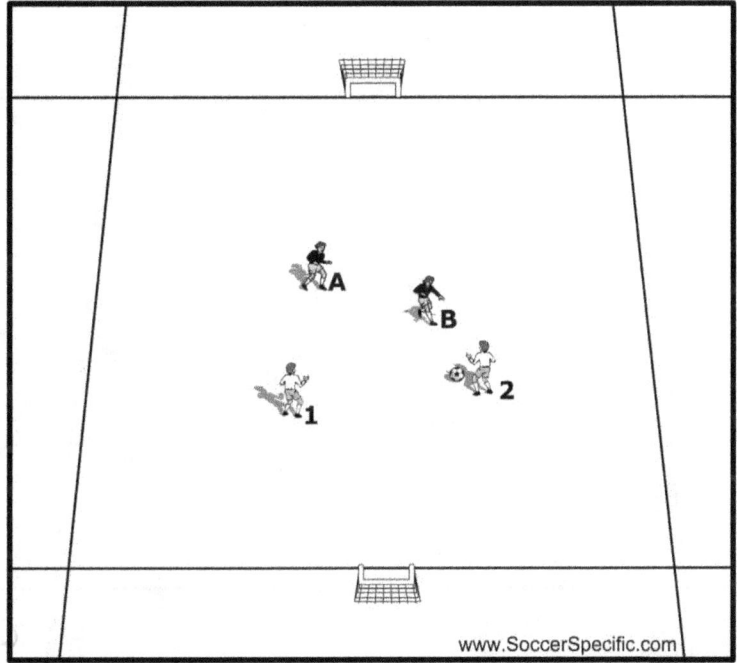

A highly competitive 2 v 2 situation now where combination plays are what the players need to produce to help them score goals. This can include takeovers, overlaps, 1-2's or diagonal runs in front of the ball.

If a player is particularly good at dribbling, the movement of the support player could be away from a support position to take the other defender away too. This will leave a 1 v 1 situation with no support for the defender.

The player on the ball must consider each movement of his teammate and act accordingly. There are two choices: a) pass to the supporting player, b) use the movement of the supporting player as a decoy to create space for the player on the ball. Which choice to make can depend on the reaction of the opponents and where they move to.

You can have a keeper in each goal so it is a 2 v 2 and both sets of two can attack and defend.

PASSING AND SUPPORT PLAY IN A 2 v 2

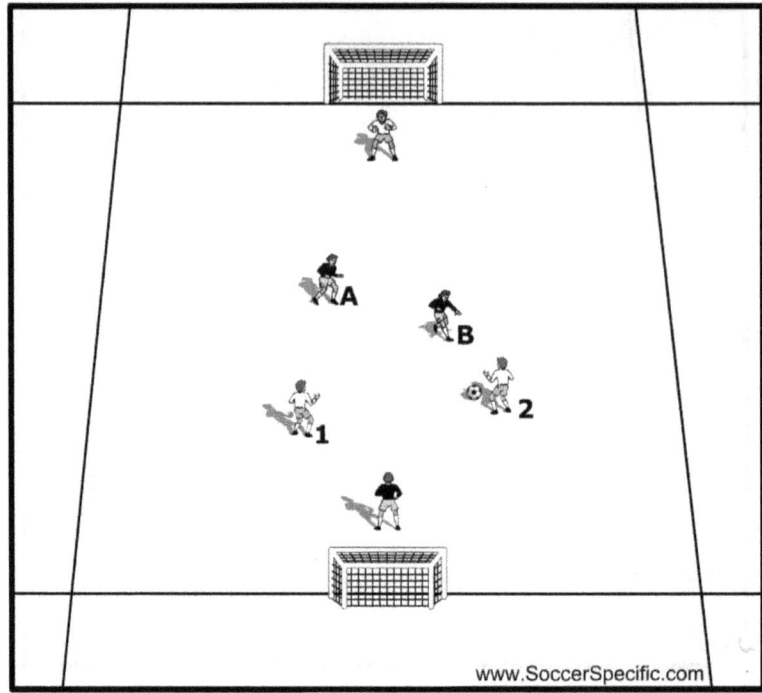

Here we have added 2 keepers to the 2 v 2 game situation. You can apply this set up to all the following diagrams showing 2 v 2, 3 v 2 and 3 v 3 set ups and what technique they are practicing in each one.

This means it is more game related and both teams get the chance to attack and work on the technical situation they are practicing.

The reason I show the set ups without keepers is to show how you can train with small numbers of players. If you have two extra you can use them as keepers and rotate the players so each has a go as an outfield player.

A 3 v 2 SITUATION

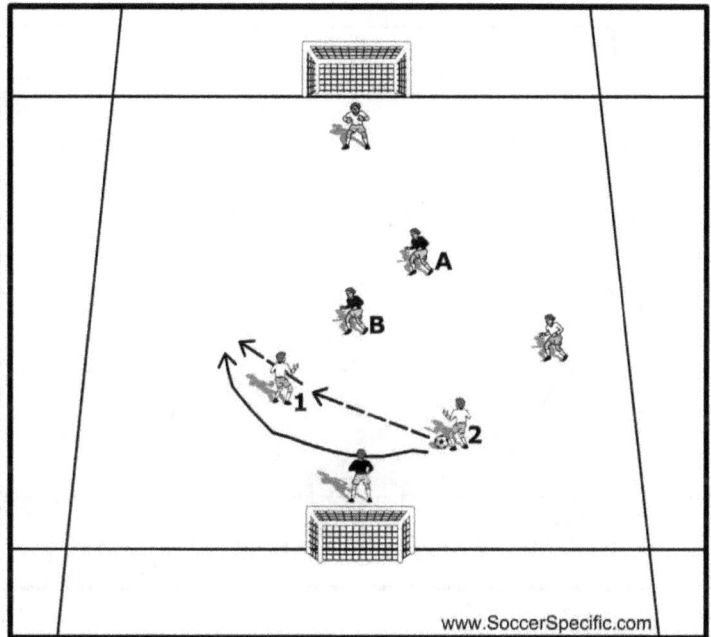

This overload situation provides a good opportunity to practice overlaps, 1 – 2's, diagonal runs in front of the ball and takeovers.

(A) or (B) pass the ball into any of the three attackers and close them down as the ball travels. Try to create a 2 v 1 set up somewhere on the field of play from the 3 v 2 situation. If it proves difficult to set up and execute successfully, start with a 3 v 1 situation then go to a 3 v 2 when it starts to work regularly.

Players can make their plays using each other's movement as a decoy as well as an exchange of possession of the ball.

Playing offside makes this set up more realistic.

Condition the attacking players where they can only score with two touches (or only one touch if possible).

The above set up shows a typical overlap situation. (1) has two choices: to pass to (2) on the overlap or use (2)'s run to take (B) out of position and come inside with the ball, creating a 2 v 1 against (A).

It is important for players to realize (in this case player 2) that they make runs to create space for themselves and also for their teammates.

COACHING STRIKERS

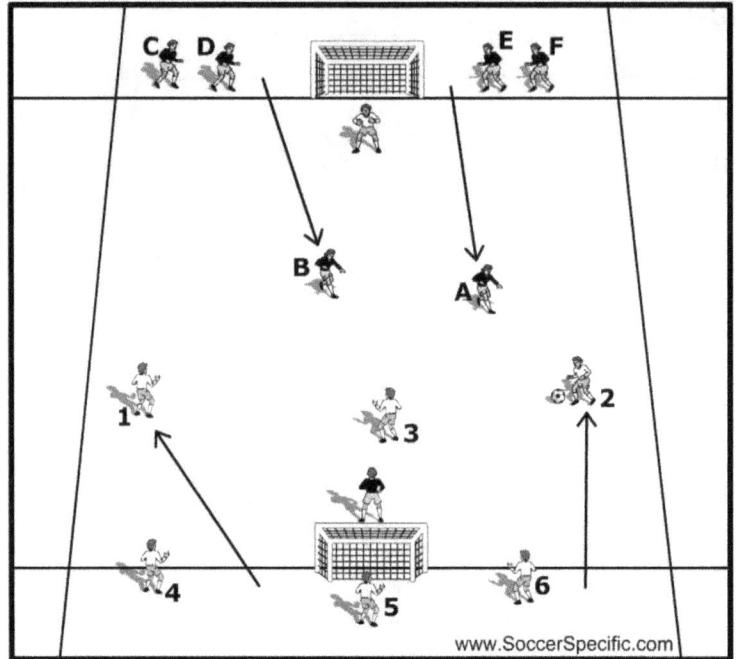

Introduce keepers and increase the size of the goals to make the set up more realistic. You can have keepers in from the beginning also if you wish. With more numbers have the players rotate on and off in 3 v 2 situations. You may need to make a 4 v 2 situation depending on the ability of the players. You can show them tried and tested ways to create overload situations (as previously shown) to begin, then let it go free and see them use their own imagination. Rotate players so defenders get the chance to be attackers and attackers to be defenders. Rotate keepers.

Competitive: Each team has 10 chances to attack and score. An overlap must be performed in each attack, either used as an overlap or used as a decoy. Which team can score the most goals?

Develop: Change the game to a 3 v 3 where it is equal numbers but only when the players are ready for this and can have success with it.

A SHOOTING GAME FROM DISTANCE

1. Technical Training

2. Three teams of 5 with the grid now broken into thirds.

3. This activity is preparing for the next one looking to get a shot hit quickly

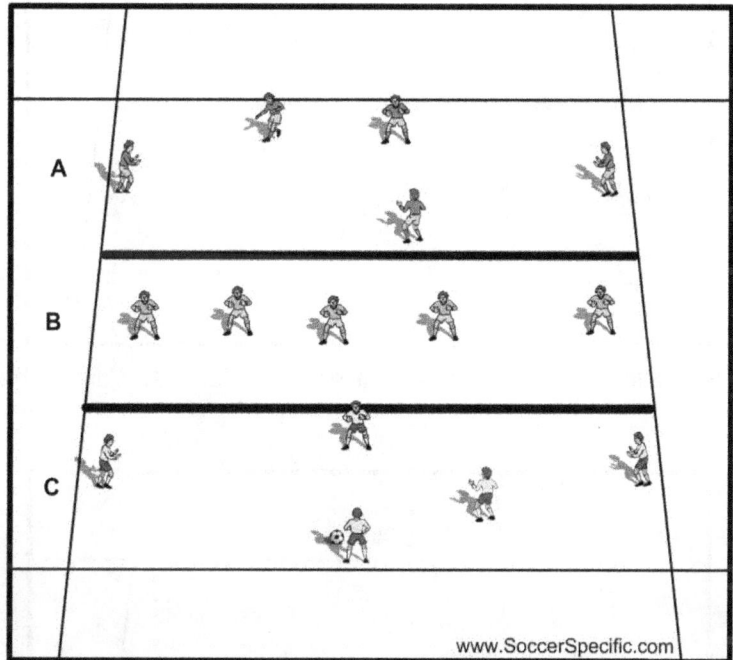

If Team C has the ball one Team B player goes and defends and the rest of the B's spread out and try to block through passes. Team C needs 3 passes and then tries to pass through or over Team B to Team A. If there is a successful through pass, this would count as a point for Team B (points are bad).

Team A is moving, looking to create passing angles. Team C is looking to maintain possession while also looking to penetrate behind the defense and Team B is looking to support defensively.

If Team C loses the ball, a new ball is played to Team A and Team B and Team C swap zones. Team C is now the defending team.

COACHING STRIKERS

Two teams of 5 with a keeper in each goal on a 30 x 40 field. Teams are in their defensive half of the field.

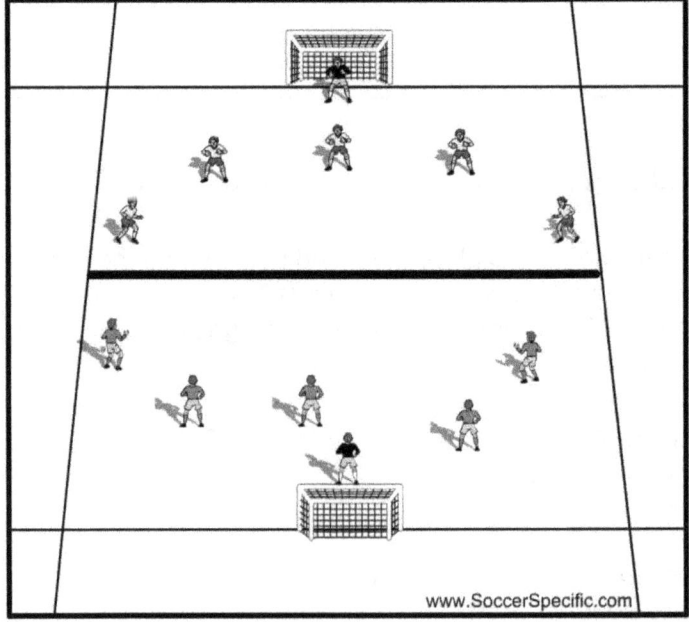

The idea here is for the players to look for quick shots and not try to dribble the ball into the goal.

Each team sends one player into their offensive half of the field. That player stays up there for a two minute period then they rotate another player up top.

Except for during the transition periods, no one can cross midfield. Players can pass to a teammate up front or shoot from behind midfield.

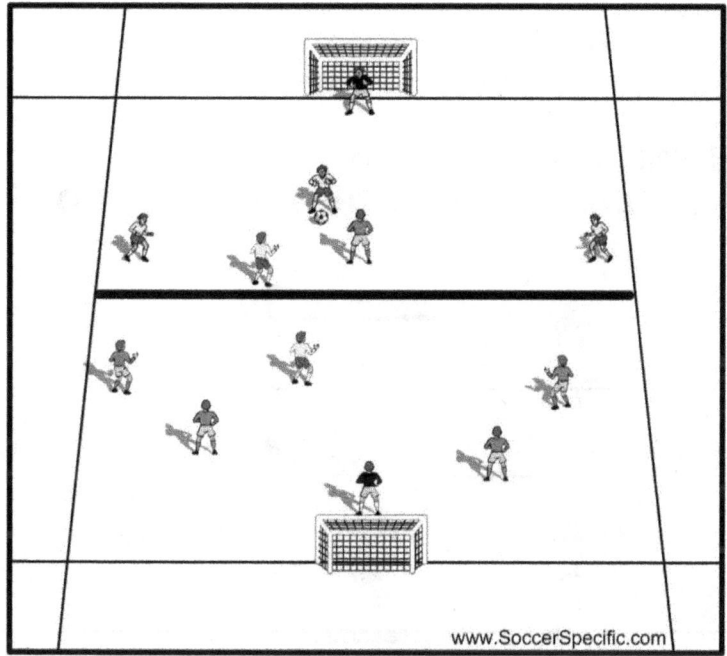

The idea is to either find the player up front for a quick shot or to move the ball around to get a shot from behind midfield.

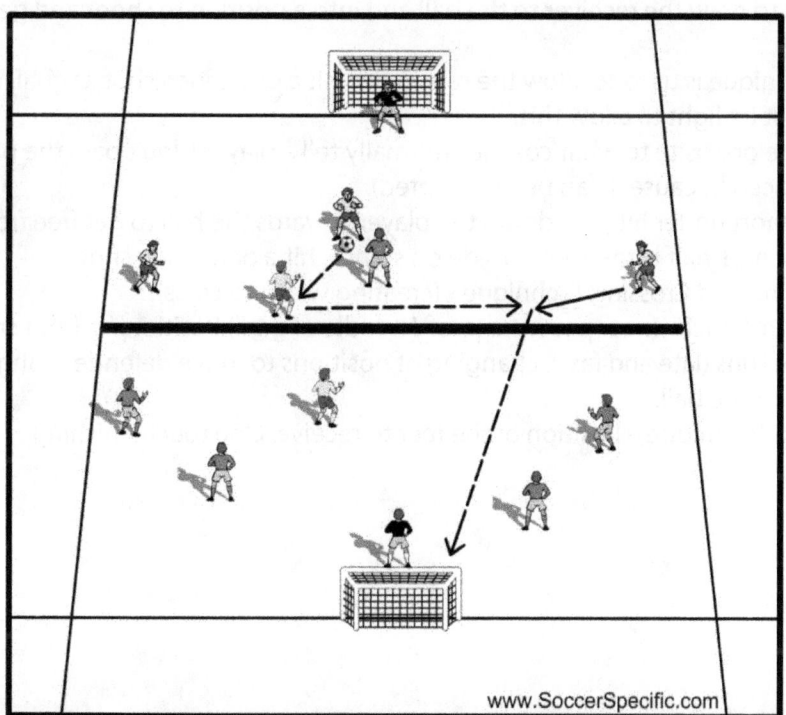

There are two games going on at the same time and each game lasts 10 minutes. Each team will play each other team once.

Small Sided Games
Same field and teams but now the midfield line is removed and it's unrestricted play with an emphasis on quick shots and being willing to shoot from a distance

ONE TOUCH FINISHING IN THE BOX
ANGLE, WEIGHT AND TIMING OF THE PASS IN THE BOX

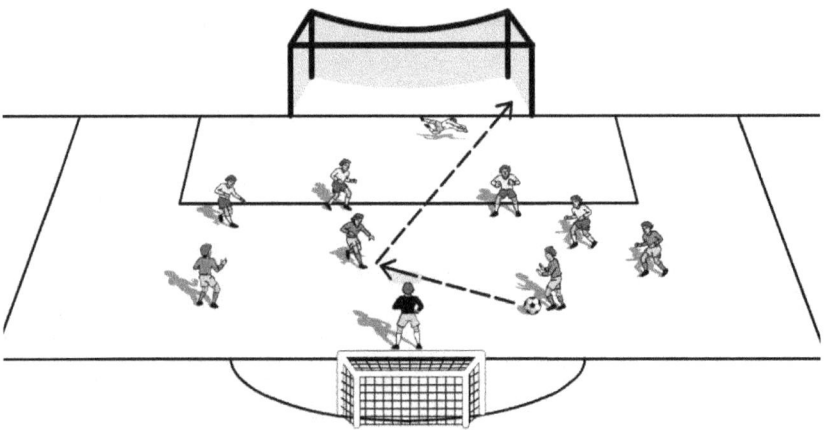

Coaching Points :
- Quality of Passing: Concentrate on the weight, timing and angle of the pass. Under-hit the pass to draw the receiver to the ball and into a position to shoot and get free of the defender.
- This technique is used to allow the receiver to hit a one touch shot at goal. Weight of pass must be light to allow this.
- This is the opposite to what coaches normally tell a player (don't pass the ball short or under paced because it can be intercepted).
- Above; short under hit pass draws the player towards the ball to get free from the defender and, half turned with a side on stance, hit a one touch shot.
- Positioning and Crossing Technique - (creating width to cross).
- Balance in Attack - (near post / far post / middle of goal).Positioning from crosses, timing of runs (late and fast), changing of positions to move defenders, angles of runs, contact on the ball.
- Finishing Technique – Position of the feet to receive. One touch finishing

POSITIONING FROM CROSSING #1

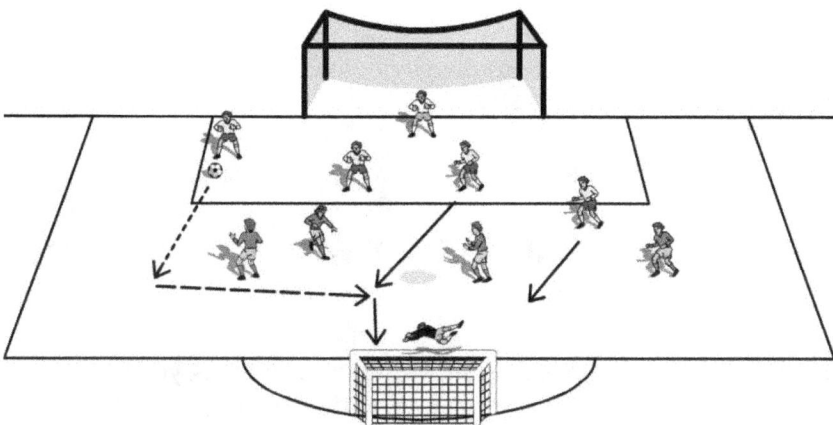

The keeper plays the ball wide and the attackers get in position to meet the cross near post, far post and centrally behind them for the pull back.

Try to finish one touch.

The game is constant attacking play both ways. To make it competitive, count the number of goals scored. Encourage the players to shoot on sight.

Teaching transitions from one moment defending to the next moment attacking, this exercise improves the concentration of the players.

POSITIONING FROM CROSSING #2

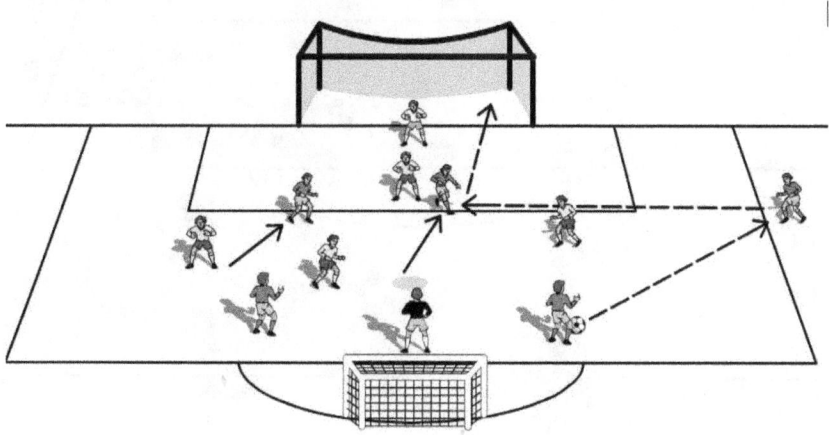

Introduce 2 players on the outside who stay outside the playing area. No one can tackle them so they are guaranteed to get a cross in.

COACHING STRIKERS

This could be a quick play session focusing on crossing and one touch finishing, the emphasis being on a two touch maximum in wide areas to ensure a quick cross into the scoring area.

Players know they only have 2 touches when it goes wide so they work quickly to get into position, expecting the early cross.

This should improve quick decision making as everything is done at pace.

FINISHING IN AND AROUND THE BOX WITH THE 4-2-3-1 DIAMOND ATTACKING SET UP

Use the players on the team in their specific positions at all times, you could have two sets of 3 and 3 as attackers so they learn to switch on to defend also; like defending from the front. A 3 v 3 + 1 attacking and defending game.

Emphasize that the diamond set up, as in the attacking phase of the 4-2-3-1, is between the opponent's back players and their midfield to gain an overload advantage.

Good for teaching strikers how to switch on immediately from attacking to defending. So have 6 attacking players in there unless you want to work on defending.

Build up can be slower using the outside players until the right moment appears. Then it has to be as fast as possible with quick combination plays by the attacking team.

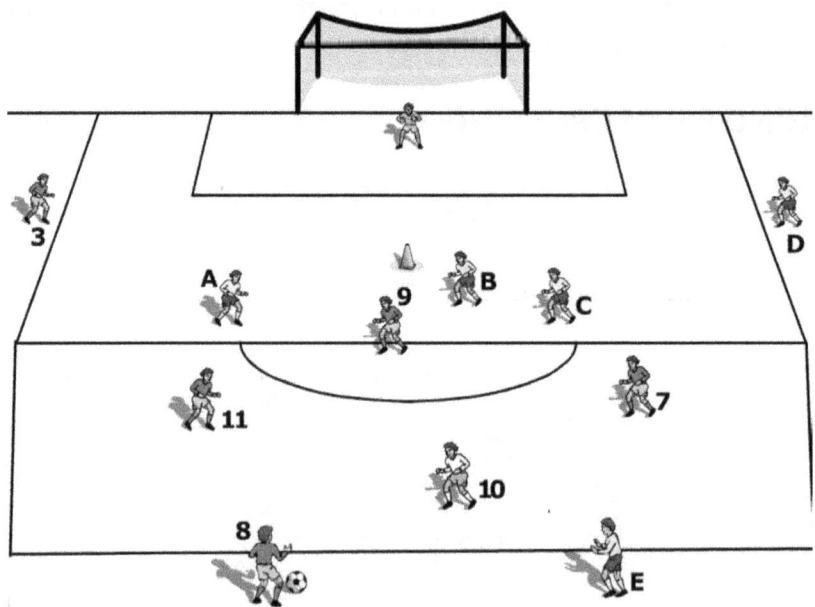

This is a Functional practice, a 3 v 3 + 1 with support players involving Receiving, Turning, Dribbling and Shooting. First priority of the striker is "Can I shoot?". Composure in the box is the key factor. Defenders don't want to concede a penalty, so strikers have more time than they realize.

No conditions to start, but support players stay outside the box. When defenders win the ball they play to the coach or just clear it to outside players. Start again with a new ball to the strikers. Strikers try to receive the ball at an angle so they are half turned and facing the goal so they can get a quick shot in. Others take up positions off this for rebounds etc.

Outside players can be passing a ball around between each other to keep active and when the play is finished inside the box whoever is on the second ball passes it in to restart. They should be looking for quick shots, working off rebounds, combination work, 1 – 2's, quick movement to create space, support play.

Use the cone for an offside line, likening it to the deepest defender, so that inside attacking players can time their runs off it.

So one team attacks the other defends. How many goals can the attacking team score in 5 minutes?

If the defending team win the ball they pass to their own players on the outside (same as winning and keeping possession in a game) who then give the ball to an outside attacking player and the sequence begins again.

Rotate the teams and each team gets a chance to attack for 5 minutes. Add up all the goals scored for either side in the 20 minutes for a combined winning team. Alternatively have two goals at opposite ends so it is more like a game situation.

Rotate the players within each team.

Coaching Points in Shooting and Finishing:
- Make it a competition between two teams. Each team has 15 attempts at goal, see who can score the most goals. Attacking team continue each attempt until the ball is out of play or a goal is scored or the opponents win possession. Rotate the defenders to keep them fresh.
- Here the coach passes to (8) who lays it off for (9) who shoots and scores. (8) and (10) follow the shot in for any rebounds.

Coaching Points in Shooting:
- Positive attitude to shoot, and shoot quickly. On every opportunity try to get a shot in.
- Receive on the half turn if possible (create space for yourself), take the chance
- Accuracy and Power (accuracy first). Be composed.
- Shooting High or Low (low is best because it's more difficult for the keeper)
- Selection of Shot (driven, chip, side foot, swerve etc). You can use defenders to shoot around for placement. Check keeper's position (if time!)
- Near Post or Far Post (can depend on keeper's position. If you shoot and miss at the near post the ball is out of play. If you shoot at the far post, even if it's going wide, a number of positive things can happen: the keeper may palm it to a striker following up, a striker may intercept it on its way and score, (it may hit a defender and go in off them)
- Rebounds (follow all shots in)

COACHING STRIKERS

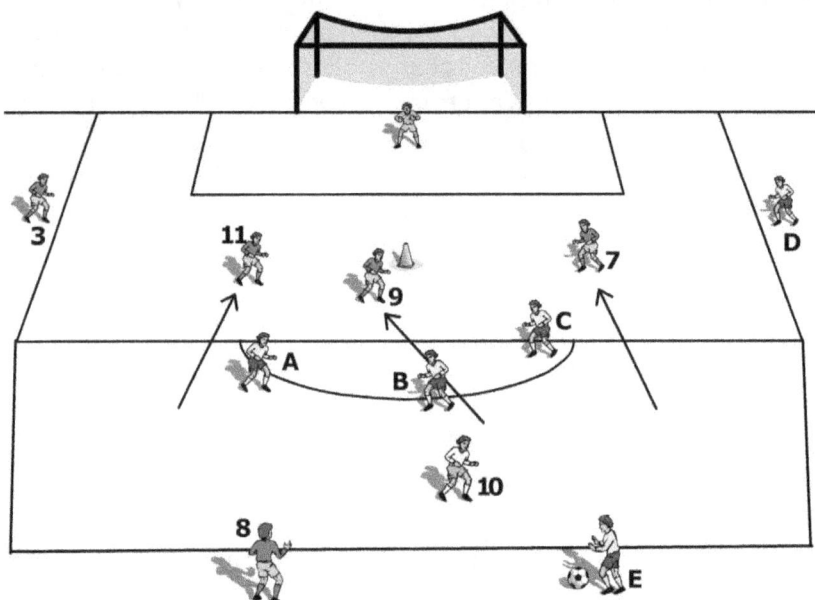

Progression: A 3 v 3 + 1 game but both teams have the chance to score a goal. The coach serves the ball in to each team alternately so they know if they have to create space or mark up. They can use the outside players as support but only their own teammates.

On regaining possession, the ball has to go outside first.

Both teams can attack and both teams can defend, hence constant transitions from defense to attack and attack to defense.

The three moments in the game now come into play; when we have the ball, when they have the ball and when the ball changes hands.

This play is good for quick decision making because of the constant transition. Server passes alternately, telling players first so each team knows how to position (defensive or attacking positioning).

Here we show the transition moment when the ball changes hands and the attacking team immediately switches on physically and mentally into a defending team.

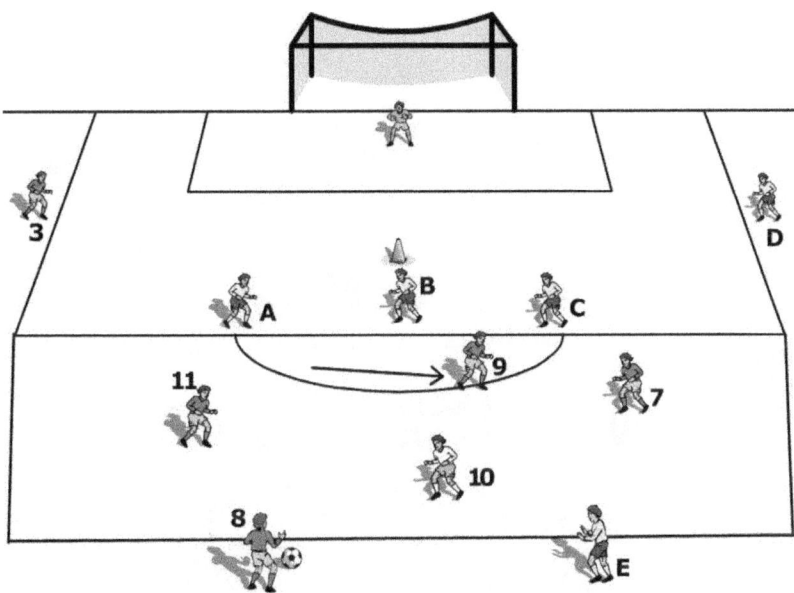

A first simple movement AWAY from the ball by (9) to get "off the shoulder" of defender (B) and find space. It may only represent 1 or 2 yards here but it poses the defender a problem.

Does defender (B) follow and leave the space open where he came from, or does he stay in the space but let (9) go free?

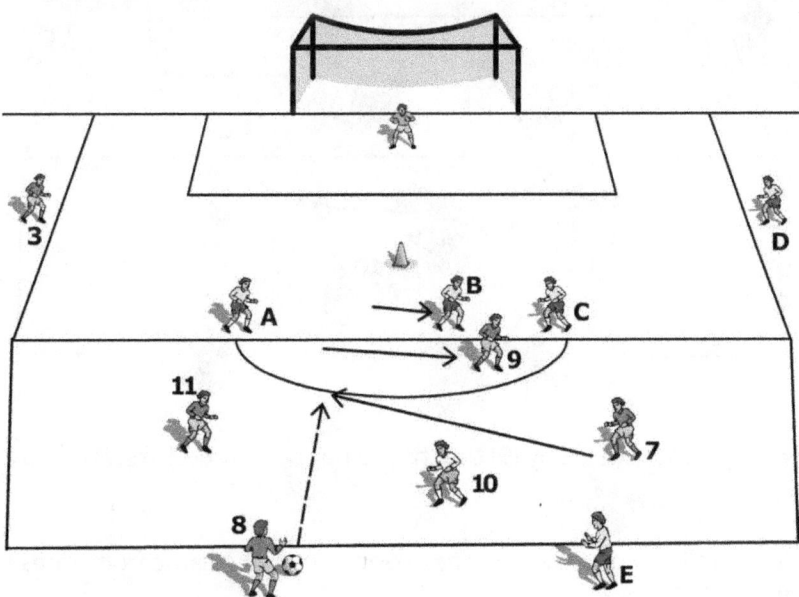

The defender (B) makes an instant decision to stay with (9) and (7) makes a great outside to inside run into the space created. Practice this particular move in training until in the moment of the game itself it becomes instinctive between (9) and (7). Likewise with (11) on the other side.

Alternatively, (9) can check back into the space he created for himself to receive the pass.

COACHING STRIKERS

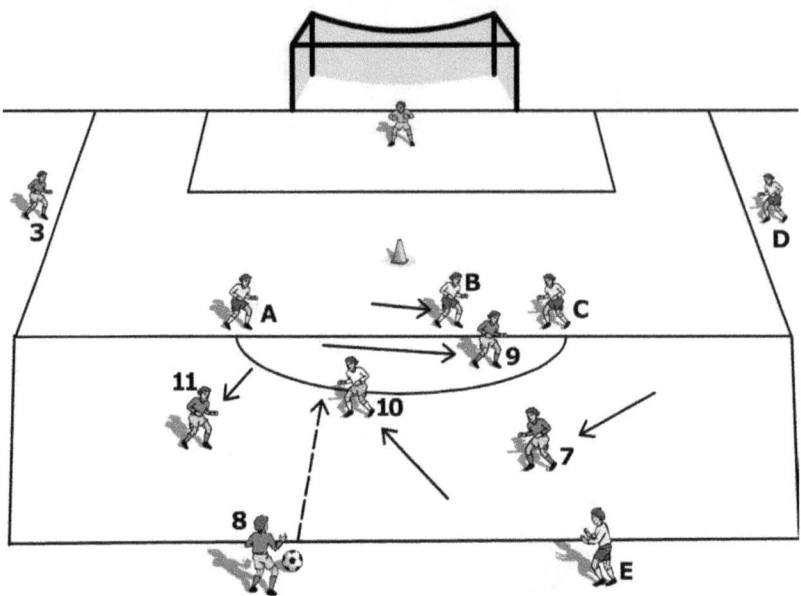

This time it is attacking midfielder (10) who makes the run into the space created by (9).

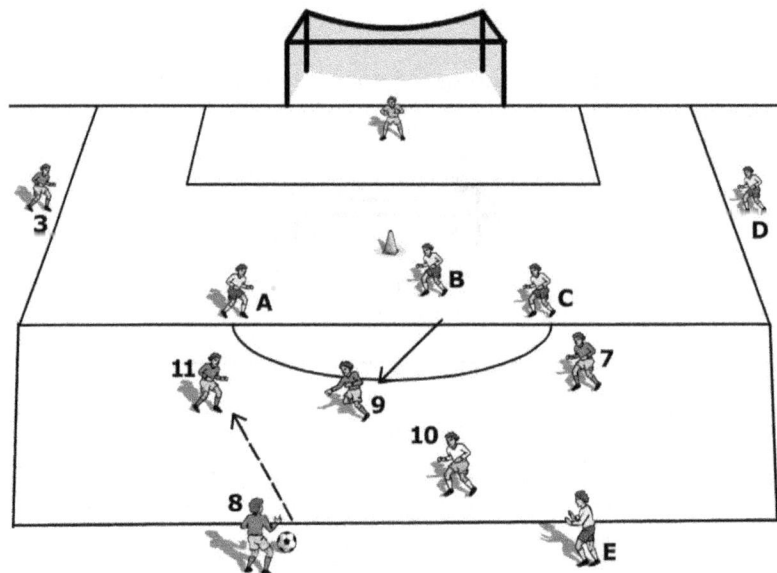

Another very simple movement by (9) that has to happen immediately to find a yard or two of space.

Does defender (B) follow and leave the space open where he came from, does he stay in the space but let (9) go free?

All attacking players, where they can, should be side-on to the goal and the ball to open up their peripheral vision.

COACHING STRIKERS

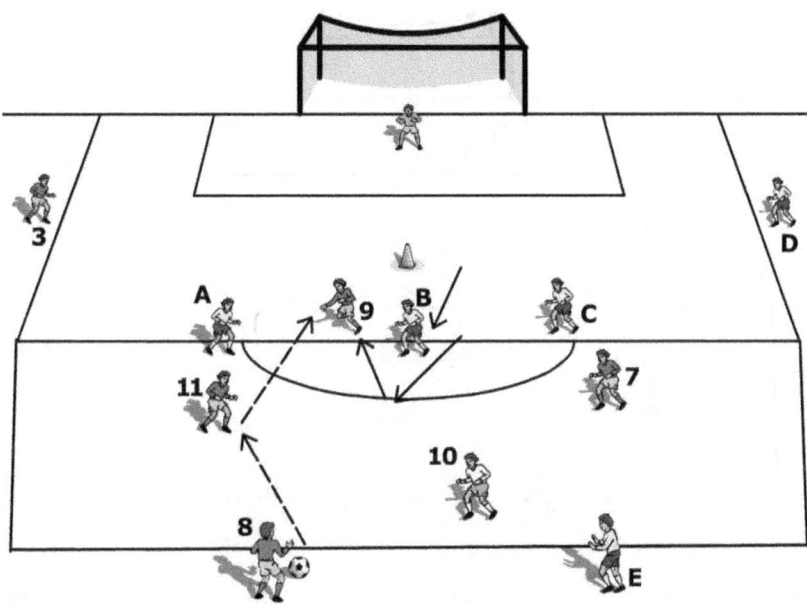

Here defender (B) follows (9) but (9) checks back across the shoulder of (B) into the space left to receive a one touch pass from (11). A short and sharp 2 step movement is required here. This is the Vialli opposite checking run.

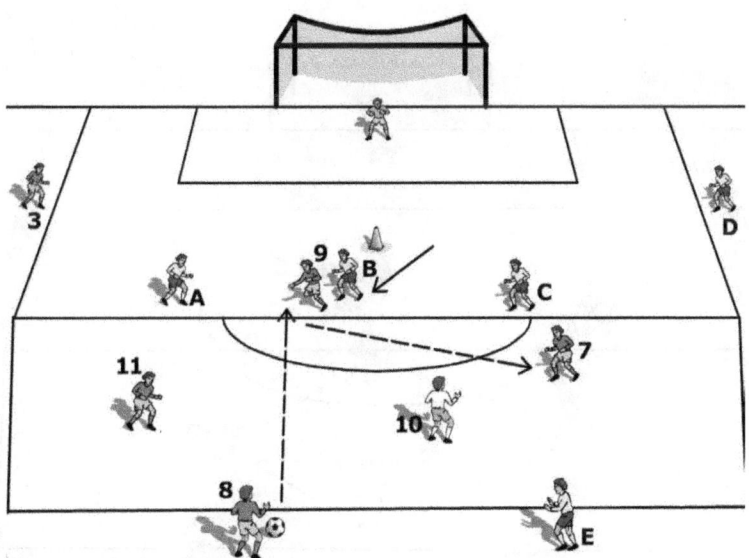

Movement away from the defender and towards the ball to get free, the player is preferably side on as they receive it.

Looking to create 1 – 2's in and around the box and isolate defenders 2 v 1 in our favor. Here (7) and (10) can combine quickly to attack (C).

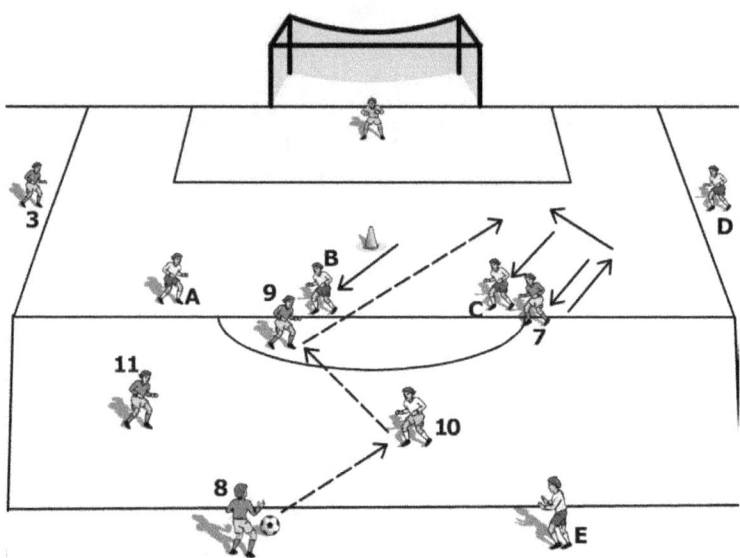

Here, as the ball moves from (8) to (10), player (7) takes defender (C) towards the ball then checks away. At the same time (9) comes off defender (B) to be able to play an angled pass into the path of (7).

Again, something you could work on in training as a set movement between 4 or 5 players.

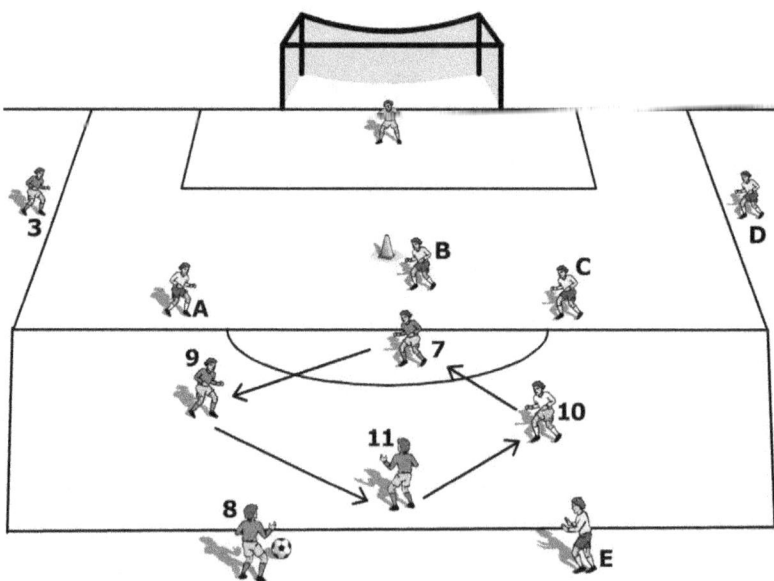

Showing potential interchanges between the 4 attacking players without showing the movements of defenders for clarity.

But you can expect someone somewhere will find some space moving defenders around when it all happens so quickly.

ATTACKING FROM CROSSES

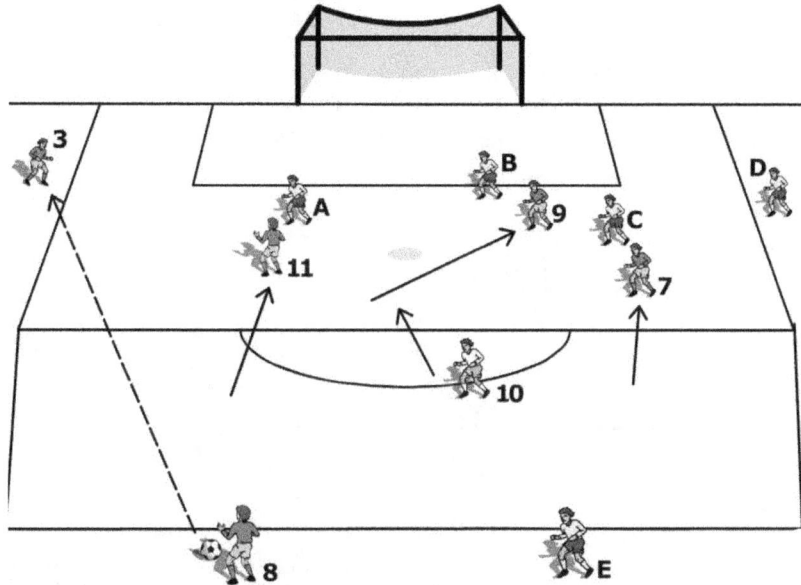

Now crossing and finishing using the wide players. Movements to attack the goal, near post far post, beyond the far post and on the edge of the box for a pullback.

Here the players are well marked by the defenders so how can they get free?

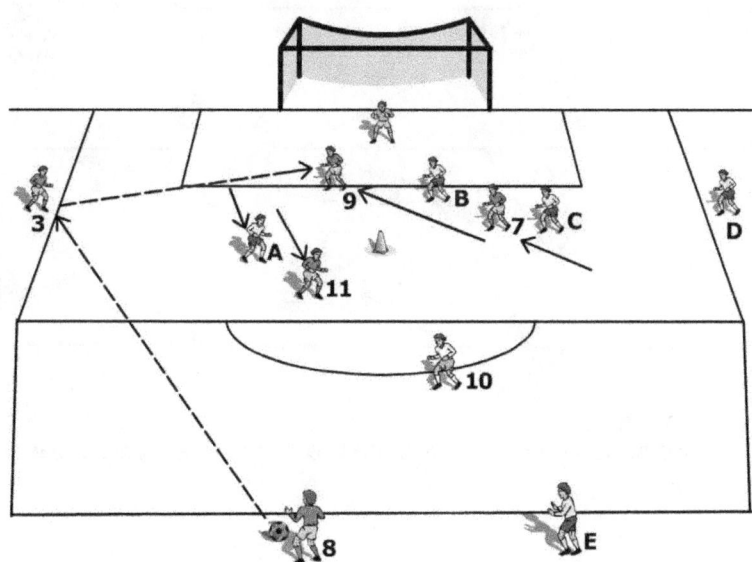

One idea: (11) comes out, takes defender (A) out and leaves the space for (9) to attack far to near. (7) fills the space left and can attack the far post should the ball go past (9).

COACHING STRIKERS

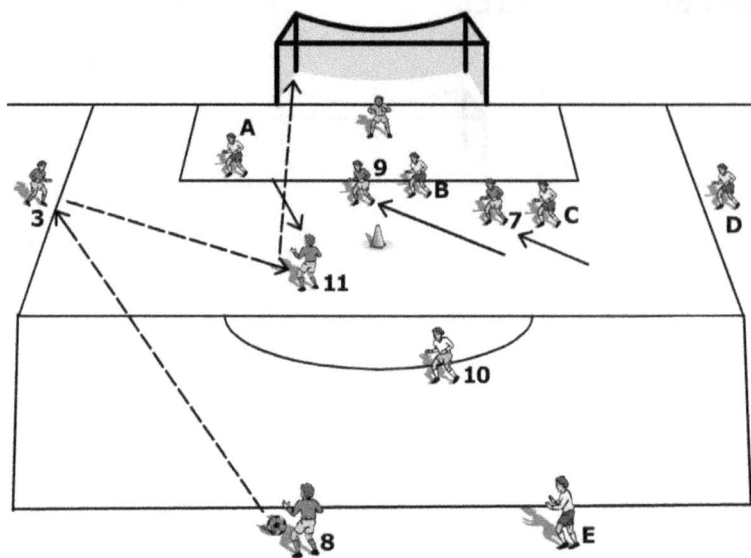

(A) decides to protect the space so there is a chance (11) may get free for a finish as above.

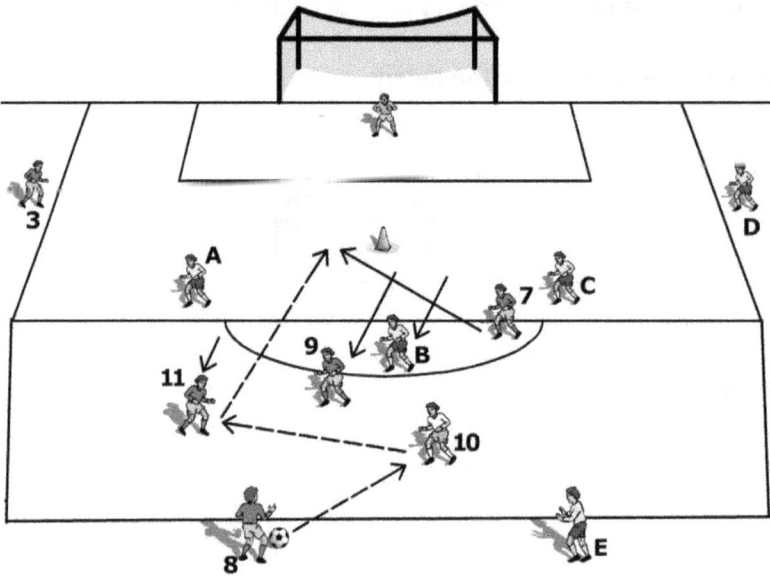

Another idea of combination moves around the box to get free. Everyone working and moving for each other

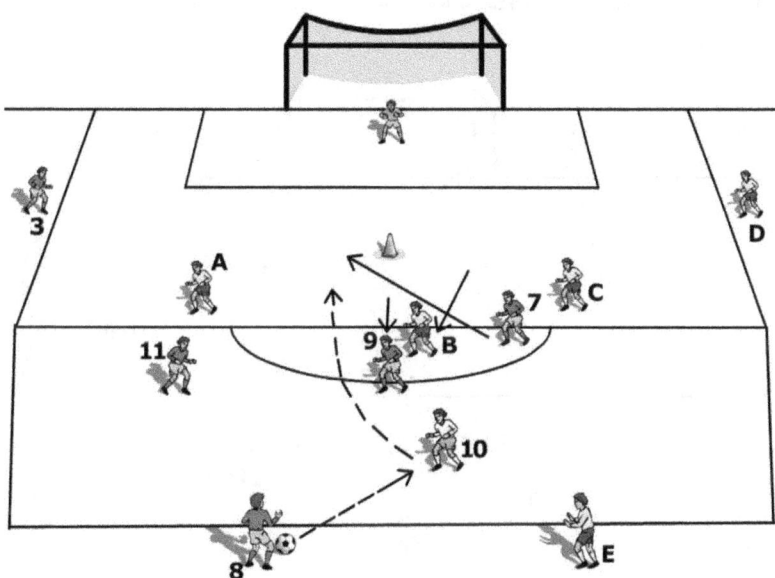

Defender (3) goes with the run of (9) and leaves space in behind. (10) receives and plays a one touch bending pass into (7), exploiting the space created by (9). (7) makes a now familiar outside to inside run across the line of the defenders to stay onside.

Progression: Support players on receiving can pass to other support players to change the direction of the attack. They can also shoot directly at goal and strikers work their positions off this, again for possible rebounds.

As you gain success in a 3 v 3 + 1 situation, even with one and two touch conditions, bring another defender in and play a 4 v 4 to increase the difficulty. Rotate players regularly to ensure quality as this session can be tiring.

Develop: Support players have a ball each and are numbered off. The coach calls a number of a server and the players react. Thinking processes are remembering where the ball is coming from and what to do when you have the ball or the opposition have it. Quick decision making.

Outside players can shoot for themselves. Develop the idea of switching positions from the outside to inside and vice versa. When the pass is made the players switch positions, one going out the other coming into play to link up with the other inside players.

One and two touch play condition to speed up decision making. This now really tests the foot and body preparation as well as the awareness principle of looking before receiving.

MAKING TRANSITIONS AND SWITCHING POSITIONS

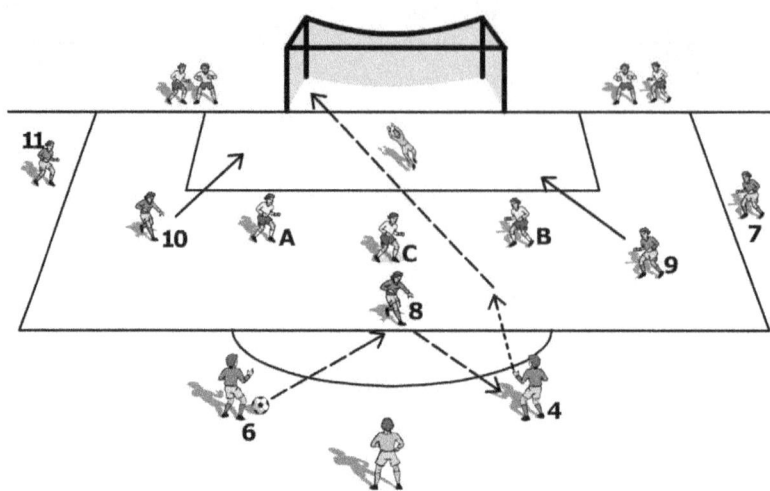

Outside players can shoot for themselves. Develop the idea of switching positions from the outside to inside and vice versa. When the pass is made (for example (8) to (4)), the players switch positions, one going out the other coming into play to link up with the other inside players.

(4) may come into a good position to shoot at goal as above. This is particularly good because the switching movement happens in a game, but also from a coaching point of view it keeps everyone involved in the game.

Overview:
- 3 v 2, 2 v 2, 3 v 3, varies depending on success. Vary number of touches on the ball.
- Outside players can pass another ball whilst action is inside (two balls working).
- Having both teams attacking the goal emphasizes transition/changing of possession
- Outside players can pass to each other and also shoot for goal (support the strikers).
- Outside players transition positions with inside players on receiving a pass from them.
- Bring in outside players so e.g. 4 v 4 or 5 v 5 inside the box, intensive work, good for seeing who can make quick decisions, who has good control of the ball etc.
- Position players inside the box, two strikers centrally and two players wide and supporting midfielder inside the edge of the box centrally for layoffs so they are working from a shape.

A 3 v 3 ATTACKING AND DEFENDING TRANSITION GAME

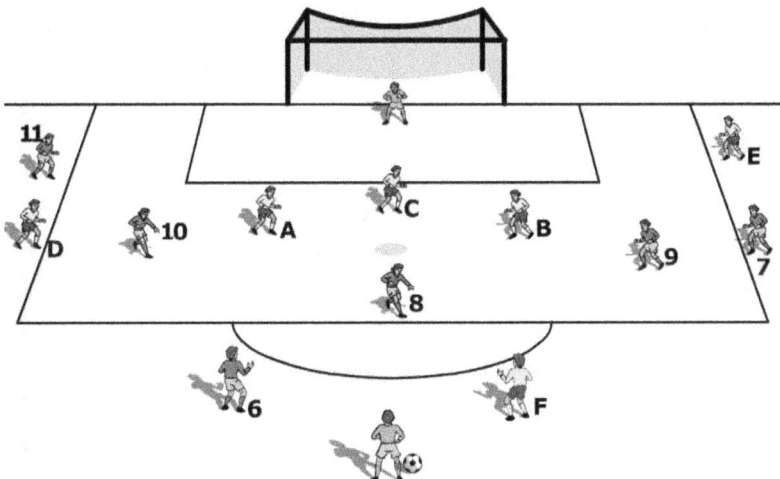

A 3 v 3 game in the middle, one team attacks the other defends. How many goals can the attacking team score in 5 minutes?

If the defending team win the ball they pass to their own players on the outside (same as winning and keeping possession in a game) who then give the ball to an outside attacking player and the sequence begins again.

Rotate the teams and each team gets a chance to attack for 5 minutes. Add up all the goals scored for either side in the 20 minutes for a combined winning team. Alternatively have two goals at opposite ends so it is more like a game situation.

Rotate the players within each team.

Good for teaching strikers how to switch on immediately from attacking to defending, so have six attacking players in there.

Progression: One touch play condition to speed up decision making. This now really tests the foot and body preparation as well as the awareness principle of looking before receiving.

Further Progression: A 3 v 3 game but both teams have the chance to score. The coach serves the ball to each team alternately.

They can use the outside players as support but only their own teammates. Both teams can attack and both teams can defend, hence constant transitions from defense to attack and attack to defense.

The three moments in the game now come into play; when we have the ball, when they have the ball and when the ball changes hands. Develops quick decision making.

Server passes alternately, telling players first so each team knows how to position (defensive or attacking positioning).

COACHING STRIKERS

CHANGING THE POINT OF ATTACK THROUGH THE DIRECTIONAL FOUR GOAL SWITCHING PLAY SMALL SIDED GAME

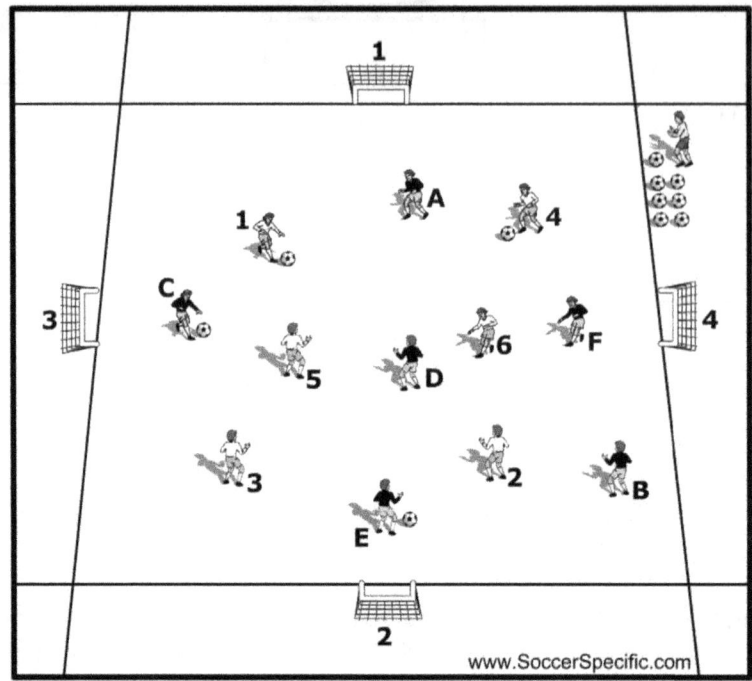

40 x 40. Two teams passing and moving with a ball each team. Initially have one team attacking goal (1) and the other team goal (2). Coach calls "switch" and they attack different goals.

Progression One:
Team (1) to (6) passes trying to score in goal (1) then (2). Team (A) to (F) passes trying to score in goal (3) then (4). Still playing through each other but going in different directions. Next each team can attack two goals (opposite goals) at once.

Looking to switch play attacking two goals, players decide when to switch the ball, and which goal to attack. Have a one or two touch shooting condition so the timing of the passing and the timing of the movement into position to shoot are correct.

Progression Two:
- Use two balls per team so they can attack two goals at once if necessary.
- Introduce goalkeepers in each of the four goals to make it more competitive. Have a constant supply of soccer balls to keep the game moving.

We are looking to include all the main coaching points in this awareness session. Call "switch" as they are playing so they attack the opposite two goals. We are developing quick thinking decision-makers. Ultimately have a competitive game between the two teams using the various rules and conditions above.

COACHING STRIKERS

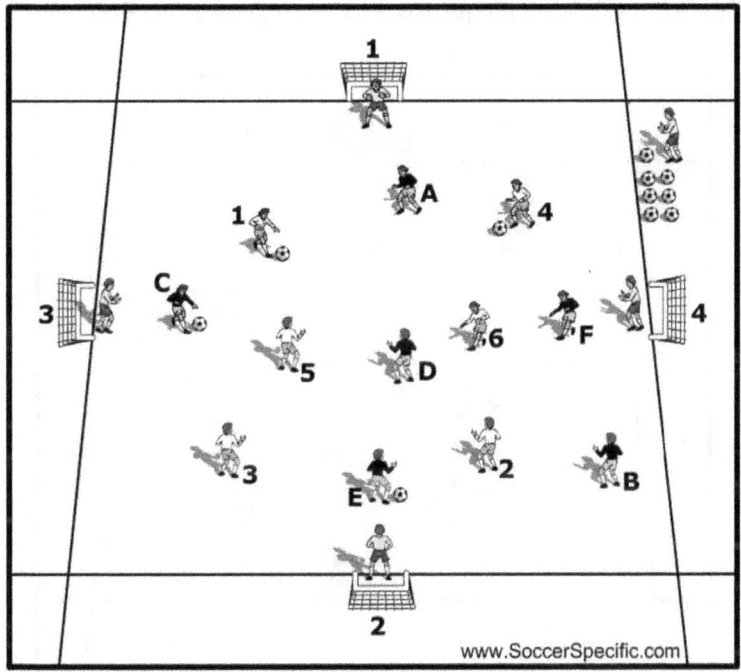

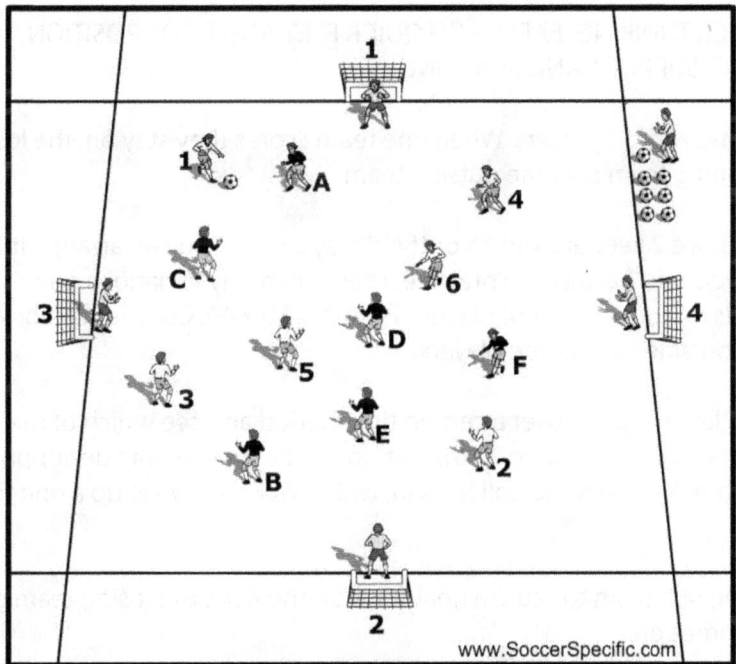

Coaching Points:
- Two directions to attack so quick decisions needed as to which one to go in
- Awareness of space in front and behind (if the player needs to change the direction of attack)
- Quick transition. Having scored in one goal, players must now change direction to score in the other goal.
- On gaining possession there is a choice of going to either goal, so quick decisions on which one to attack.

COACHING STRIKERS

AN AWARENESS THREE TEAM PASSING AND FINISHING GAME

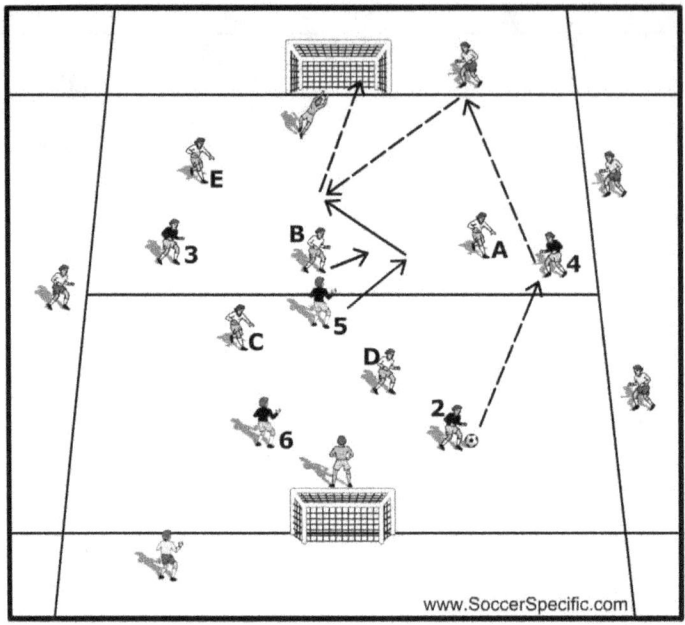

FOCUS ON QUICK THINKING, EARLY AND QUICK FEET AND BODY POSITION, 1 AND 2 TOUCH PASSING; SUPPORT AND FINISHING

Three team game with 17 players. When one team scores they stay on, the losing team go off and the winning team play the outside team.

It's great if you have 2 keepers and 15 outfield players but you can arrange it based on the number of players you have at the practice. There are many variations on this theme. Size of field depends on the number of players. Here it is 50 x 40. Coaches can be one touch players on the outside to help the players.

Competitive: Play the game over a certain time period and see which of the three teams scores the most goals in that time. In this set up it is best if the outside support players have only one touch to pass the ball back in, which will usually set up a one touch finish to goal.

Alternatively the first team to score a goal stays on the field, the losing team goes off and the 3rd team comes on.

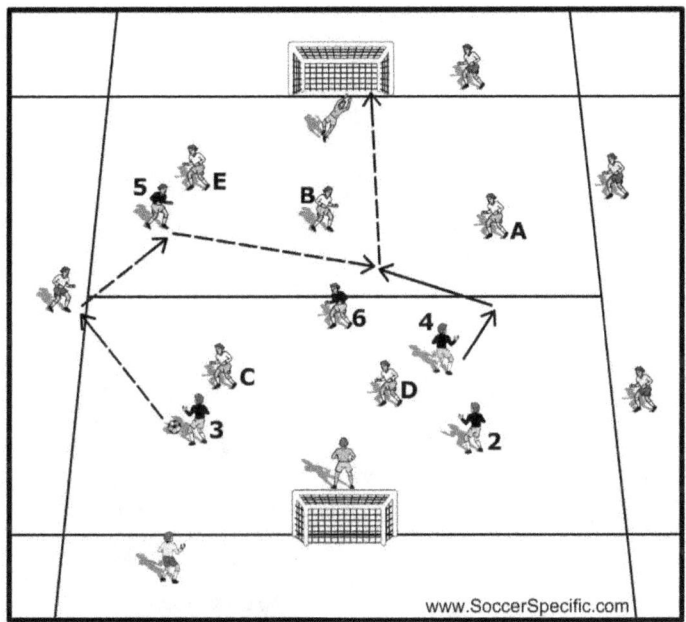

15 players to work with so 5 on the outside, one of which will be a keeper for this outside team when they get into the game.

Here (C) blocks a pass to striker (5) from (3) so the outside player is used in a support position to get the ball to (5). (4) loses the defender (A) and gets a layoff pass from (5) to score. This is just one example of many situations that can be created by this game plan.

Coaching Points:
- Thought processes on and off the ball
- Feet and Body positioning before receiving the ball
- Quality of Passing especially weight of pass if a 1 and 2 touch condition
- Quality of Support and Movement "off the ball"
- Quality and Speed of Finishing
- Effective Team Play

COACHING STRIKERS

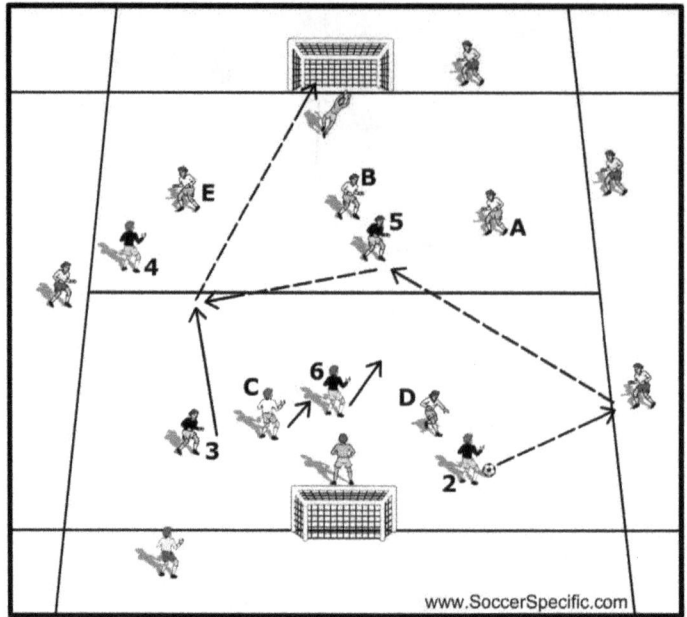

Outside players have two touches to begin, then we go to one touch only. Inside players begin with three touches, then go to two touches, then go to one and two touches (one touch is encouraged but only if it is on to do so).

As the outside players have only one touch, the inside players passing to them have to think, before they pass the ball, about weighting the pass and making it accurate, so the outside player can pass it back in successfully with one touch.

To be successful, the outside player must, before receiving the ball, view the field and see where the players are (own players and opponents).

The player or players able to receive this next pass back inside from the outside player must make sure they are available to receive the next pass by getting into an open position to receive in front, behind and to the side to help the outside player, knowing the outside player has only one touch.

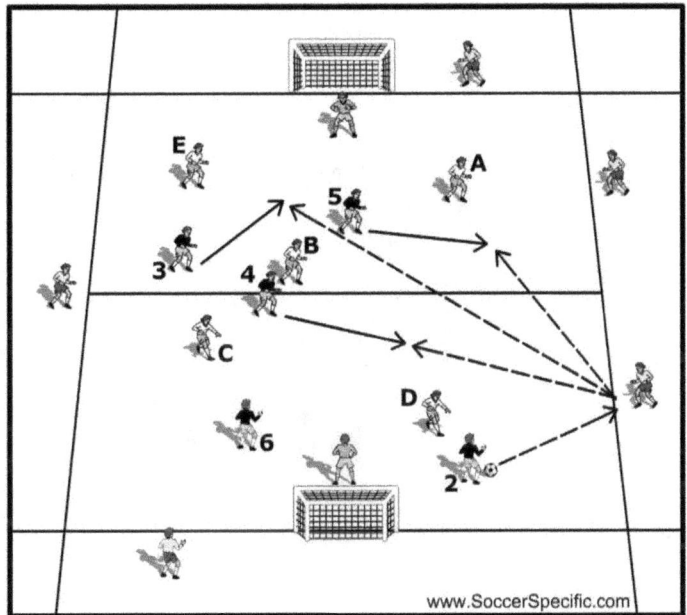

Player 2 has two touches so must pass the ball quickly to the outside player who is available to receive the pass. The outside player has only one touch so to make the next pass successful, three things have to happen:
1. The pass has to be accurate, but more importantly the weight of the pass has to be such that it is easy for the player receiving the pass to make a one touch pass on;
2. The player receiving the pass has to know his options for the next pass before receiving the ball;
3. The players in the team need to get open to help the player receiving the pass, knowing he'll only have one touch to move the ball on. So they need to be on the move to find space to receive before the outside player receives the pass.

Good communication is essential between the players here.

In the diagram, players 3, 4 and 5 have given the outside player three options, but also the passing player 2 can receive the pass back, so he must also be available.

Alternatively (if allowed depending on the rules for the game you impose) the outside player can pass directly to another outside player; though this for me makes it a little too easy.

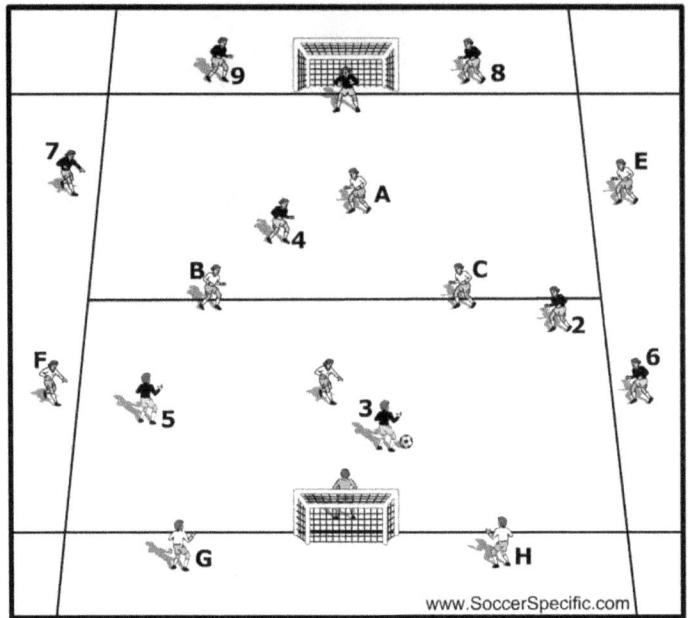

18 players and a 4 v 4 game with side players to support and goal line players for 1-2's to set up shooting chances. You can vary the number of players playing in the game.

Players on the outside need to keep on their toes. Game lasts until players begin to tire (or first team to score, losing team off). Rotate outside players in, inside players out.

Progressions:
- Outside players 1 or 2 touch restriction on the ball.
- Inside players touches restriction on the ball.
- Player passes to outside player and switches, gets the players thinking especially if it is when the player coming in has only 1 touch so must immediately find a player.
- Occasionally bring in all the players so it's a 9 v 9 with the keepers. This tests how they play in a restricted space with more players to deal with.
- Reduce the size of the area to 40 x 20 and go 4 v 4. This gets more shots on goal.

A CROSSING AND FINISHING SMALL SIDED GAME

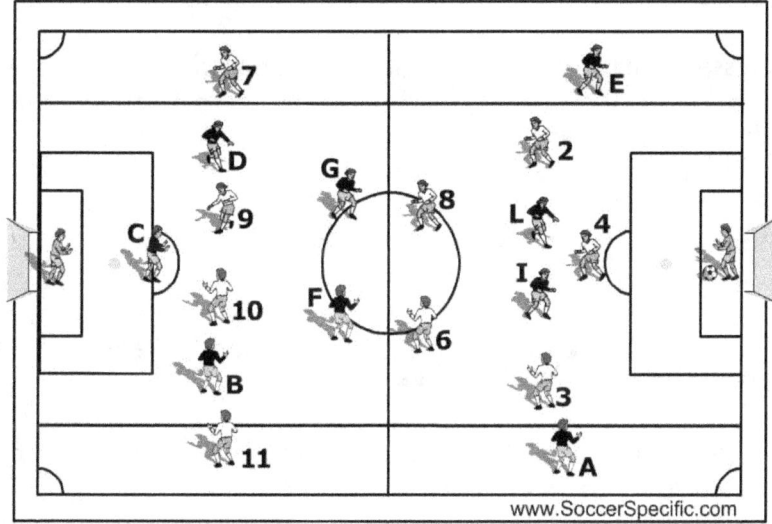

Working both ways. This is a quick transition play session using wide players as the focal points to ensure we get lots of crosses in.

You can overload areas. For instance, if your players are particularly poor in finishing have only one defender against two attackers and so on.

You can determine any strategy you like and tailor the session to the number of players you have to work with. Here we have 20 players working constantly.

Wide players perform in channels and no defenders can encroach into these zones, ensuring a constant supply of crosses both ways.

They stay in the attacking half of the field. The field is short and tight to make sure lots of crossing and finishing takes place at both ends of the field.

Coaching Points in Crossing and Finishing

Head Up – Glance from the crosser to know where the players (attackers, defenders, and the keeper) are. Sometimes they don't have time to do this, they just get the ball into the danger area and expect players to be there.

Decision – When, Where and How to cross. Cross as early as possible to give defenders as little time as possible to get into a good defensive position.

Technique of the Cross –
- A good first touch out of your feet to set the cross up but looking also to where the ball is going and where the attackers are to receive the cross.
- Balanced position with the non kicking foot alongside the ball pointing in the direction you want the cross to go. Use of techniques to produce the type of delivery below, kicking through the ball with correct timing.

Types of Cross –
- Crosses that are driven low with power (usually to the near post).
- Swerved crosses. For example, around a defender using the body position as a guide (near or far post).
- Chipped crosses from the goal line (usually to the far post).
- Longer, higher trajectory crosses to the far post and past it (to opposite wide player who can shoot at goal or head or pass it back into the danger zone).
- Pull back crosses or passes to a midfield player coming in late.

Runs of the Players – Near post / Far post, away from the ball initially to come back if possible (to lose markers). When a striker runs away from the ball the defender has the problem that when he looks at the ball, he can't see the player he is marking or that player's movement; when he looks at the player, he can't see the delivery of the ball. Anticipation of where the ball will arrive is key.

Timing of the Run – As late as possible and as fast as possible (so you are difficult to mark plus you don't get into the correct position too early). The player making the near post run must use the post as a guide. If he runs past the near post to receive then it's difficult to get a shot or header on target. Try to time the run so the ball is arriving as you are arriving, then it's a straight shot or header. The only time the near post runner should run beyond the near post is when he is trying to pull a defender out of position to create space for a teammate coming in behind.

Angle of the Run – Into the line of the crossed ball, not across it.

The Attacking Finish – Contact on the ball is probably one touch only using the head or foot. Use the momentum of the crossed ball for power. Almost let it hit your foot rather than aggressively swinging at it.

EXAMPLES OF TYPES OF PLAYS

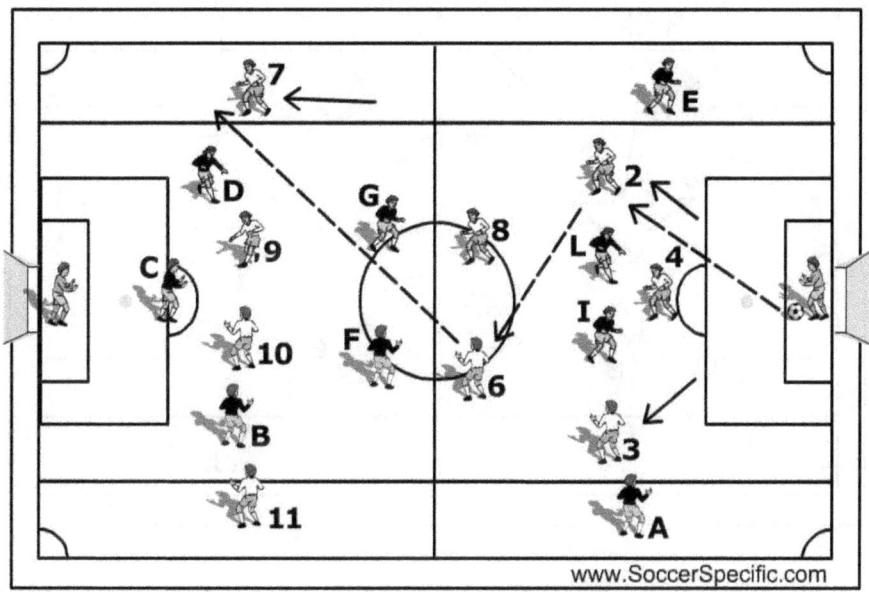

Here we see the following passing sequence: Keeper to full back, a diagonal pass to a midfielder who passes to a wide player to cross.

Another possibility: Keeper to full back to a striker who is closed down and can't turn, so he plays the ball wide for a cross. Look at movement of strikers and support players.

If the ball is played into a striker who can shoot, even if it hasn't gone wide yet, he should shoot as that is the right decision.

Generally work the session using width but not to the extent where decisions become false.

COACHING STRIKERS

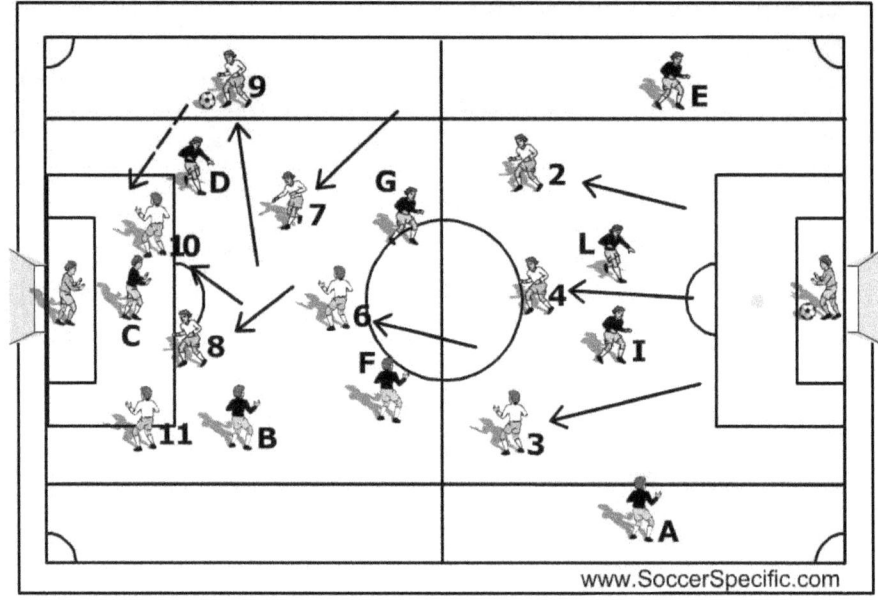

Here is an example of a striker (9) moving wide to receive a pass to end up crossing the ball.

(8) runs to attack a far post cross. Striker (10) becomes the near post area player.

(11) attacks beyond the far post, the initial passer (6) attacks the central area around or just inside the box, (7) moves into an anticipation area around the box also, and the attacking defensive players (2), (3) and (4) all move up the field as does the keeper, maintaining their compactness as a team from the back to the front.

GAME CONDITIONS
- Start with the keeper who serves the ball to the wide defenders creating space breaking wide. They must find a wide player with a pass; it can be a player on the same side or a diagonal pass to the other side. Wide player gets a cross in.
- The ball to midfield players then to wide players.
- The ball to forwards, then to wide players.
- To forwards who must link with midfield with a pass who must then pass to wide players. You can mix this up depending on how you want to play. It helps focus the players' minds on how to pass and support and who to pass to and support. Finish with free play and see how they do it for themselves.
- Teams must stay in their thirds to get an idea of team shape but can work up to the edge of each third of the field. Once a clear shape is established, let it go free and observe movement between the thirds. See if players fill in for one another. For example, if a defender makes a run forward does a midfield player fill in? Where does the defender recover to when that team loses the ball?
- To ensure teams work up and down the field, condition the game so the team in possession can't score unless the defenders of that attacking team are up and over the defending third line. Play offside from this line. This pushes midfield players forward into anticipation area positions closer to goal, thus creating a better chance to regain possession should a defender head the ball clear.

- Crossers only have two touches to make them concentrate more on their first touch, which sets them up for the cross.
- Have no one in wide areas but when they go in to receive a pass or run the ball in they are unopposed. Once the cross is made they come back into the game. This ensures most players get a chance to get in wide areas to cross. For example, if a forward makes a run wide, the second forward and wide midfield player become the two forwards to receive the cross (or maybe a full back gets into a crossing position).

SIDEWAYS ON / FACING UP STRIKER POSITIONING IN A SMALL SIDED GAME

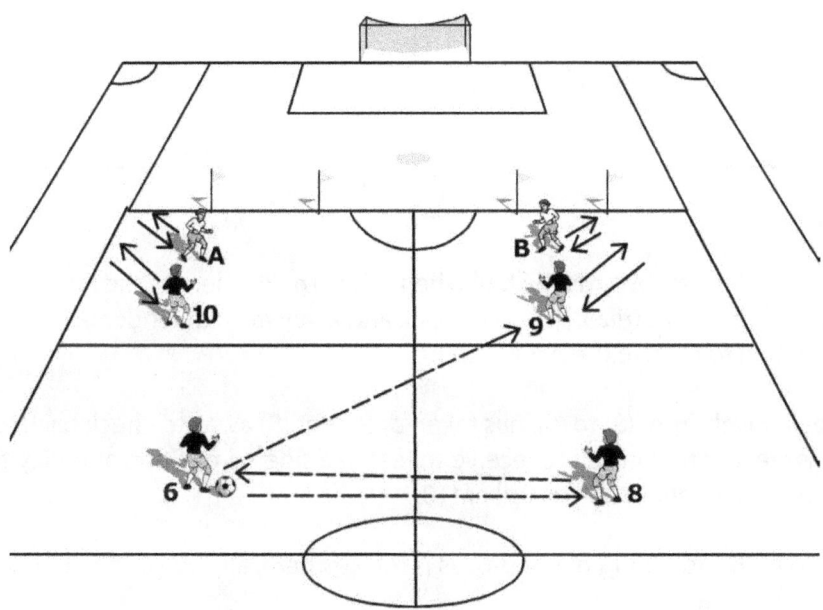

Playing to two small goals. Passing forward has to be diagonal.

Coaching Points:
- Simple movements; checking away to come back; create space to run back into and take the defender away from the space.
- The strikers' first priority is to get faced up to their defender and to the goal, not with their backs to goal as they normally set themselves up.
- Their movements OFF THE BALL help create this space for themselves.
- Too many strikers do not move until the ball is delivered. They should have already moved defenders around before the pass is made.

DEL PIERO MOVE:

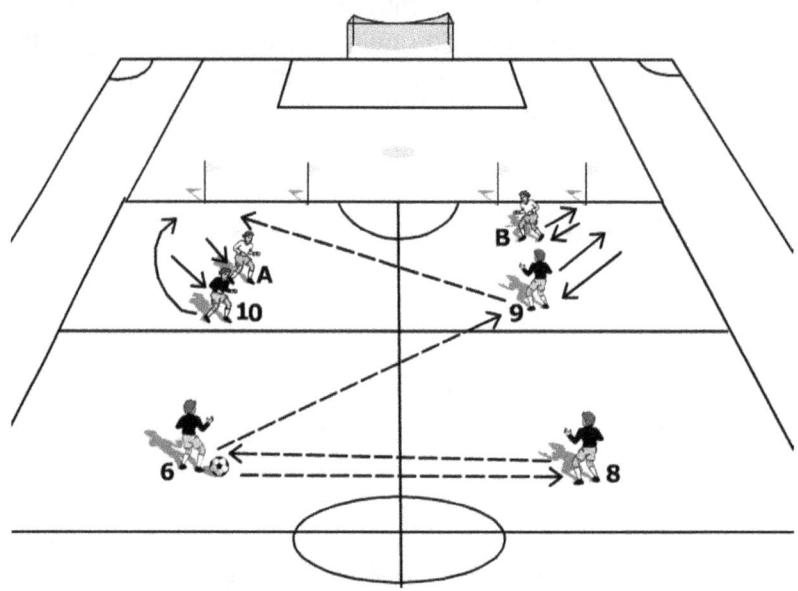

(10) draws the defender towards the ball when it is with (8). Then, as the ball is passed to (6) and is traveling to (9), striker (10) spins back and away from defender (A) and into the space behind him to receive the pass from (9).

(9), as the ball travels from (8) to (6), has taken defender (B) away to check back to the space he has created for himself to receive to feet in a side on position and play the ball inside and behind defender (A) for striker (10).

Timing of the runs and timing of the passes is the key here, all have to be in sync with each other.

COACHING STRIKERS

VIALLI MOVE:

(10) checks away, taking (A) with him, then checks back to receive the ball to feet facing forward (if he has created enough space for himself to do so).

This is happening as the ball is traveling from (6) to (8), as previously mentioned but worth mentioning again to reinforce the point. Too many strikers do not move until the ball is traveling to them and so fail to create space either for themselves or, as we will see later, for their teammates.

If they move defenders into unfavorable areas one or two passes before it gets to them, they will have more chance of success.

(10) gets free to lay the ball off to midfielder (6), and again (6) has had to move OFF THE BALL to be free to receive (in a game situation).

(9) in the meantime also has moved towards the ball, taking defender (B) towards the ball, creating space behind and off the shoulder of (B). Now (6) plays a pass over the shoulder of (B) for (9) to run onto and score a goal.

This OFF THE SHOULDER movement is a classic movement all strikers need to learn.

Striker (10) checks forward to come back, striker (9) checks inside to go outside.
If they can play quickly, one or two touch maximum, they are more likely to have success as it gives the defenders less time to think and react.

COACHING STRIKERS

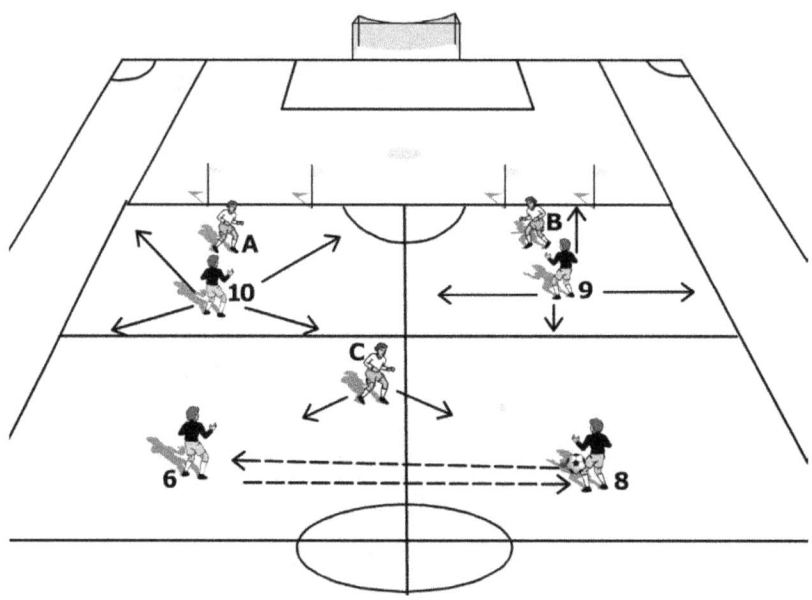

Now we have a defender (C) in the game to pressure the two central midfielders.

COACHING POINTS:
- Midfielders passing but looking at the movements of the strikers (Awareness)
- Movement of the strikers off the ball
- Types of runs
- Timing of the runs
- Angles of the runs
- Timing of the passes
- Angles of the passes
- Combination plays between strikers
- Combination plays between strikers and midfielders

FOUR GOALS

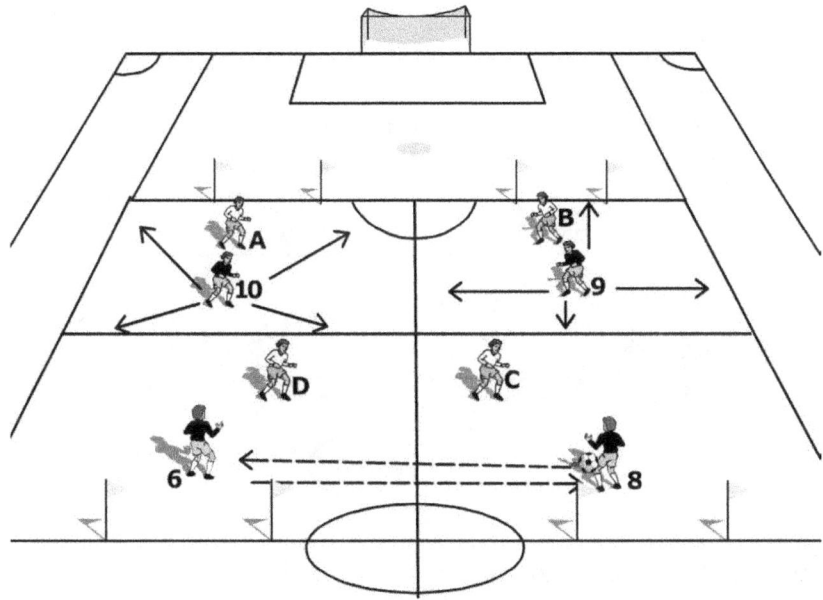

Bring in two more small sided goals. Now you can develop this idea with two sets of strikers so you are educating 4 strikers at once going both ways. Plus you are training central midfielders (or center backs) to both attack and defend.

COACHING STRIKERS

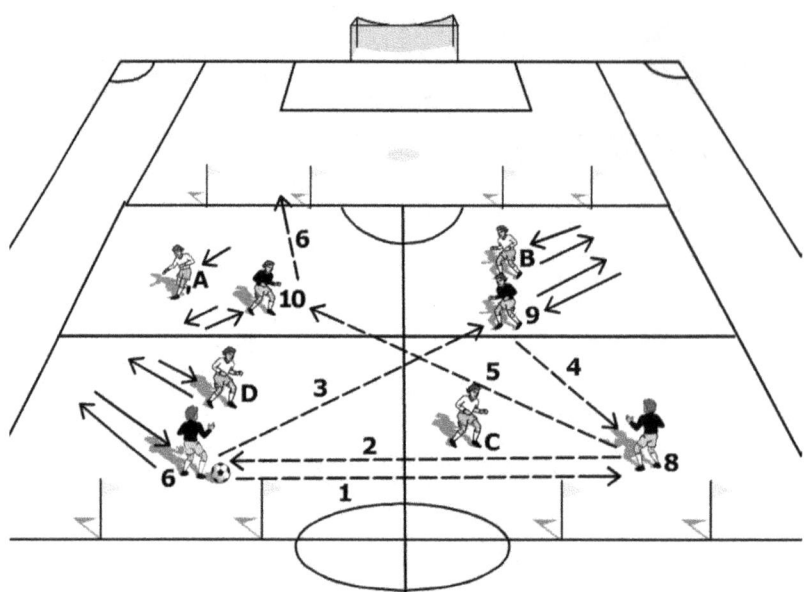

All players moving OFF THE BALL to create space. I have numbered the passes for clarity, going from 1 to 6.

(10) takes defender (A) wide to create space inside to check back into. First he moves OFF THE SHOULDER of (A) to invite a pass into his feet or behind (A). (A) then checks to (10), leaving space inside. (8) sees this run and passes inside to (10) who is now in space to receive the ball and score.

So the routine of passes is (6) to (8), back to (6) until a space opens to pass forward. (9) creates space to receive to feet half turned and sideways on, but let's say (B) stops the forward pass to (10) directly. In this case, (9) lays the pass off to (8) who plays the ball into the path of (10) to score.

ALL TIMING OF RUNS AND PASSES HAS TO BE PRECISE.

USING FULL SIZE GOALS

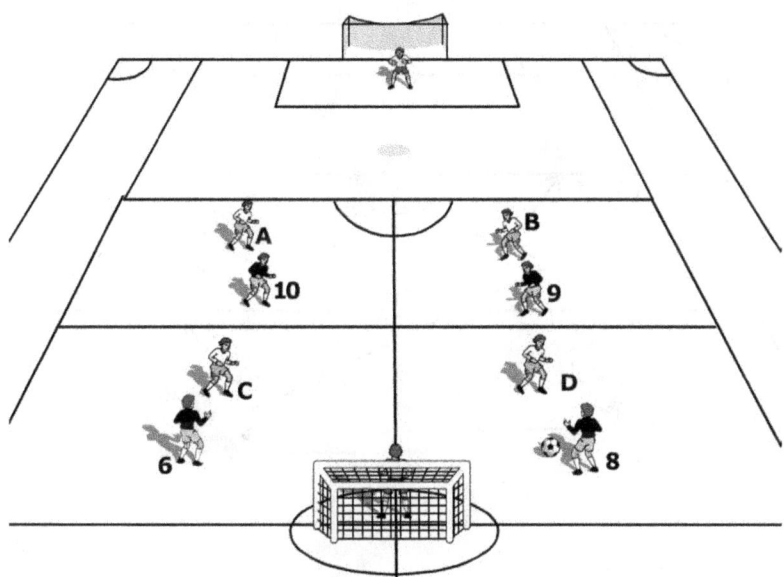

Now we bring two full size goals in; or if you want you can do one full size goal and two small goals going the other way if you want to focus on one particular pair of strikers.

In this case two goals with keepers so we are now game realistic.

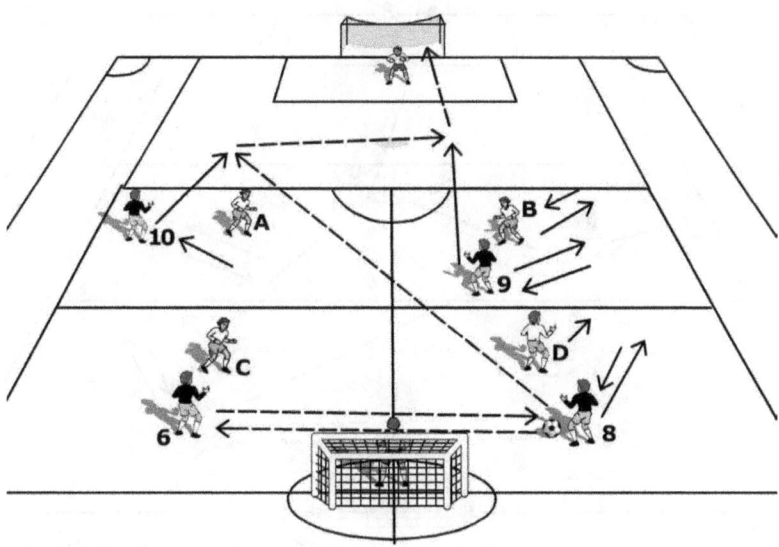

OFF THE SHOULDER MOVEMENT of (10) works well here as (A) stays centrally and is vulnerable to the ball over his shoulder and in behind.

In the next phase of play (9) has gotten free of defender (B) with good movement and is facing forward, allowing him to make a forward run and link with (10) to score.

DEFENDER DROPS OFF TO PROTECT THE SPACE BEHIND

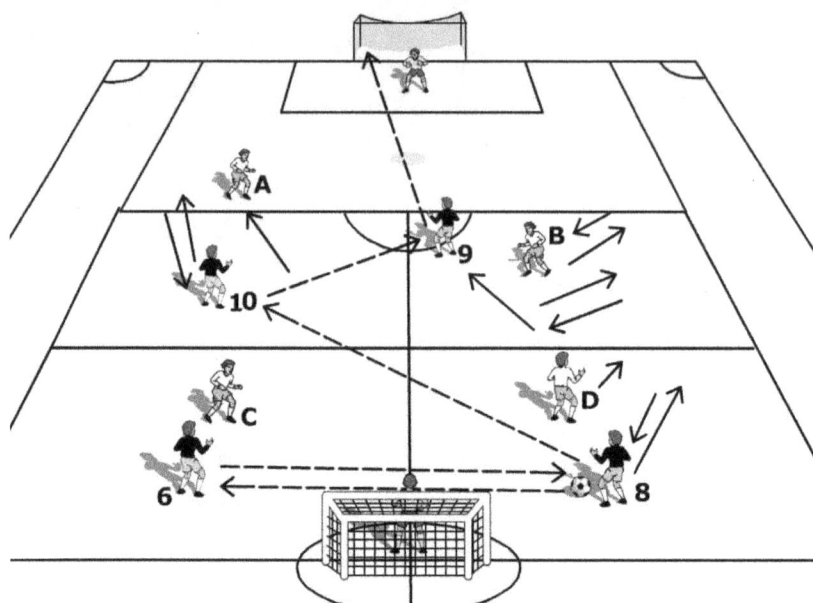

(10) again checks away to get OFF THE SHOULDER of defender (A), this time defender (A) realizes he is vulnerable to the ball in behind and DROPS OFF INTO THE SPACE to stop the pass there.

This is the cue for (10) to check back and receive the ball to feet to both face up and pass forward to (9).

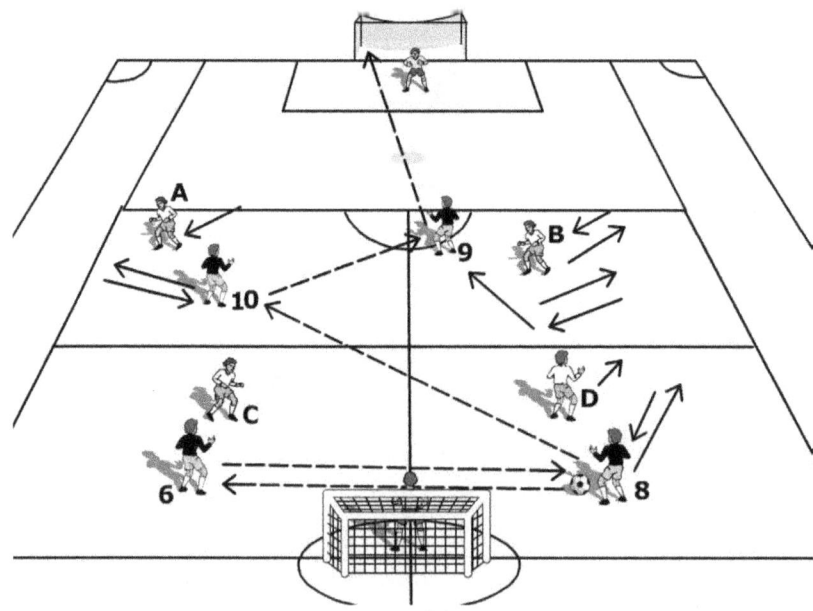

(10) now takes defender (A) wide to create space inside to check back into. First he moves OFF THE SHOULDER of (A) to invite a pass into his feet or behind (A); (A) then checks to (10), leaving space inside.

COACHING STRIKERS

Develop 1: Add more corridors (zones) so you can have three strikers and three midfielders supporting them, and more variety of movements. Now using 14 players.

Have 4 corridors (zones) to play in with 18 players total.

Develop 2: Have it game realistic with a back four and 2 strikers going both ways and now movements by strikers are between fullbacks and center backs.

STRIKERS CAN NOW INTERCHANGE AREAS

RULES:
1. Diagonally forward passes only
2. Movements in front but defenders man-mark
3. Movements in front and defenders mark zonally
4. Movements in front, players make runs short and long (opposites)
5. Movements in front, players make runs wide and inside (opposites)
6. Before the switching runs, the first striker goes short to go long (or long to go short) for himself in behind or in front to receive the pass.
7. Same movements but now doing it for the 2nd striker with the switch
8. Develop 1: If they make the switching run in front then the midfielder can make a straight pass (timing is imperative).
9. Develop 2: Switch from the front to the back and from the back to the front
10. Develop 3: Can switch diagonally from the front to the back, or back to front
11. Take out the zones and let it go free and let players work the runs and passes out without any conditions.
12. Man marking to show how movement can affect players

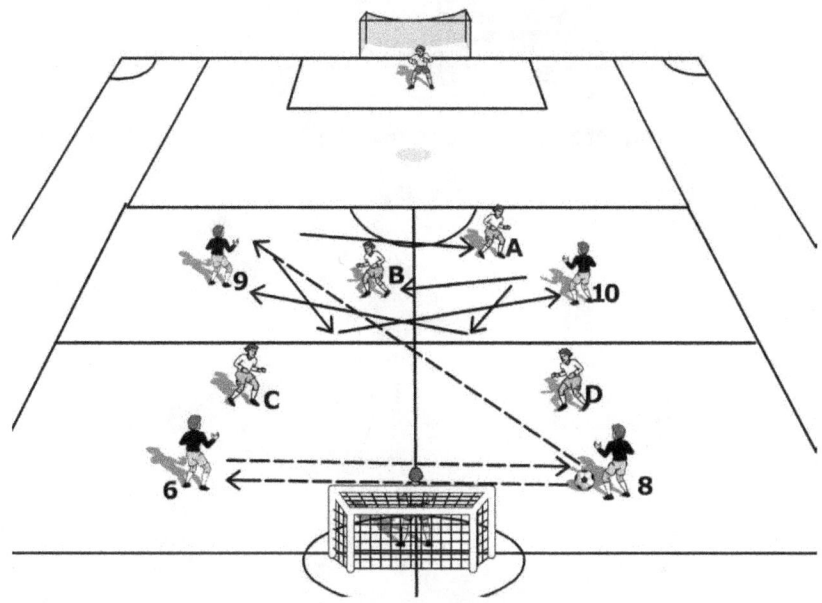

Develop 1: Players can change corridors but the same passing rules apply; no straight passing in your own corridor. So, midfield two do not change corridors, front two can change corridors to begin; then all players can.

COACHING STRIKERS

This opens up even more opportunities for diagonal passes into side-on receivers and diagonal and short and long movements, especially when it is attacking players (strikers) making the movements. They may work long and short between each other.

Develop 2: Have the defenders stay with the strikers so they man-mark them.

This creates all sorts of options for the strikers when they make their movements. (5) can play to the feet of (3) or into the channel and space to (4).

If they both lose their markers they are in. Each player's movement creates space for the other one to run into.

Timing of the pass and the run are important as always. Here (10) makes the first run, leaving the space for (9) to run into in order to receive the pass.

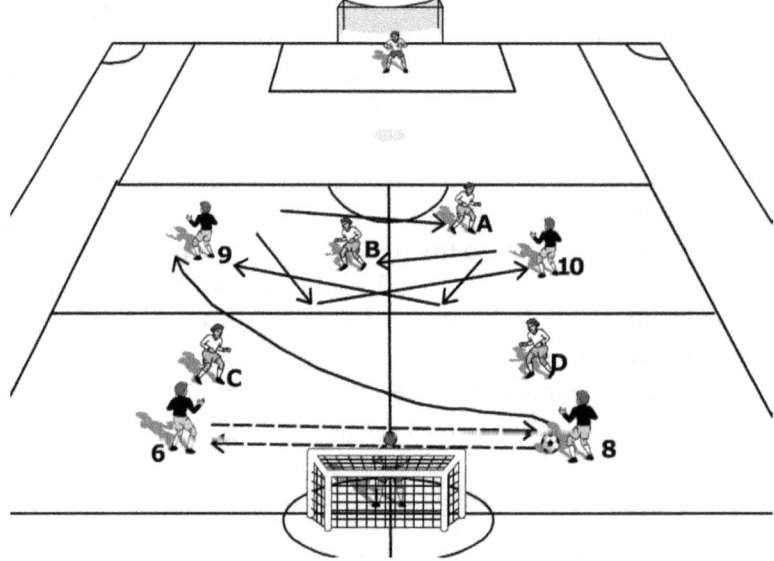

Player (8) can bend the ball around into the path of striker (9).

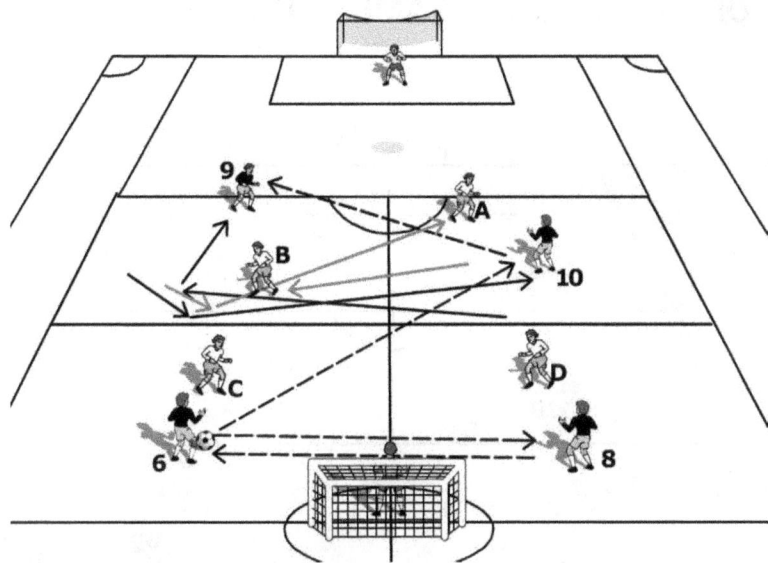

We have a finishing game incorporating movement of the strikers.

(10) goes inside, defender (A), per the rules of the game, must go with him. This opens up the space centrally for (10) to run into for a pass from (8) and make a diagonal pass to (9) who continued his run to score a goal.

Develop: Zonal marking so players have to make more intelligent runs now. Simply exchanging positions won't affect the center backs as they will just pass each player on. Runs must be away or towards the ball, or even into wider positions to begin in order to move the defenders initially and then they can switch positions.

Eventually let them all go free to see if players continue to make switching movements with each other.

COACHING STRIKERS

SIDEWAYS ON TRAINING IN A GAME SITUATION

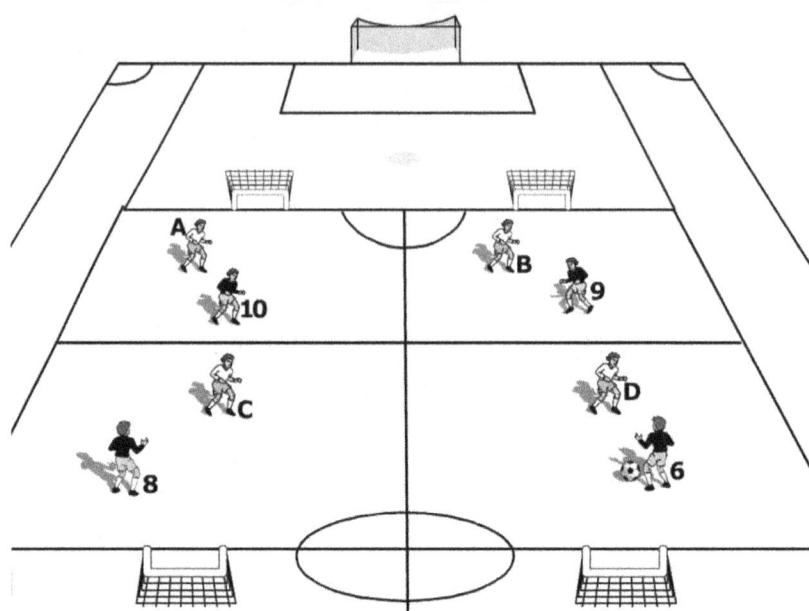

Two corridors to play in; first touch is free for in this case (10) and then on the first touch defender (A) can close him down.

FUNCTIONAL AND PHASE OF PLAY STRIKER WORK

A CROSSING AND FINISHING FUNCTION

This session is a functional practice aimed at improving and developing attacking patterns from wide positions. It starts off with no opposition and gradually builds in numbers as the patterns progress. Each progression is performed for 5-10 minutes continuously. Eventually an 8 v 8 game is played.

It is not recommended that this session be used with young or inexperienced players since a high level of skill execution and tactical awareness is required.

Players are organized on a half pitch as shown. Groups are: (B, C) central midfield players, and (A, D) wide midfield players. A supply of balls is placed with the coach. A goalkeeper(s) is positioned in goal.

The setup is replicated on the other half of the pitch so that 2 groups are going simultaneously. The assistant coach maintains the flow of this second group.

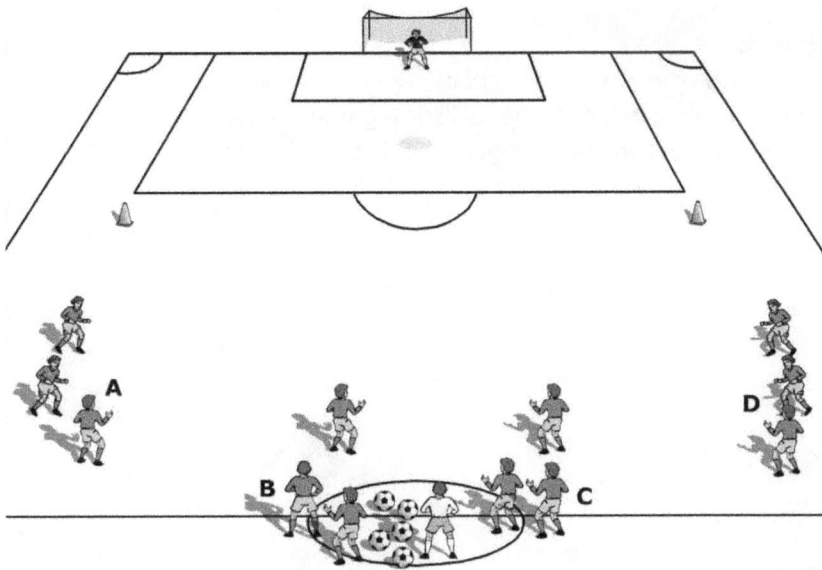

The pattern begins with a pass from the coach to either central midfield player.

The central midfield player must receive the ball in a half-turn and quickly pass to the wide midfield player.

The wide midfield player must "drive" down the line before crossing into the box.

COACHING STRIKERS

The central midfield players and opposite side wide midfield player must attempt to get in the box for the cross.

The next group of players begins on a pass from the coach. Alternate sides – play is continuous on coach's command. This pattern is illustrated on the next diagram.

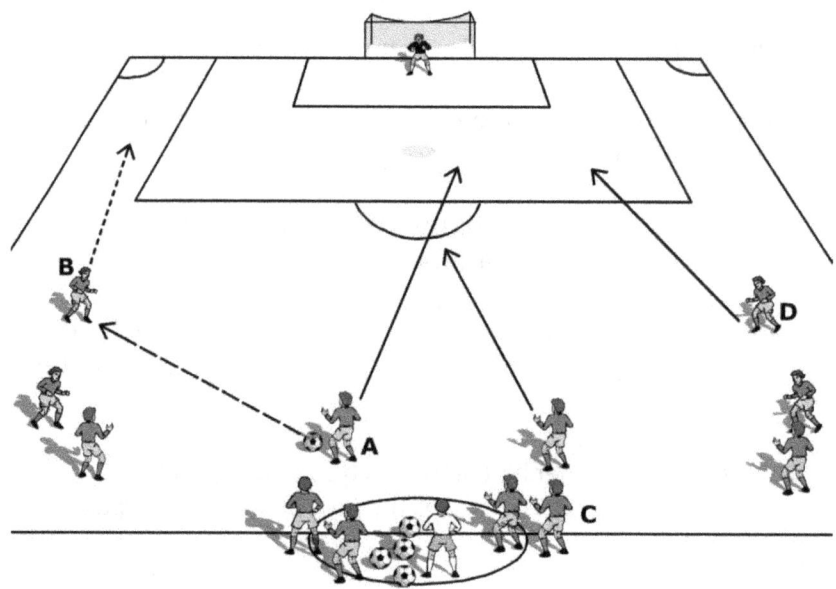

Coaching Points:
- Sharp accurate passing in build-up play.
- Movement to receive ball must be realistic – game speed.
- Wide midfield players are encouraged to deliver balls with pace into the box.
- Finishing must be of high quality.

Progression 1:
Same setup as above but 2 cones have been added slightly outside the corners of the 18-yard box as shown below.

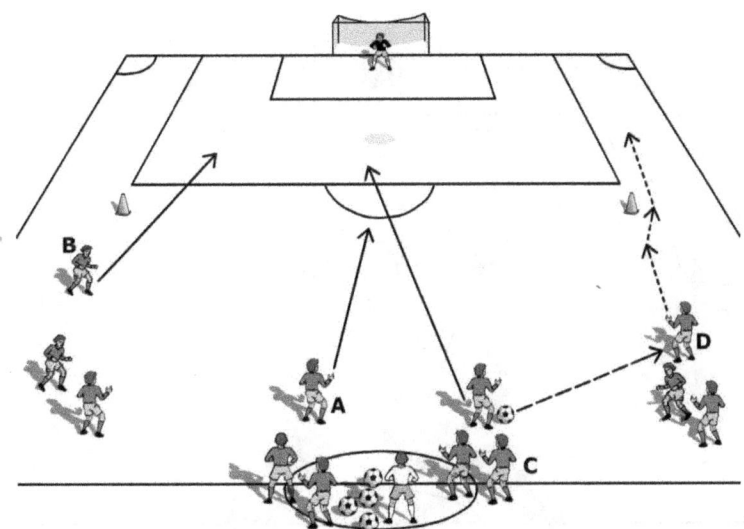

The pattern begins with a pass from the coach to either central midfield player (A, C).

The central midfield player must receive the ball in a half-turn and quickly pass to the wide midfield player.

The wide midfield player must "drive" inside at the cone (imaginary opponent) before cutting back down the line to deliver a cross into the box. The central midfield players and opposite side wide midfield player must attempt to get in the box for the cross.

Coaching Points:
- Wide midfielder must be encouraged to be "positive" – drive at the cone with pace!
- Sharp accurate passing in build-up play.
- Movement to receive ball must be realistic – game speed.

Progression 2:
Same setup as above with the addition of 2 center forwards (B,F) and 2 central defenders as shown below.

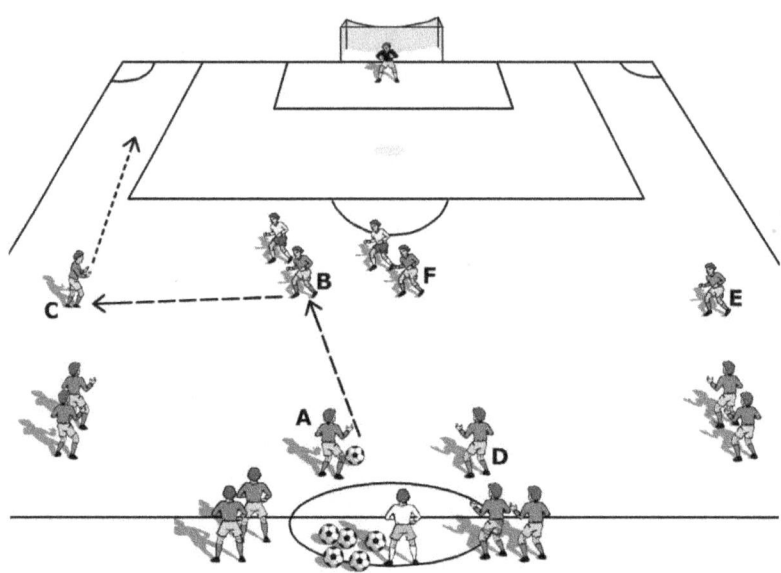

Key concepts:
- The ball must be played to either center forward prior to going wide. Play begins with a pass from the coach to either central midfield player.
- The central midfield player must pass the ball to either center forward.
- The center forward may pass directly to the wide player or lay-the-ball-off for the central midfield player to pass it wide.
- Wide players are encouraged to take a limited number of touches before crossing – cross early. The diagram above illustrates the center forward passing directly to the wide midfield player.
- Both center forwards, the opposite side midfielder and one central midfield player must get in the box for the cross.
- The other central midfield player can "hold" outside the box.

COACHING STRIKERS

The diagram below illustrates the movement and the runs into the box for the cross. Central midfield player (A) can be seen "holding" outside the box.

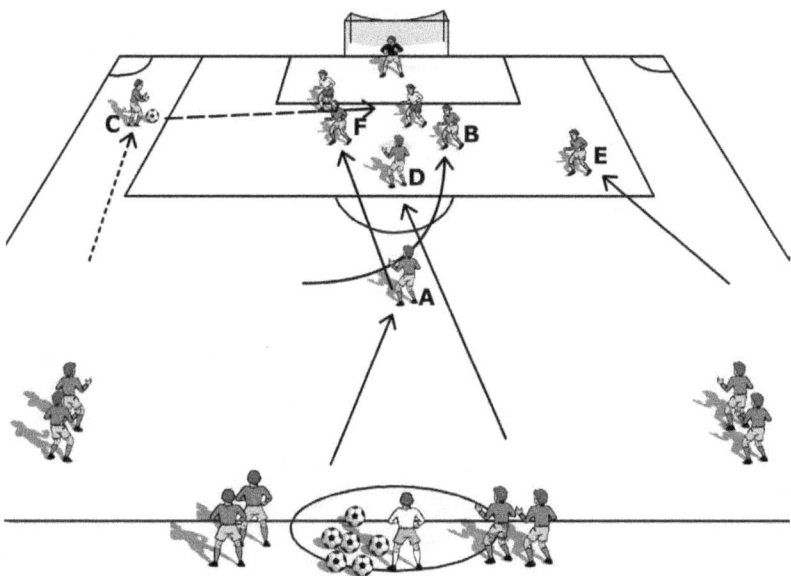

Coaching Points:
- Movement of center forwards must be sharp – game realistic to create passing lanes/angles for the central midfield players.
- Sharp accurate passing in build-up play.
- Movement to receive ball must be realistic – game speed.
- Early cross from wide players is encouraged.
- Timing and angle of runs into box.

Progression 3:
Same setup.

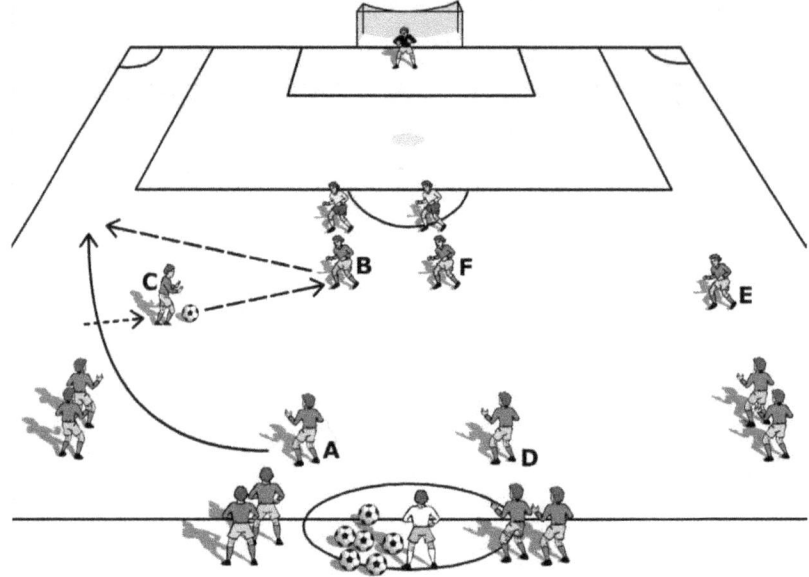

Play begins again with a pass from the coach.

The central midfield player must pass to either wide player.

The wide player must "drive" inside to create a lane for the central midfield player to overlap.

The ball is played to the nearest center forward who plays it out wide for the overlapping central midfield player.

The central midfield player now delivers the cross into the box.

Coaching Points:
- Timing and angle of run inside by wide player must be coordinated with central player.
- Center forwards must make realistic game-like runs to receive the ball.
- Sharp, accurate passing on all build-up play.
- Quality crossing/finishing.

Progression 4:
Same setup with the addition of 2 full-backs as shown below.

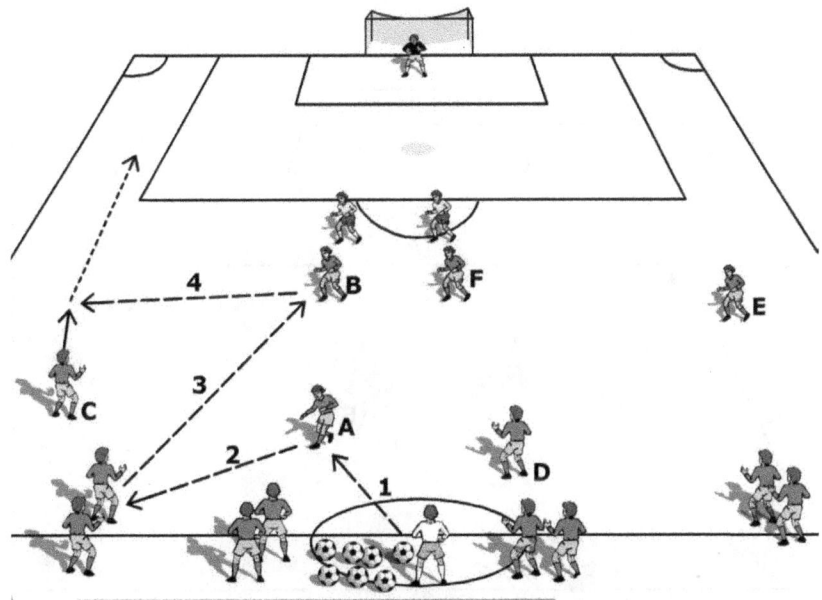

The coach begins the pattern with a pass to either fullback.

The coach does not play the ball directly to the full-back. The ball is played behind him, forcing him to go back and turn before playing forward. This is to create a game-like situation.

The fullback now has the freedom to pass to the central midfield players, the wide player or the center forwards.

Once the ball is played to any of the targets the previous patterns are encouraged.

At this phase of the session players are told to "play what they see" and don't force things. The setup of the activity caused the previous patterns to repeat.

COACHING STRIKERS

Final Activity:
- Goals are placed on the 18-yard lines as shown in the diagram below.
- For illustration purposes only half the playing area is shown.
- A 6 v 6 with 2 channel players (8v8 game) is organized as shown below.

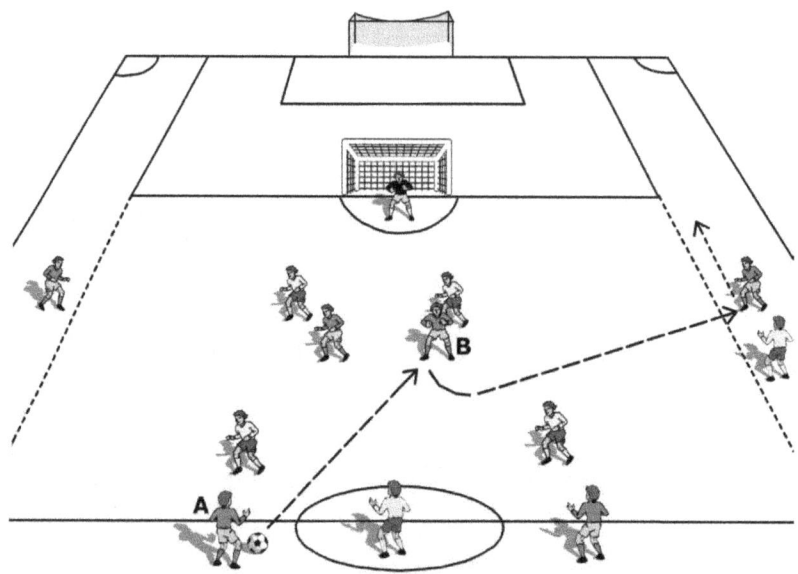

Both teams compete for possession of the ball and attempt to score in their opponent's goal.

Players are encouraged to "get the ball wide" for crossing opportunities.

Wide players are encouraged to cross "early" by using a 2-touch restriction. Goals are worth 2 when scored from a cross.

Play is continuous.

Coaching points:
- All previous points and patterns are encouraged.
- Sharp passing in central area to create opportunities to play wide.
- Early delivery into the box.
- Quality of finishing must be high.

ANOTHER FUNCTIONAL CROSSING AND FINISHING SESSION

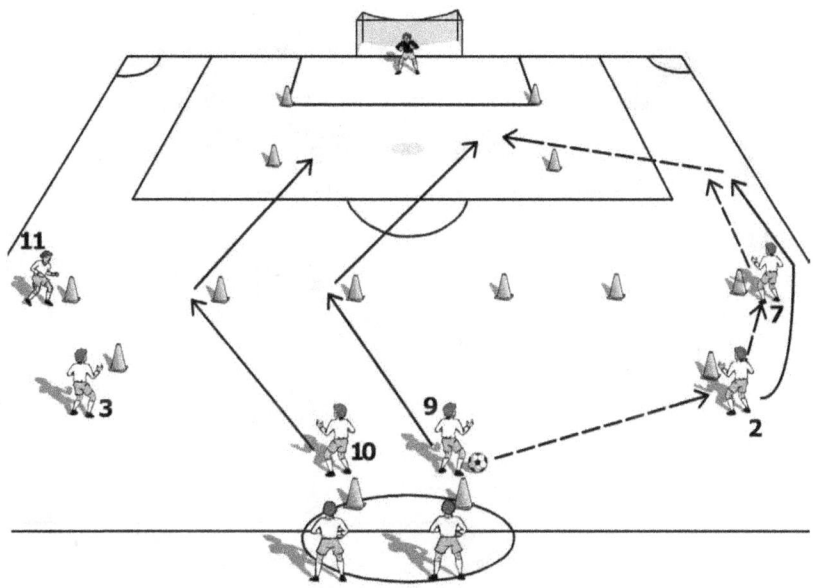

Shadow Play to begin. Attack in two's to begin. Movement away from the ball initially if there is time in the buildup. We are working on the timing of runs. Attack near post and far post areas. Cross from both sides.

Position off the near post, don't go beyond it to meet the ball, unless drawing a defender out of position for the second striker to attack. Winger plays a 1-2 and crosses as early as possible. Strikers know this and must get in position to meet the cross. The cross should be between knee and head height. Service could be a driven pass from a striker to a wide player or the play starts wide (timing is better).

THE SET UP

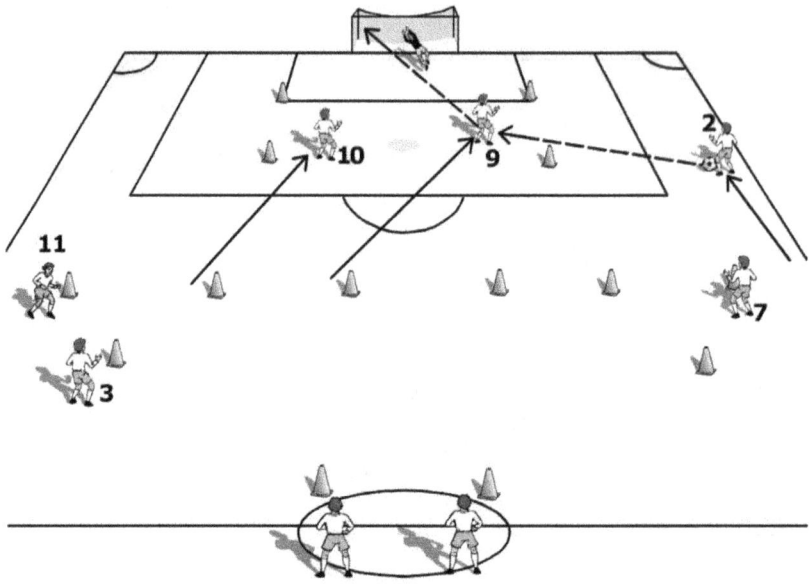

Introduce a defender who must choose a striker to mark. The defender starts from the same area as the striker as if retreating back towards goal. The crosser finds a free player.

Introduce a third attacking player in behind the front two for the pull back.

Have the opposite wide player coming inside as an additional attacker to cover the area beyond the far post and give the crosser another player to pick out (now it is a 4 v 1 situation).

Introduce another defender to mark up another attacker (4 v 2).

DEVELOPMENT

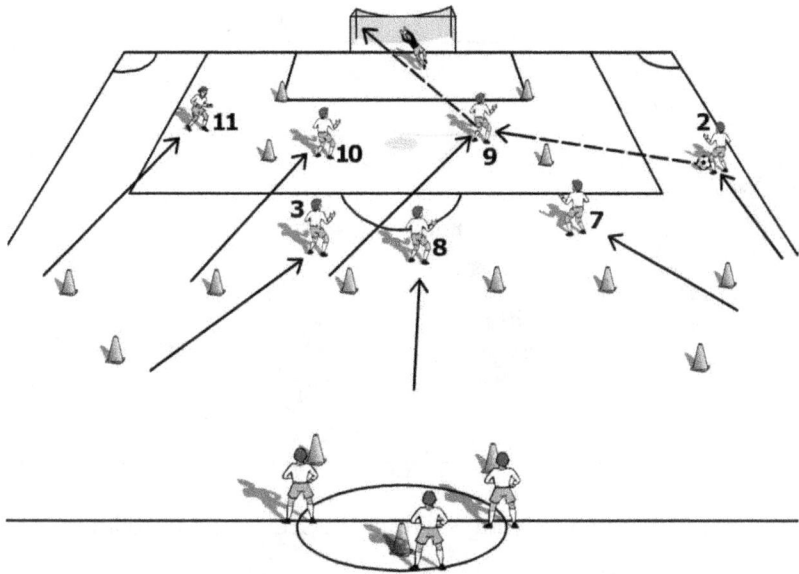

Once (3) and (7) have played the wide player in to cross, they can take up anticipation area positions around the box to receive any second ball possession from defenders' clearances. They can shoot or pass to someone in a better position (this keeps the pressure on).

These are the positions they need to be in to make it easy for the crosser to deliver the ball.

This provides four options, so wherever the crosser plays the ball in there could or should be someone fairly close to the ball to affect a finish on goal.

THE END PHASE

The final set up for a functional crossing session. The scenario is as follows:

We have a 4 v 2 overload situation with wide players working 1 – 2's or receiving diagonal passes from central strikers to create a crossing position.

Strikers make runs away from the ball initially to confuse defenders. By running away from the ball, defenders who mark them can see either the player or the ball, not both at the same time. This gives the striker the edge. Defenders must pick a player out and track his run.

Four players are attacking the cross expecting to receive it, so they make sure they get into the correct attacking positions.

An attempt is made to score a goal. Whatever the outcome, the central attackers and the defenders move back around the outside of the practice to start again and the next two lines begin their attack. We are generally working on one touch finishing from the attackers.

Develop this session by opening it out into a phase of play and bring in a back three or four plus a midfield to defend, taking it into a game situation, but only when you are getting constant success with the overload situation.

COMBINATION PLAYS CREATING MOVEMENT AND SCORING OPPORTUNITIES

You can develop this the same way with the second striker in behind the first striker as many teams play this way now.

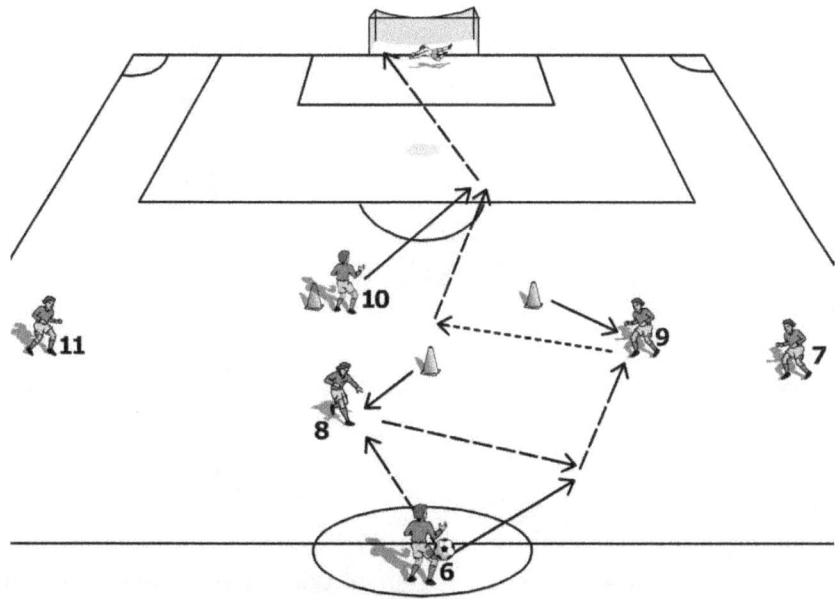

(6) passes to (8) who has come off at an angle to receive, and gets the pass back. (9) checks and receives a pass from (6).

(9) then turns and moves infield with the ball and plays an angled pass to (10).

Coaching Points:
- Communication.
- Receiving the pass "side-on".
- Timing and angle of the run from (10).
- Timing and pace of the pass from (9). Try to pass with the outside of the front foot for deception.

During any of these progressions you can include defenders if you feed it is more realistic. You can have them defending passively to begin. Sometimes players can make their movements more easily if there is a defender as a reference point.

COMBINATION PLAY LINKING WITH THE FIRST STRIKER

First Striker In

You can do this without defenders to begin, then introduce passive defenders, then progress to full scale defending. This applies to all the upcoming sessions in this segment.

Combination work using the wide midfielder to link with the front players. Pass to the wide player on his left foot away from the defender. Defenders always show the player inside.

Slide the first striker in down the side with a pass off the front foot of (7) for deception.

Coaching Points as before but also the first striker must create space to go into before the ball arrives.

COMBINATION PLAY LINKING WITH THE SECOND STRIKER

First striker (9) goes short and deep to pull the defender out and create space behind for the second striker (10) to get in off the through ball.

If the defender doesn't go short with (9) then (7) can play the ball to the feet of (9) to receive, turn and attack.

Coaching Points as before but also the timing of the run by the second striker (10) is crucial. He must not run offside or get ahead of the ball being played in.

LINKING PLAY BETWEEN THE FIRST AND SECOND STRIKERS

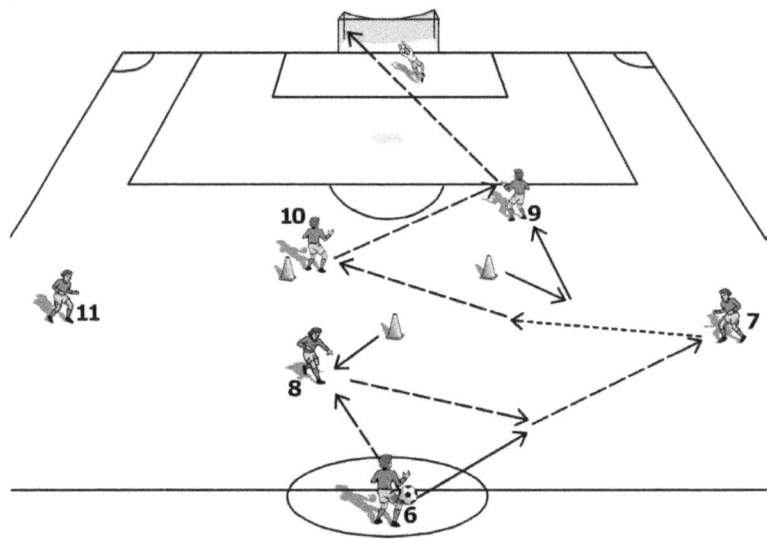

Same build up getting the ball wide. (7) brings the ball inside to attack the space. (9) goes short as if to receive the ball and lets it run across and inside his body away from the defender to (10). As the ball passes, (9) spins forward to receive the through ball from (10) who has played it one touch in behind the defense.

As (10) receives the ball another option would be to shoot directly on goal and (9) can follow up for any rebounds.

A variation on this can be (9) going short and turning away from the goal (opposite to above) and (10) setting up a shot from behind instead of in front. If it's tight, (9) can play the ball wide to (11) to change the direction of play and everyone adjusts off (11)'s cross.

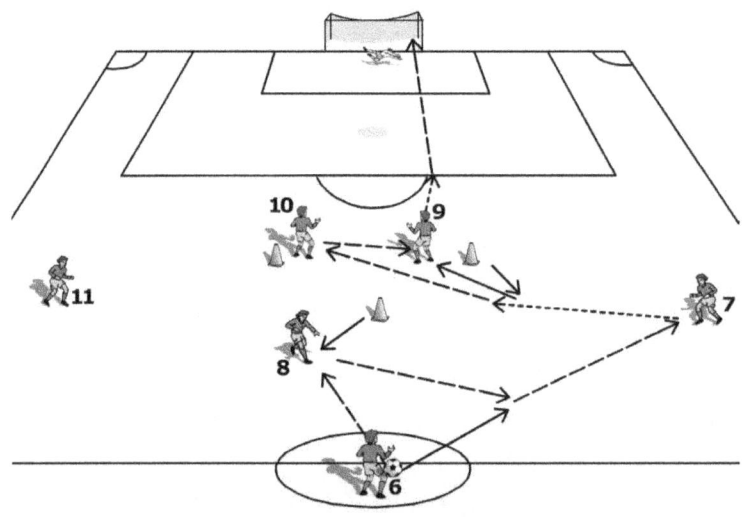

A CENTRAL MIDFIELDER LINKING WITH A WIDE MIDFIELDER

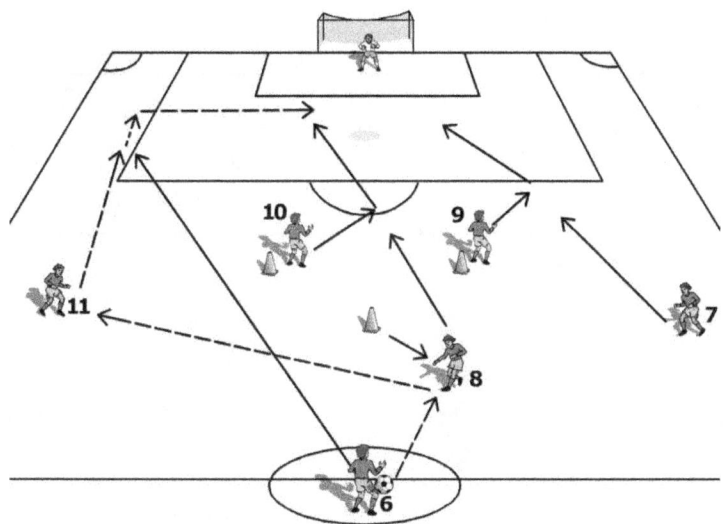

(6) begins the play with a pass to (8) who checks off at an angle to receive. (8) plays the ball wide to (11) and (6) makes a third man run beyond (11) who plays the ball into the path of that run. (6) must decide if there is an angle to shoot or cross the ball.

You could call this an "under-lap" rather than an overlap.

(7), (9) and (10) make runs into finishing positions to receive the cross.

This is also a good example of a "third man run" off the ball to receive. This is a harder run to pick up defensively.

The end product of the move is shown in the diagram below.

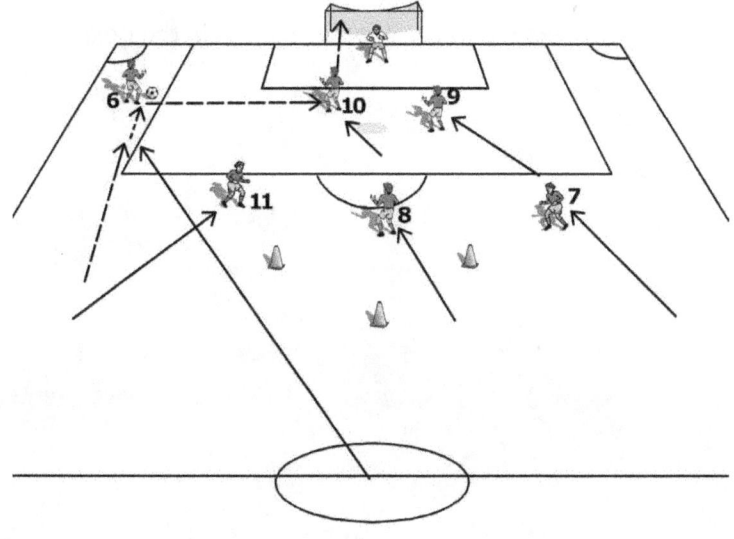

A MIDFIELDER LINKING OFF THE FIRST STRIKER'S PASS

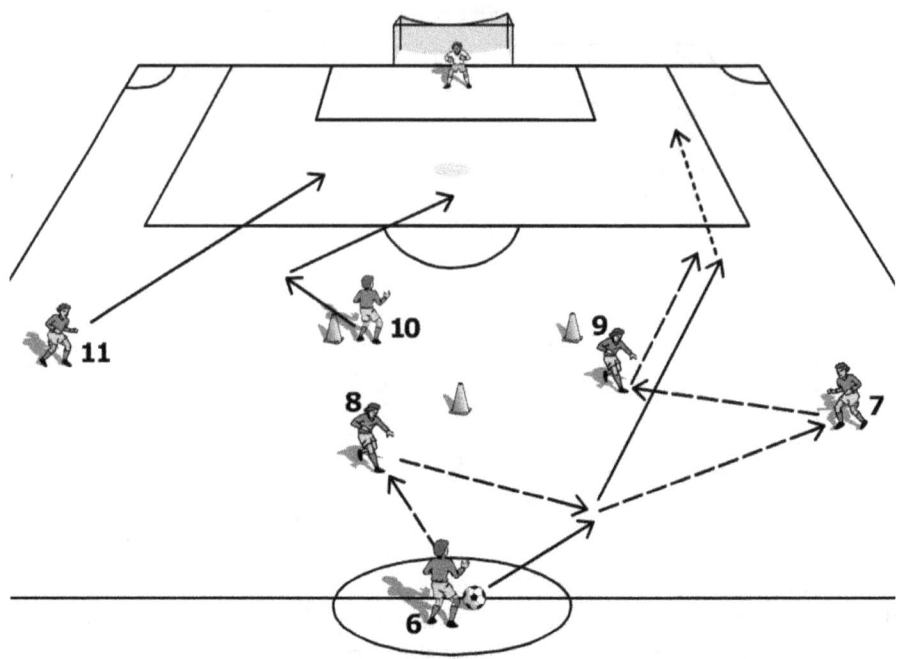

A midfield player passes the ball wide and continues the run forward. The first striker (9) comes short, pulling a defender out, and receives a pass from (7). (9) plays a first time pass into the path of midfield player (6). (6) can shoot or cross.

In this kind of run (6) is very hard to pick up and a defensive midfielder has to be disciplined and track the run.

The first striker must check the position of his marker because he may spot the run and go with the midfielder (6). In such a case (9) can hold the ball, turn and attack instead of playing the through pass.

Second striker (10) and (11) become the two target players in the box.

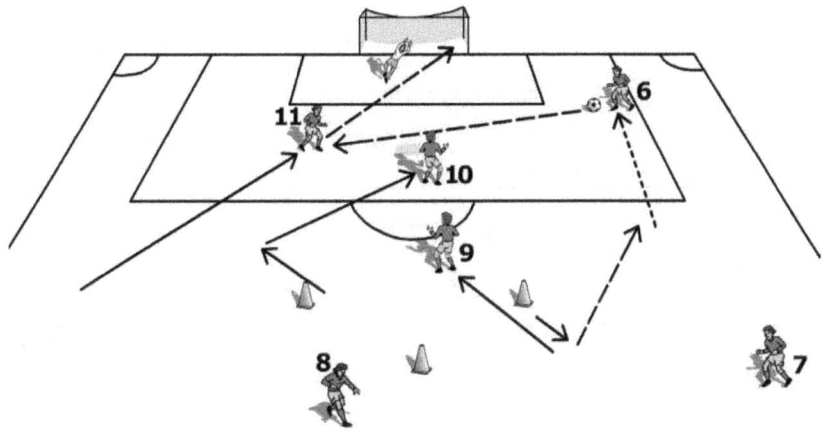

Here is the finish with (11) at the far post meeting the ball from the cross and scoring in the far corner of the goal.

One near post (10), one far post (11) and one in behind them for the pull back (9).

A MIDFIELDER LINKING OFF THE SECOND STRIKER'S PASS

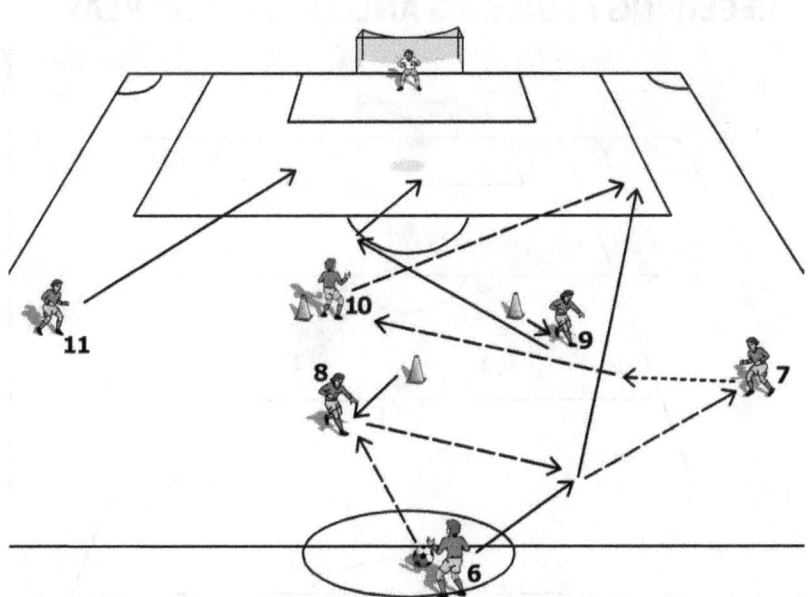

(6) begins the move again and passes to (8) who plays the ball wide to (7). (6) continues the run forward (third man run), (9) comes short and pulls the defender out of the space created for (6) to run into.

(7) comes inside and plays the ball inside to the second striker (10) who plays the ball in one touch to (6).

The other option for (10) is to have a shot on goal if there is enough space.

The final movement with a finish and score on goal with a header by (9) attacking the near post, (11) attacking the far post.

(10) follows in behind for the pull back behind the two front attackers.

A SMALL SIZED FUNCTION AND PHASE OF PLAY: STRIKERS RECEIVING / TURNING AND LINKING UP PLAY

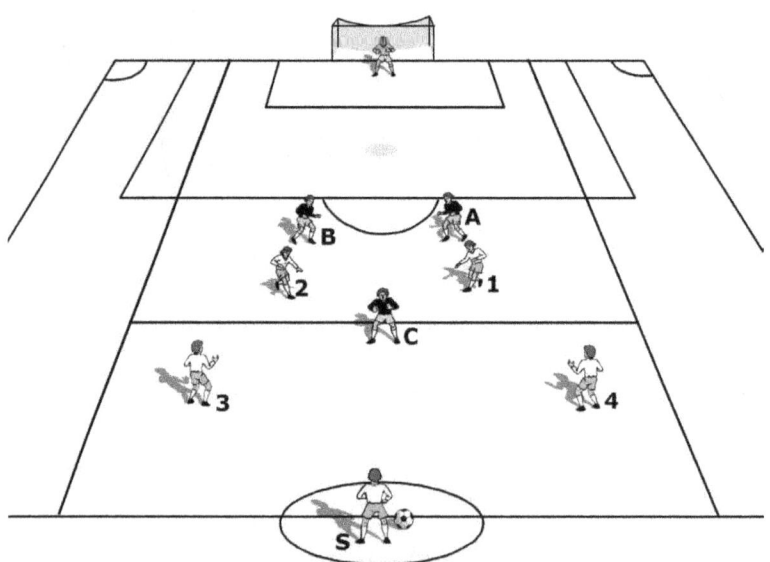

The game is two touch in the outer zone where the midfield are and free play in the strikers' zone.

We have a 2 v 1 in this area where there is pressure to pass but also an overload to ensure passes are able to be made into the strikers.

Strikers try to get free from defenders to receive and turn and get a shot in or make combination plays to set up a shooting chance.

If the defenders win the ball it goes back to the server (S) to start again.

Coaching Points:
- Create Space (movement, R and T, short and wide)
- Support Positions (1-2's, crossovers, diagonal runs, one short one long)
- Shots on target and rebound positions.

FUNCTION: CENTRAL MIDFIELD PLAYERS RECEIVING AND TURNING

A server passes the ball into the central midfield players and the play begins (to keep the practice in eights the coach can be the server if necessary).

Coaching Points:
- Creating Space by movement off markers (e.g. a crossover).
- Decision – When and where to Receive and Turn with the ball.
- Technique – How to receive and turn (see previous points).
- Quality of pass into receiver (angle, accuracy and weight).
- Support positions of teammates behind and in front of the ball.

Server who plays the ball in can join in the play.

Develop: Introduce another attacker and another defender. Introduce wide attackers and wide defenders. Develop into a phase play but still play into central midfield to begin the practice.

CENTRAL MIDFIELD AND STRIKERS RECEIVING AND TURNING

Always working the ball into central midfield first to (7), (8) and (11)

Start Position 1: (6) passing in to all three in turn. Receivers getting body half turned to receive. Midfield players must move and create space to receive to feet or down the side.

SP2 - (11) and (7) crossover and (6) plays the ball down the side.

SP3 – A wide player passes into (7) or (11) who passes one touch into a striker.

SP4 – A wide player into (8) to receive and turn, working with strikers or bringing central midfield into play.

MOVEMENT OF THE STRIKERS AND MIDFIELDERS IN A SHADOW PLAY

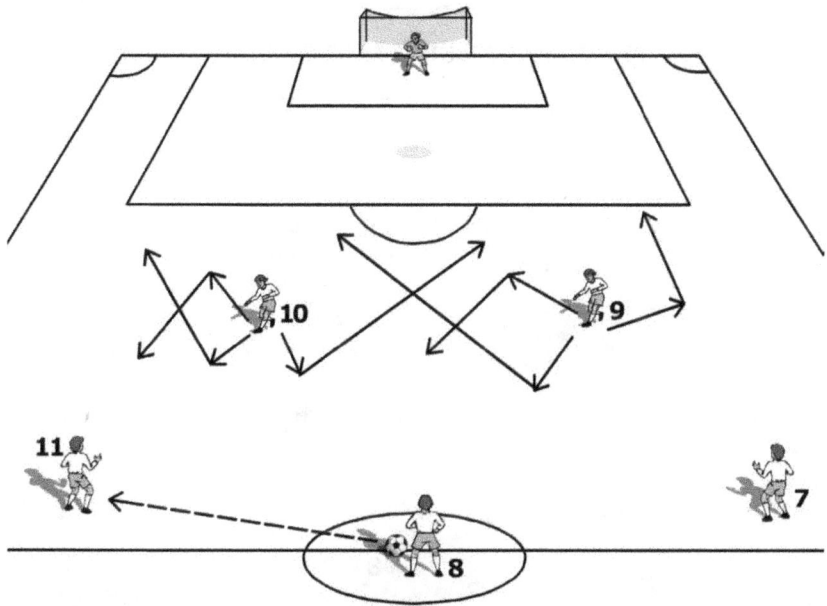

First striker (10)'s run options to receive or create space for another player to receive.

If the player on the ball has time, it is better for the striker to initially run in the opposite direction to draw the defender away from where the ball is going.

As above, (10) comes short to go long and goes long to come short. This will create an extra few yards of space to work in.

To avoid running offside, the run away (opposite diagonal) should not be a straight line run. A lot of this depends on the time the passer has on the ball. If no time then come short or go long or just make the diagonally opposite run.

The two strikers need to understand each other's runs and (8) must work a position off them. (8)'s movement mirrors the three basic runs.

There are many options but these three are the easiest to use and result in creating space for the runner and/or others to exploit. Plus, they move defenders into positions they don't want to go (especially man-marking defenders).

STRIKER MOVEMENT STARTING FROM BEHIND DEFENDERS

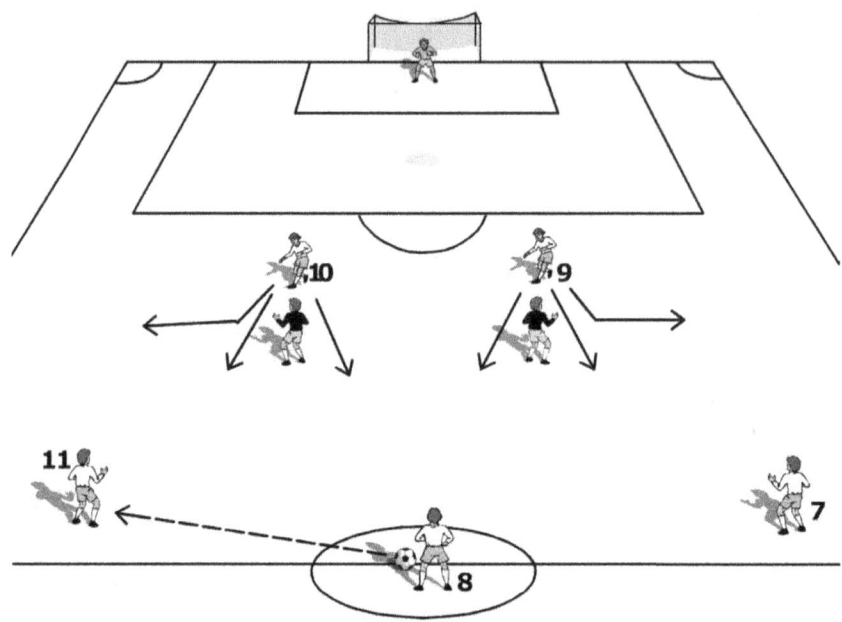

Most strikers work in front of defenders but as the ball is played into the striker a defender can see the striker's movement and get in front of him to intercept the ball. The use of this tactic occasionally can disrupt the defender.

Encourage strikers to work behind the defenders (away to come back). They must not go too far away because of offside. They have to time their run back in front or to the side of the defender just before the pass is made.

From this position the defender can't see the striker behind him and consequently can't see the run he makes. If he looks at the striker he can't see the ball and where and when it is passed.

This gives the striker an advantage whichever way the defender looks. The striker must move short and sharp to get the advantage. He can receive and turn and face up to the defender or receive and lay the ball off to a teammate.

SPLIT RUNS OF STRIKERS TO GET CENTRAL ATTACKING MIDFIELDER IN

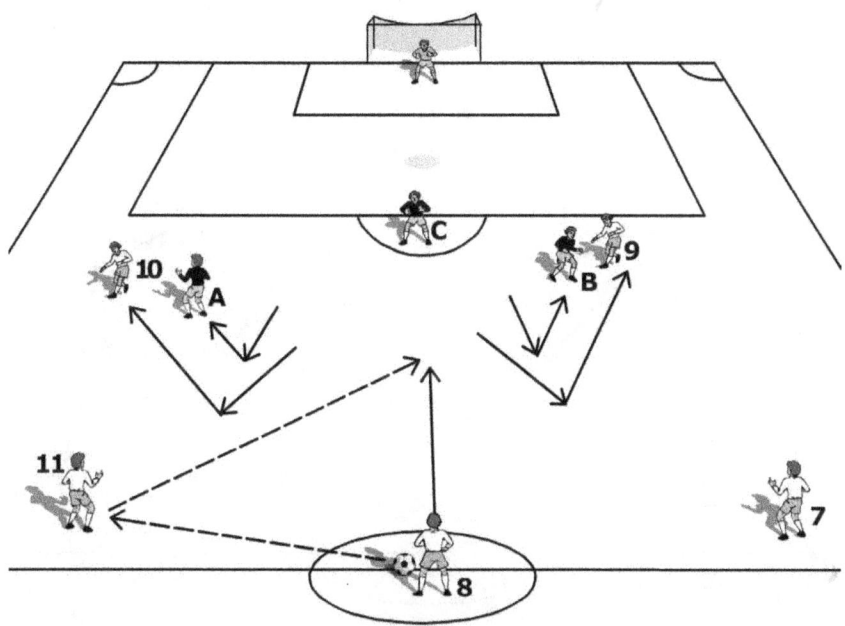

Man-marking defenders go with the strikers, creating space centrally for a 1 v 1 situation to develop.

(11) may have another option such as a straight pass down the side to (10) or a longer diagonal pass to (9) who has come off the shoulder of the center back marker.

(10) comes short to go long to pull the defender away from the space he is trying to exploit (i.e. behind the defender). Players aren't always able to make the perfect run and may just have to get there to receive the pass because there is no time to work a move.

L – SHAPED SPLIT RUNS OF STRIKERS TO GET CENTRAL ATTACKING MIDFIELDER IN

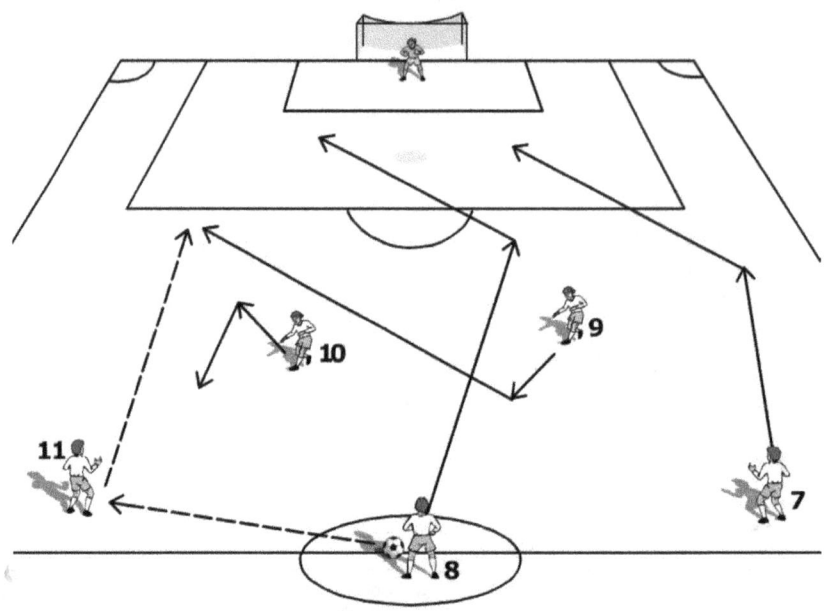

Player on the ball may have other options such as a pass to (10)'s feet, a long diagonal pass to (9), or a pass to (8)'s diagonal run in behind.

(10) goes long to come short to create space in front for a pass to feet and in behind for (8)'s run.

Forwards only make opposite runs if the player on the ball has time, otherwise they just make the one run for the early delivery (i.e. a straight run).

Turns must be short and sharp, avoiding running in a wider curved way which is easier for a defender to mark.

IDEAL TEAM SHAPE DURING CROSSING PHASE OF A GAME

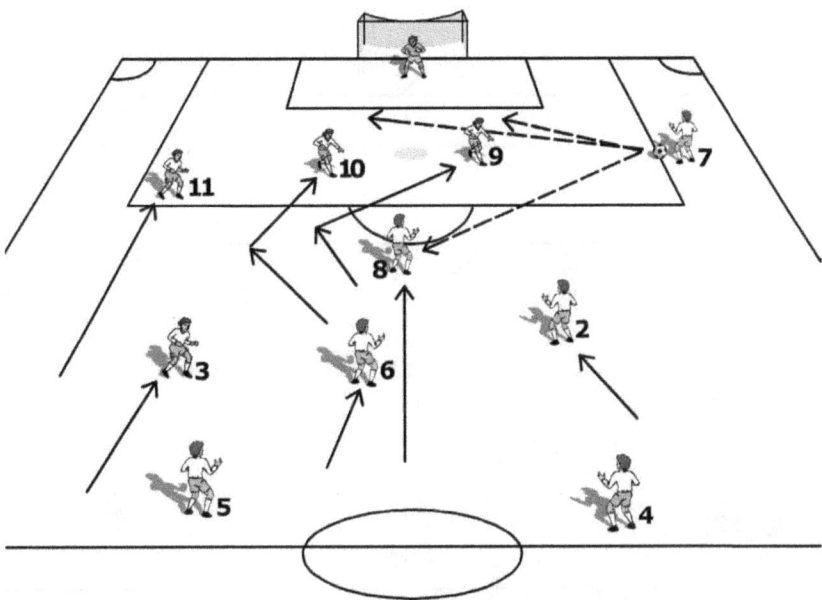

Three attackers in the box attacking near post, far post and a pull back to mid-goal position behind the defense (attacking triangle with staggered runs).

Three outside the box cover anticipation areas (if the ball is cleared by a defender) to regain possession from secondary play. (11) can also cover the area beyond the far post should the delivery be played to that position.

The back three are in position to defend a counter attack by the opposition or attack any ball that clears the second line i.e. beyond (11), (6) and (2).

Essentially three lines (units) of three players including the crosser.

PLAYING TWO UP AND ONE IN BEHIND (ATTACKING MIDFIELDER)
Initially a Shadow Play

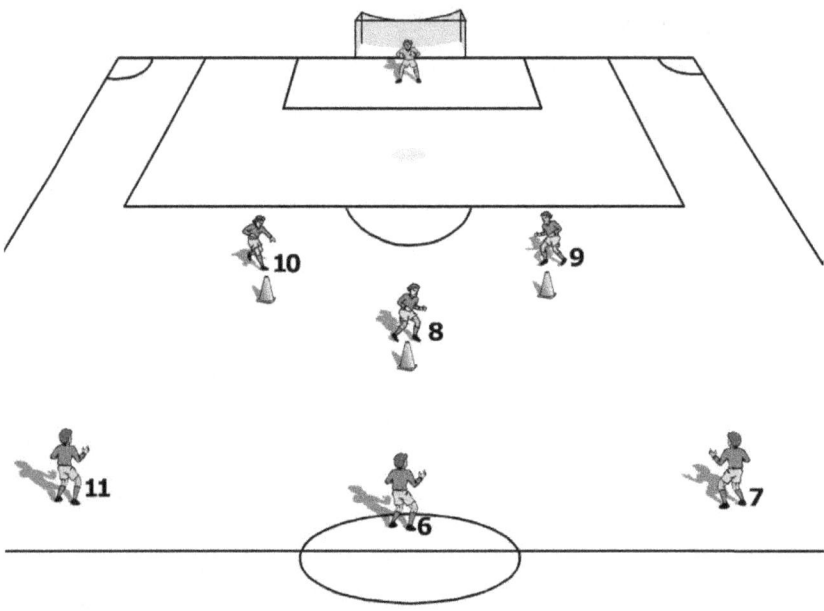

Using cones to show the basic set-up for the players.

Two strikers and one attacking midfielder. We are looking for them to make three different runs for the passer to have three passing options.

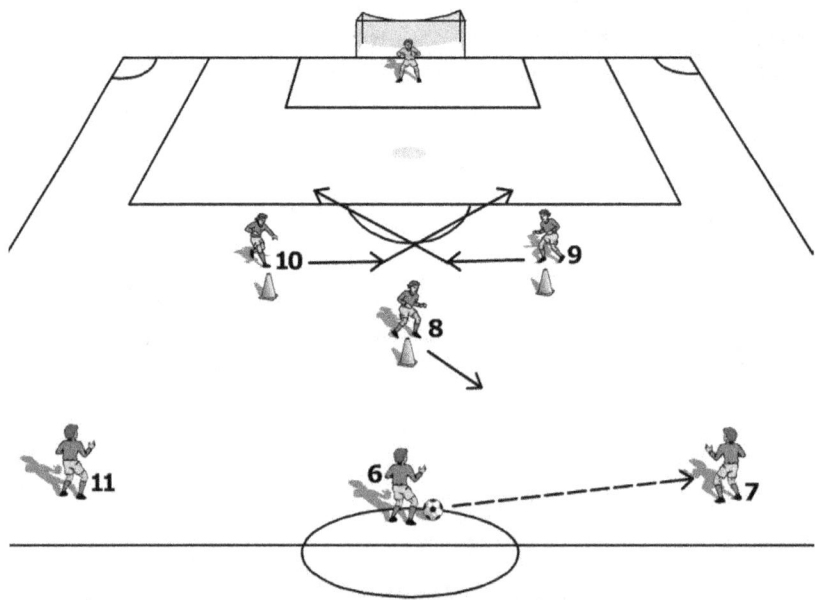

Here the start position is a pass from (6) to (7). As the ball travels, the three front players make a series of movements as shown. The coach can dictate this to begin to get them used to the idea.

The Start Position: The player on the ball always uses the first touch to move the ball to signify the game is live. Once this touch has been made, players can begin their movements.

The start position player usually passes the ball on the second touch when the players are already in motion.

So we have a run short, and two diagonally opposite runs, one down the channel for a straight pass, the other diagonally opposite for a longer diagonal pass.

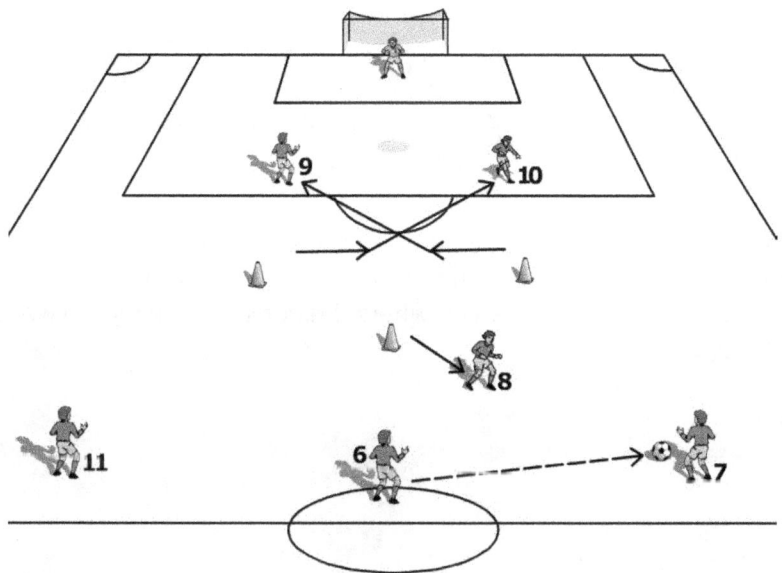

Here is the end product of the runs showing where the players will finish up, each ready to receive the ball.

All three players must expect it, only one will receive it. There are three options for the passer who must identify immediately which one is the best option.

As we progress the session with defenders included, the best pass is often determined by who gets free of their defender in the most dangerous area.

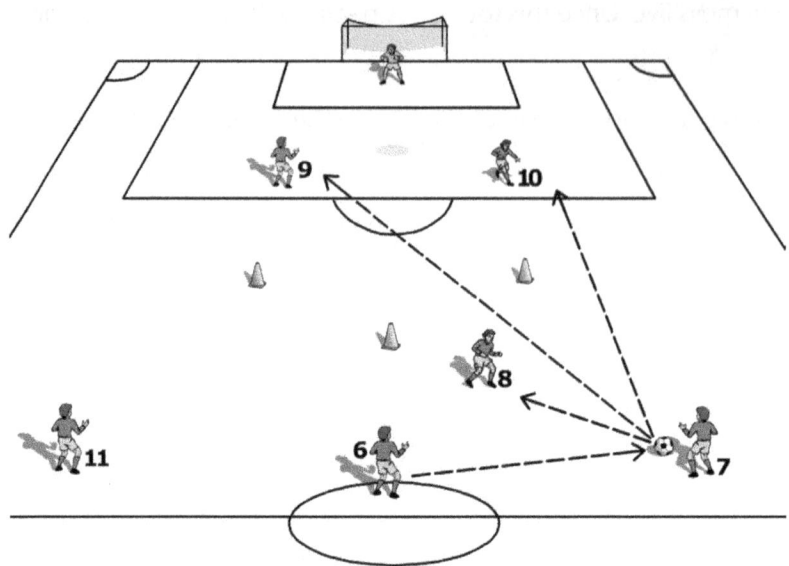

Now we show the three pass options, diagonally short into feet to (8), diagonally long into space for (9) and a straight pass down the channel into space for (10).
All three can be effective passes based on where the defenders go (which we will introduce soon for greater realism).

Coaching Points:
- Quality of passes.
- Timing of passes.
- Timing of runs.
- Angle of runs.

(8) links to get the ball to feet. If the marker doesn't go short also then (8) can receive and turn with the ball. If (8)'s marker goes short, space is created behind and (9) can make a diagonal run into that space to receive the pass. (9) can make the run in behind for a diagonal ball or to attack the goal from (10)'s cross (near post run).

(11) can join in and aim to attack the far post area.

L - Shaped runs are best to drag defenders out of position so strikers can cut back across their shoulders and gain space. Often players don't have time to do this so runs are more direct. Just avoid running offside (timing of run).

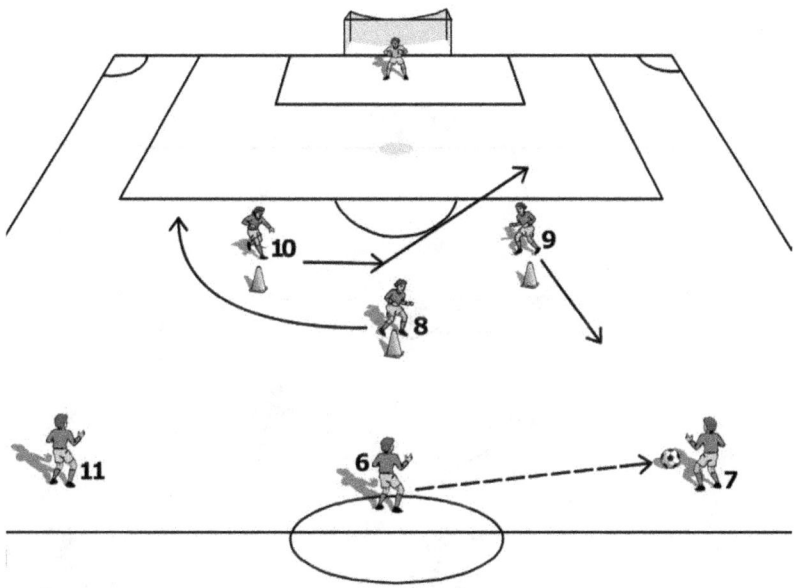

Here are other choices of runs by the three front players.

Once you have established a couple of ideas have the players decide for themselves. They will usually work off the movement of the nearest player to the ball and react off that player.

PLAYING ONE UP WITH TWO IN BEHIND

Push a player on now as a point striker so it is a reverse of the previous triangle.

Now as the ball travels from (6) to (7) the three strikers must be on the move.

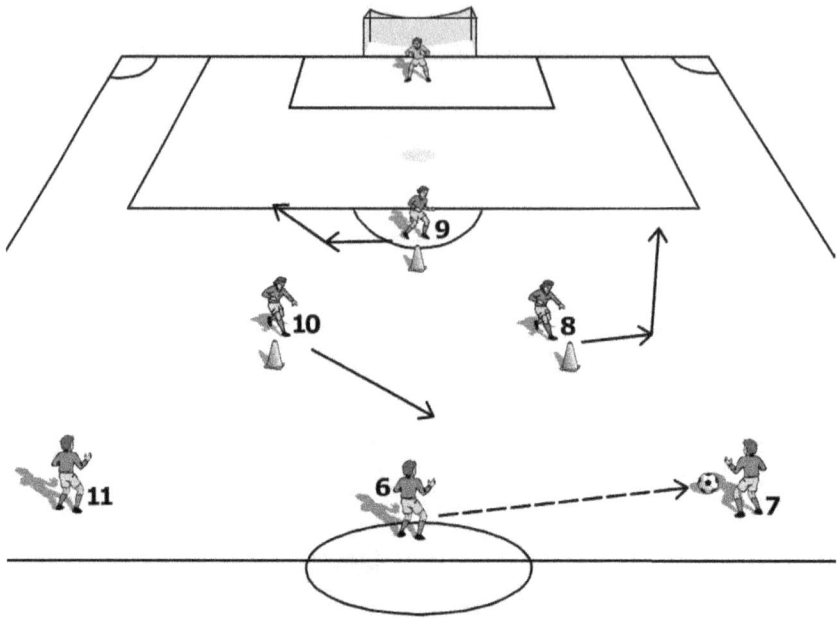

Here are some movements they can make. Again, the coach can dictate it to help them understand what they need to do.

Three players work off each other as shown.

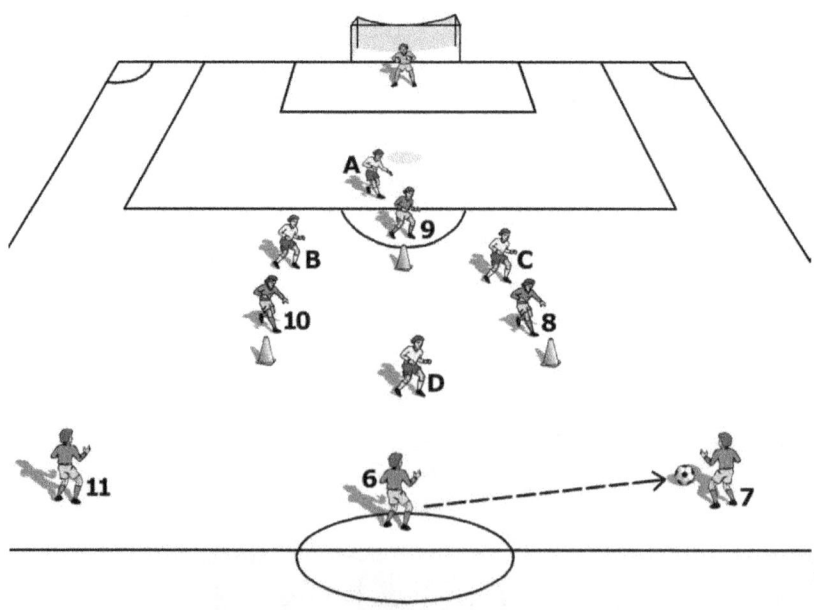

Introduce four defenders in a diamond defense set-up.

A 3 v 3 situation is the result of pushing a player onto the sweeper. Now the opposition has no cover unless they change their shape (which is unlikely to happen) so we are at an advantage.

The sweeper does not like to be man-marked and is usually the free player, so he may try to drop deeper to escape the marking. This will allow us to push up as a team, giving us an advantage.

Movement of the three front players can seriously affect the positioning of the defenders, especially if they use a man-marking philosophy. This will create a lot of space to be exploited centrally. If they marked zones, this disruption of the defense would not happen.

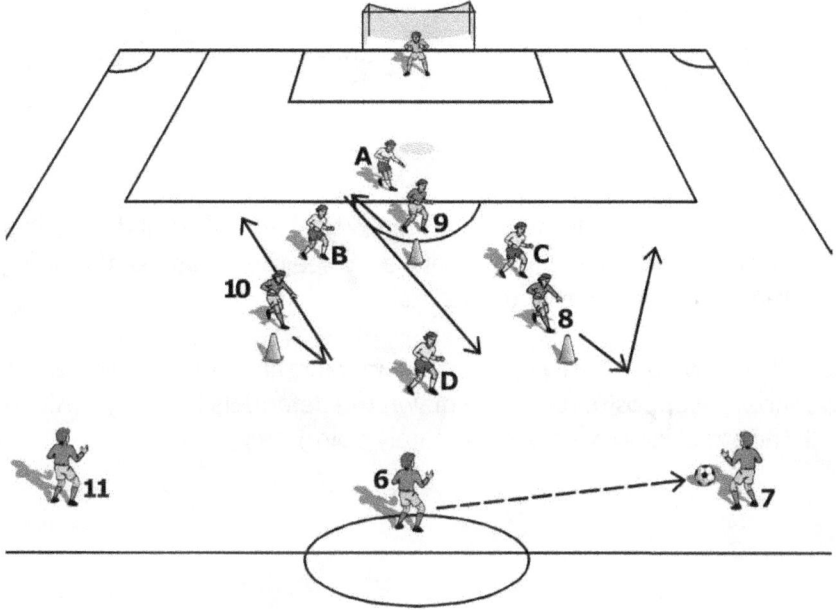

The player on the ball expects movement at pace to create options for a pass and get opponents thinking who are they marking and where are they going. We know where they are going, the opponents don't. That's the key to it all.

The striker can use a key word to let the passer know that he is making the "opposite run". "Vialli" can be the word to use as he was the great striker who perfected this move.

It may only be used a couple of times during a game. Most of the time the runs will be immediate and in the same direction and the defenders will expect this, then you throw in the Vialli and maybe that is when you get free to score.

COACHING STRIKERS

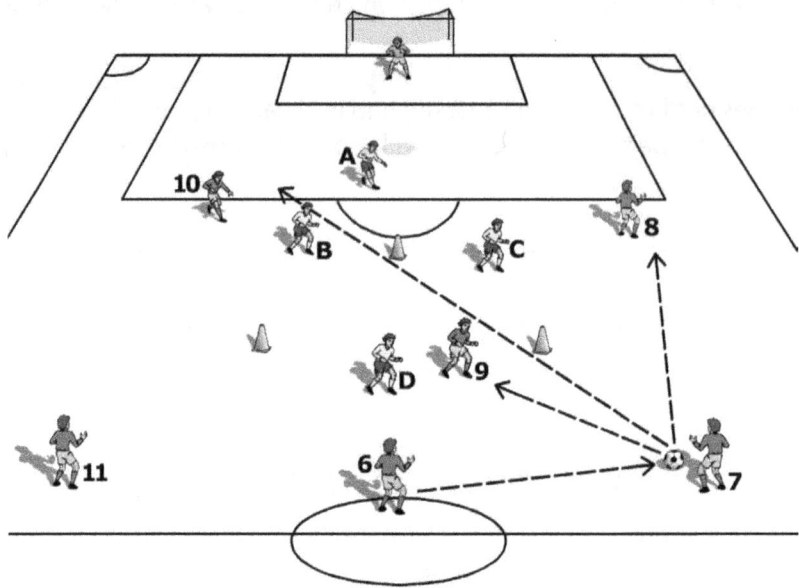

In an ideal world this is what will happen. It is unlikely, I know, that all three will get free, but if one gets free the player on the ball has to see this and make the right pass. If defenders man-mark it will be easier to establish.

So all three strikers have gotten away from their markers and are free to receive either to feet or into space. The opposite runs have drawn the defenders in the opposite direction to that which the attacking players are ultimately going.

COACHING STRIKERS

PHASE PLAY: QUICK PLAY AROUND THE PENALTY AREA

This is the basic set up with a 2 v 1 attacking overload in wide areas to allow the possibility of successful overlaps.

A 1 v 1 in central midfield and a 2 v 2 with the two strikers and the two center backs, ultimately a 7 v 6 in favor of the attacking team but within the field setting a 7 v 5.

Any variations of numbers can be used here, but this works well for a small number of players where you still create what you are trying to achieve with fast play around the penalty area.

If the defending team wins possession they have to score within 5 passes in either of the small goals and then the attacking phase starts again with (8).

Coaching Points:
- Quality Passing
- Good first touch control
- Creating overloads with Combination Plays
- Quality movements off the ball to create space for oneself and for teammates
- Play one and two touch to keep the passing and movement as fast as possible

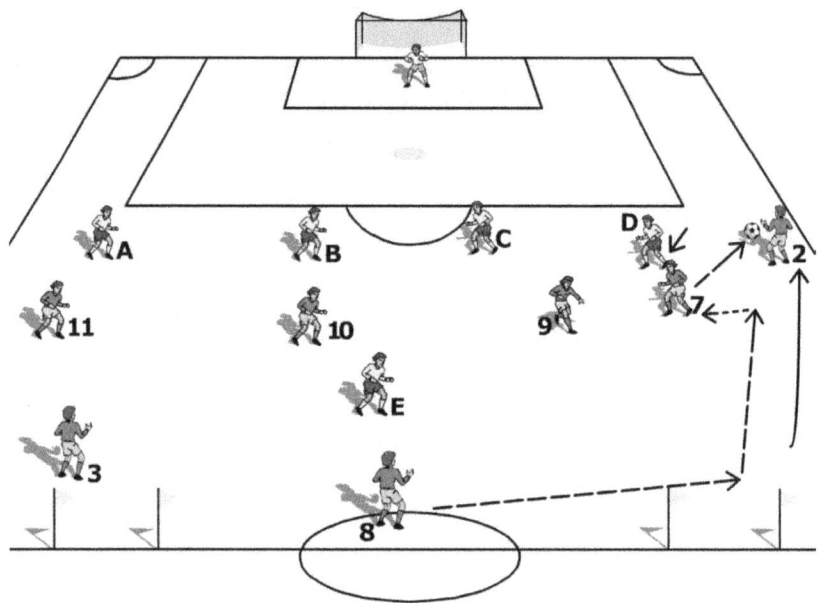

Start Position: The first development we are looking to create is an overlap in a 2 v 1 situation with (2) and (7) against full back (D). In this case (2) passes to (7) who is closed down by (D).

Fullback (2) can also run quickly at defender (D) and draw him to the ball. This will create space for (7) to receive the pass.

Encourage quick play at all times and in all situations, be it running with the ball, passing the ball or movement on and off the ball.

Coaching Points in overlapping:
- Create Space – Receiver brings the ball inside to create space outside for the overlapping player, particularly in a wide area of the field.
- Communication – Overlapping player calls "HOLD".
- Timing of the run – When the receiving player is faced forward.
- Angle of the run – Wide away from the defender
- Timing of the pass – Into the path in front of the overlapping player with correct weight so the overlapping player does not have to break stride
- Decoy or pass – Instead of passing use the run to take a defender away from the space inside and come inside with the ball.

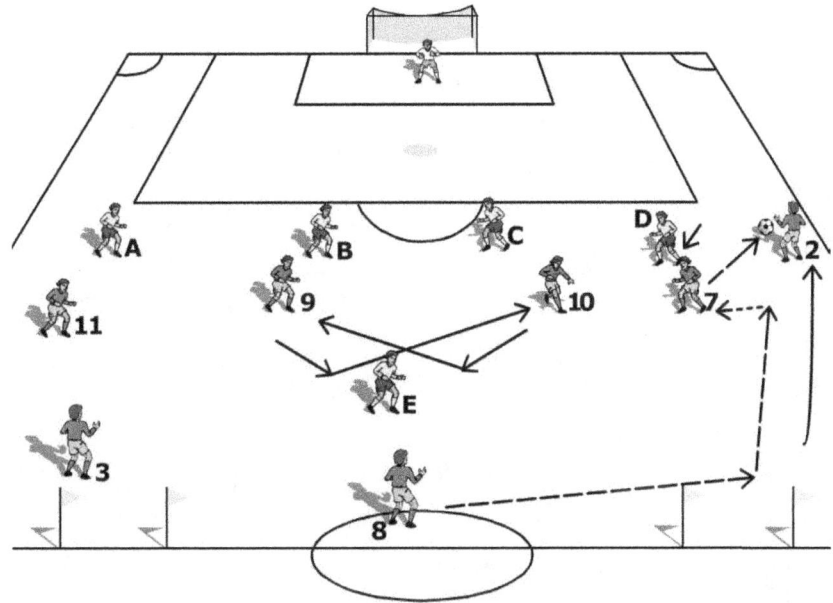

Here we start the idea of the two strikers making movements off the ball.

The center backs, if zonal marking, will pass them on. But if the movement is particularly quick they may not have time to communicate effectively and may track these runs, which may open up space more easily.

Plus, strikers do not move into the same spaces they came from when they switch as that is making it too easy for the defenders, who can simply pass them on and mark zonally.

So, if they pass them on the defenders still need to make adjustments to mark the new player coming close to their zone.

Encourage the strikers to make these combination movements to move the defenders around and try to confuse them rather than staying in the same channels and being easily marked.

If the defenders man-mark as some teams do, this kind of movement can be very effective.

COACHING STRIKERS

COMBINATION MOVEMENTS IN A PHASE OF PLAY

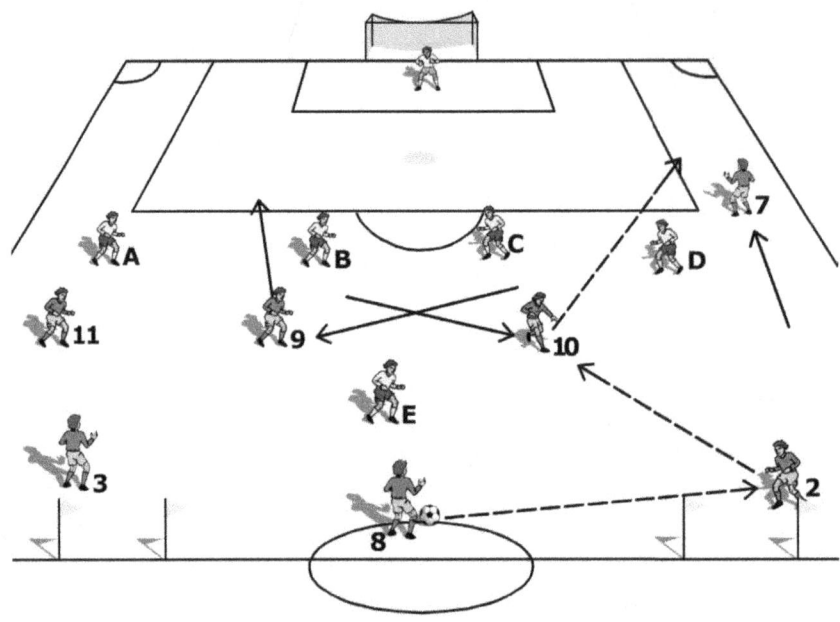

Here they interchange and the 2nd striker (10) gets free to play an angled pass into the path of wide player (7) who has gotten free in behind defender (D).

(9) is set up in a position off the shoulder of defender (B) ready to receive the cross from (7).

(9) attacks the near post as the first striker now. (11) becomes the second striker and (10) will get to the edge of the box for the pullback.

COACHING STRIKERS

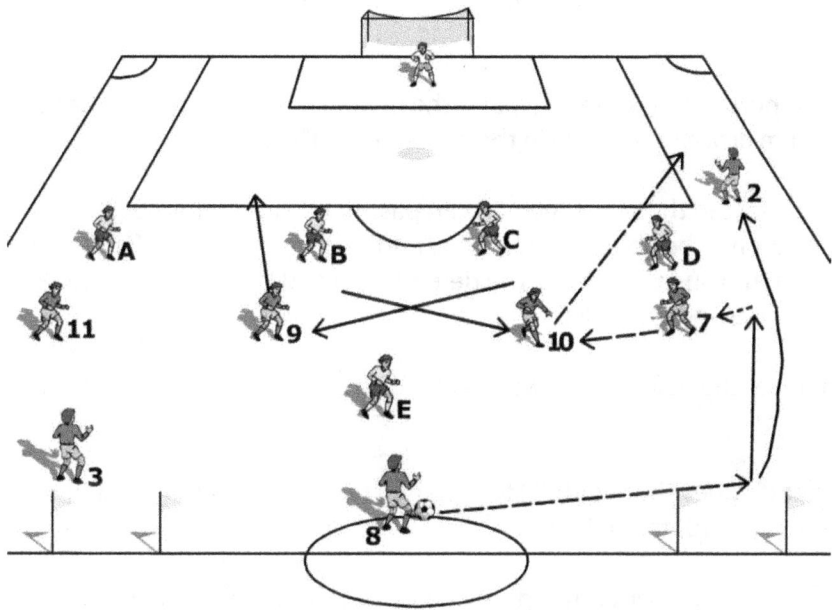

Here they interchange and the 2nd striker (10) gets free to play an angled pass into the path of overlapping fullback (2).

The same ideas as before with the aim of getting players attacking the near post, the far post and behind the two strikers just inside the edge of the box.

If players just interchange, defenders start to pick up what they are doing and simply pass them on and mark them zonally.

COACHING STRIKERS

The way to beat this is to exchange but move up and down the field, not just across the back four. So the same defensive player has to mark the same striker or he will get free to receive to feet and turn.

Here (9) goes short to receive from (2) and the defender marking him (C) has to decide "Do I go to close him down or do I stay in the space behind"?

If defender (C) stays in the space then (2) can pass to (9) and therefore (9), who should be positioned side-on to be able to turn quickly and also to see if the defender has followed him or not, can turn and run 1 v 1 at the defender (C) and leave him vulnerable, especially if this player (9) is a good dribbler.

(9) can also run at the defense and work a combination with (10) and try to create a 2 v 1 centrally.

Here defender (C) goes short with (9) to stop him receiving and turning and this creates space in behind for (10) to run into.

(2) then plays a great pass into the space and in front of (10) who can run onto the ball and get a shot on goal.

Likewise (7) could attack outside to in and inside defender (D) into the space.

Also, if defender (B) stays with (10) and stops those attacking the goal then (10) is facing wide with the ball and (7) can get in behind defender (D) to receive and cross.

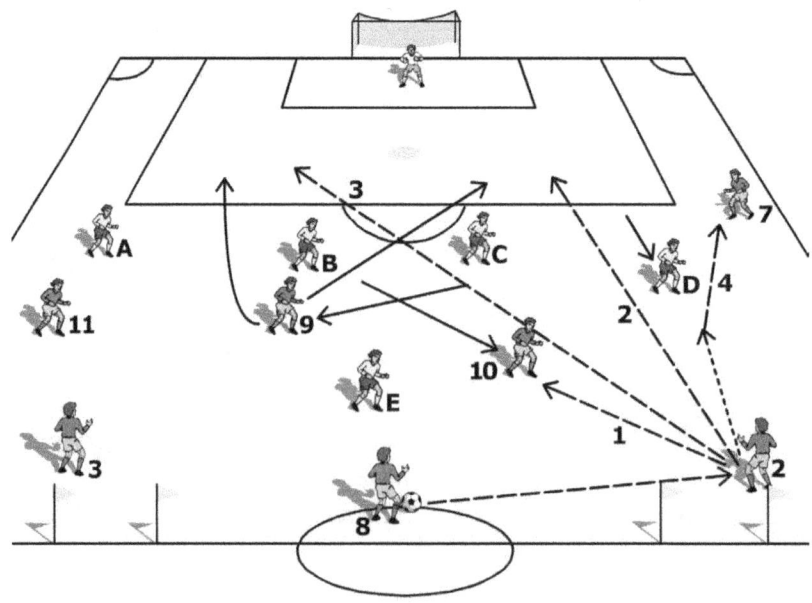

There are many combinations players can create in these situations. These are just a few you can focus on.

Play 1: A simple pass into the feet of (10) coming short to receive. Various situations can occur from this. The play is free and see what the players come up with.

Play 2: Based on great movements in front of the ball, space is created behind the back four and (2) plays a pass into that space for (9) or (10) depending on whether or not they switched positions initially.

Play 3: Strikers switch positions and (9) positions off the shoulder of defender (B), inviting a diagonal ball from (2) into the space behind.

Play 4: (2) runs at defender (D) with pace trying to commit him to a tackle and in the meantime (7) goes touchline wide to create as much space to receive the pass in as possible. This is a fine situation to create a 2 v 1 overload and get into a good crossing position.

This should give a good starting point for teams who play with two central strikers against a defensive flat zonal marking back four in terms of attacking plays to try to beat them and score goals.

All moves are replicated on the left side of the field also to develop the ideas on both sides.

Once there is good offensive success you can add defenders and make it a greater challenge.

For example, add a wide defensive midfielder on either side of the field so it is now a 2 v 2 on both sides and more difficult to create an overlap with the fullback attacking.
Have a 4 v 3 in midfield then a 4 v 4 and so on.

PLAYING THREE UP WITH A STRIKER AND TWO WINGERS AGAINST A MAN-MARKING BACK THREE

The following session and activities focus on developing attacking play through the use of 3 "strikers".

This may be in a situation where an attacking midfield player pushes on to the opposing sweeper OR where a team plays with 1 true center forward and 2 "wingers".

We offer suggestions on how to adjust your team shape as well as affect the shape of the opposition in the detailed explanations / diagrams that follow.

Half pitch with 6 attacking players against 4 defenders and a goalkeeper as shown in diagram below. Play begins with a pass from the coach (c).

COACHING STRIKERS

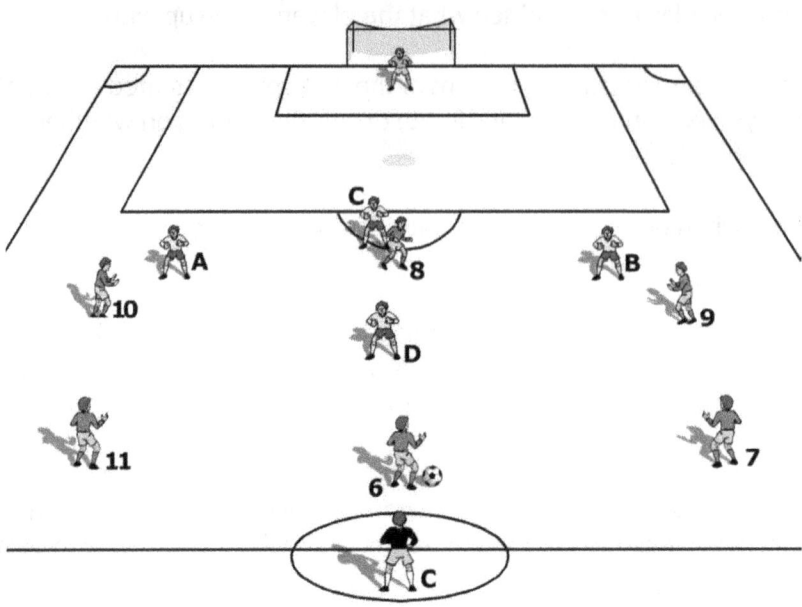

A 3 v 3 situation is the result of pushing the attacking midfield player (8) onto the sweeper. Now the opposition has no cover unless they change their shape (which is unlikely to happen) so we are at an advantage.

The sweeper does not like to be man-marked as he is usually the free player so he may try to drop deeper to escape the marking, allowing us to push up as a team and giving us an advantage.

Movement of the 3 front players can seriously affect the positioning of the defenders as they will likely follow them if they usually use a man-marking philosophy.

This will create a lot of space to exploit centrally. If they marked zones, this disruption of the defense would not happen. We are technically playing three strikers but calling them wingers plants the seed that they need to play wide.

Explanation of Movements:
Set the players up in a situation where the two strikers go touchline tight and the attacking midfielder pushes onto the sweeper.

Observe what the defenders in a diamond defense do. (next diagram)

If they man-mark them they will then we have three 1 v 1 situations in the attacking third with no cover on.

COACHING STRIKERS

Also, this has created a lot of space (shaded boxes) inside between the sweeper and the center backs for players to break into and for the ball to be passed into.

These spaces are in important parts of the field where players can exploit the man-marking ideas of the opposition. If they mark inside them (zonal) then particularly the two wide strikers are free to receive to feet in space.

The stopper (D) in this situation often does not know where to go or who to mark.

Progression:
The session below is all about diagonal movement and passing - getting away from players running up and down the field in straight lines and always passing in straight lines.

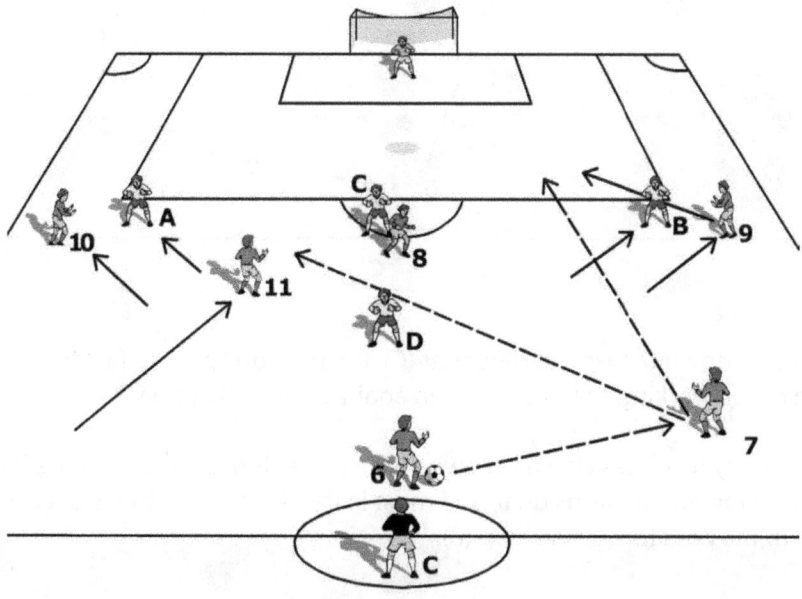

The session takes a lot of work to plant the seed in the minds of the players but it is worth seeing it through. Start position can be (D) passing to (6). Use passive defending to start

COACHING STRIKERS

and fewer defenders to gain success. In the diagram the wide players have pulled out to the touchline. This has created a channel for (11) to attack. Here (11) has no marker which highlights the movement even more.

The plan is:
a) Work with movement of the front players,
b) Work with movement of the midfield players,
c) Work with movement of the fullbacks.

Additional Movements:

See the next diagram - Movement OFF THE BALL has occurred and the man-marking defenders now are taken into areas they don't want to go. This creates space centrally for the attacking team to exploit. The defense of the opposition is pulled apart. (8)'s movement dictates to them all.

Strikers / Wingers (9) and (10) time their movement late as the ball is passed from (7) to (6). They each must expect the pass also but at the same time realize their movement may create space for someone else and they must remain unselfish about this.

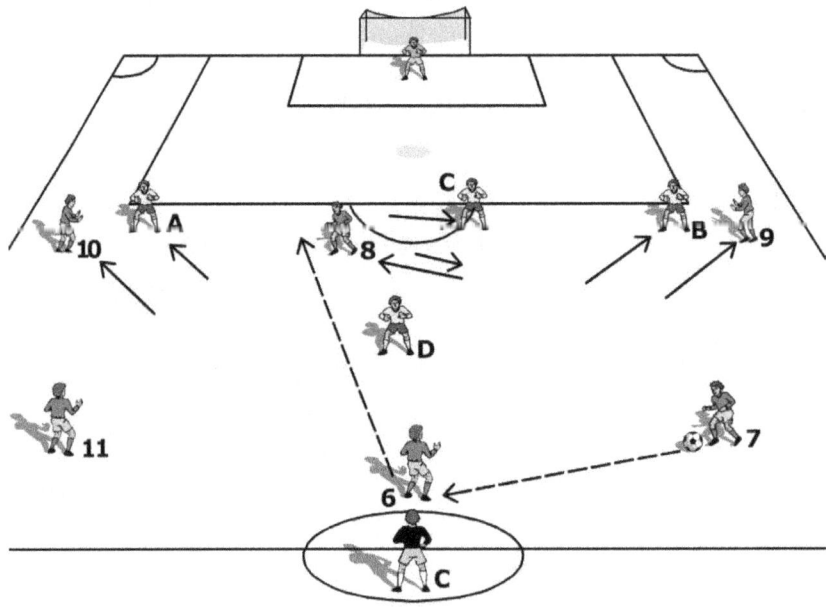

For the ball to (8) down the side of defender (C), (8) must go late and fast to get away from the marking of (C), working the opposite run again and checking back.

If (8) goes too early he closes down his own space to run into and receive the ball at least half-turned and moving towards goal, and must instead receive with his back to goal. The momentum of the pass (pace) will help (8).

See the next diagram. Here the idea is for players to make runs to create space for their teammates to exploit. If (B) tracks (9) inside, the space is then cleared for (8) to make a run into. If (8) is already on the sweeper (C)'s toes then it is a short run to get into position to receive the pass from (7) down the side.

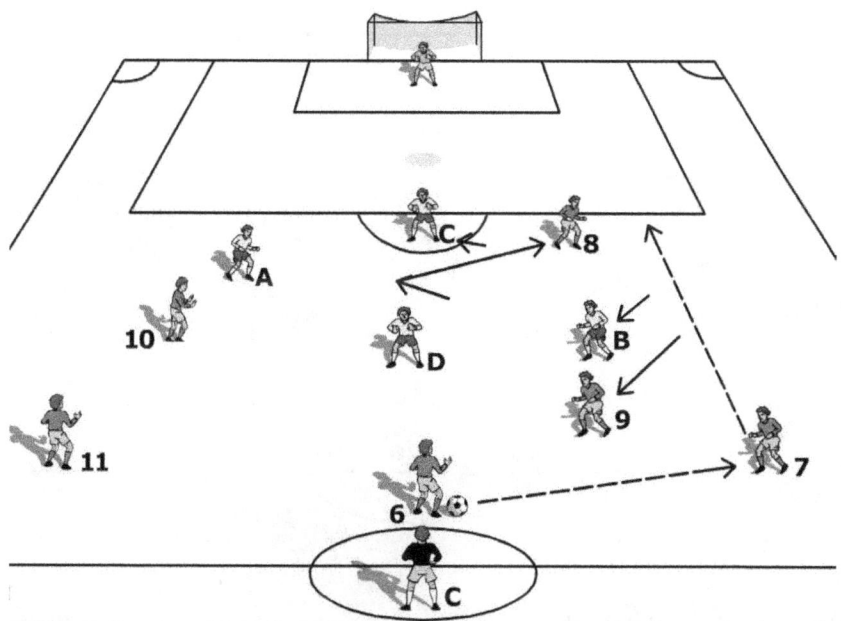

Coaching Points:
- Timing of the run by (9).
- Quality of the pass by (7).
- Timing and weight of the pass by (7).
- Timing of the run by (8) into space, late and fast to escape the marking of (C).
- Angle of runs.

If (8) goes into the space too early then (C) is taken into that space which means (8) has less room to work in. If (8) has time, move (C) away from the space to come back to create more time to receive the pass and space to run into.

Progression:
The numbers are increased to 9 v 8 as shown in the next diagram.

In this situation the attacking team has created space down the sides in the channels.

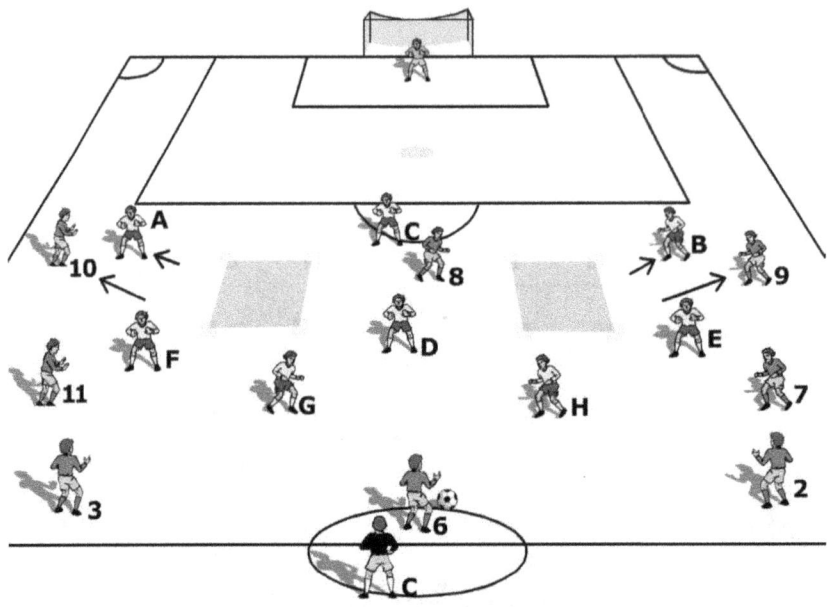

Options:
Midfield players may break into those areas or strikers may check back into those areas to receive a pass inside the marking defender.

It also creates space for a pass down the side for (8) to receive and attack the sweeper.

The strikers must be unselfish in their play to do this for the team. It can be implemented at certain times during the game to confuse the opposition defenders.

They are making runs to create space for other players, not necessarily themselves, but if defenders do not follow them then as a consequence of their movement they themselves get free.

In the next diagram it is the same situation except the central defenders stay and mark "zones".

Since the defenders remain central, marking zones, the space is now in the wide areas, not centrally as before. Midfield players can link up and support the strikers in these areas to create overloads.

COACHING STRIKERS

Defensive Team Adjustments

In the diagram below the wide midfield players have dropped back deep to mark the "wingers" of the attacking team.

Teams may do this to counter the attacking action which means full-backs (2, 3) can now attack with ease.

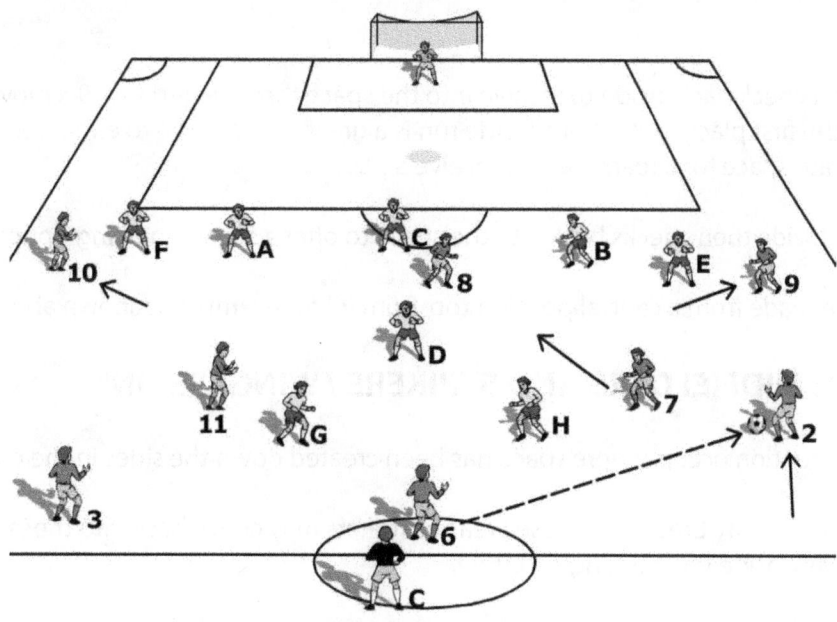

Two forwards pull out wide - Central defenders stay central and mark the space and let the two strikers go wide into winger's positions.

Two wide midfield players drop back to mark them.

The defending team become very defensive now and find trouble getting forward and attacking because they have so many players playing in deep positions.

SPREADING THE ATTACK

Strikers break wide to become wingers. They create space inside for central striker (8) in particular.

Options:
Wingers can check back inside to receive into the space they created (see 9's movement above) in the first place. Outside-to-inside run is a great run to make to either receive a pass or create space for a teammate to receive a pass.

(9) takes (B) wide then checks back into the space to offer a second passing option for (3).

Pass can be made from a central position too, from (6) for example as shown above.

GETTING MIDFIELDERS AND STRIKERS / WINGERS "IN"

The same situation occurs where space has been created down the sides in the channels.

Midfield players may break into those areas or strikers may check back into those areas to receive a pass inside the marking defender.

It also creates space for a pass down the side for (8) to receive and attack the sweeper.

It is worth mentioning again that the strikers must be unselfish in their play to do this for the team. It can be implemented at certain times during the game to confuse the opposition defenders.

They are making runs to create space for other players, not necessarily themselves, but if defenders do not follow them then as a consequence of their movement they themselves get free.

GETTING FULL-BACKS "IN"

Now we are creating space up front for fullbacks to break forward from deep.

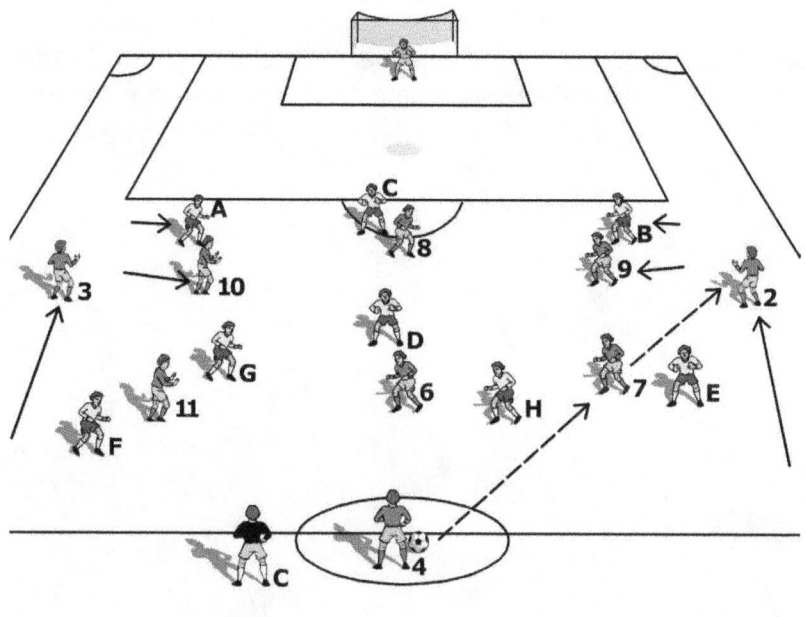

COACHING STRIKERS

Movements:
(9) checks inside, taking defender (B) inside also, creating space outside for fullback (2) to run into and receive a pass from (7).

Same situation could be worked on the other side with (3). Run has to be late and fast to catch the defenders out.

(E) may be caught out with this blindside run and not recover quickly enough.

COMBINATION MOVEMENTS OF THE FRONT THREE

This is good to play against a sweeper and two man markers and a back three which is much more prevalent in the USA than in Europe.

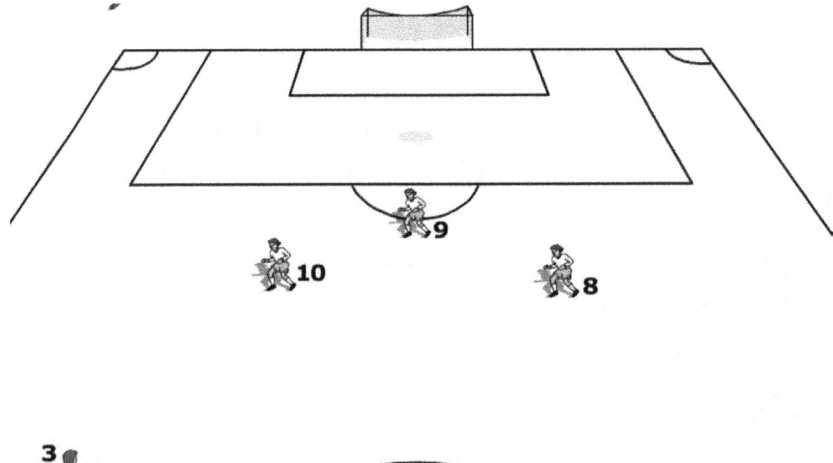

Start positions of the front three with no defenders. I am showing only the three front players and the server, and then the appropriate defenders to simplify the set up.

Finishing positions of the three movements, left striker (10) short to receive the ball to feet, central striker (9) diagonal run down the left channel for the channel pass, right striker (8) right diagonal run off the shoulder of the (imaginary) defender for the right diagonal pass.

Here (9) comes short and (8) and (10) perform a criss-cross movement.

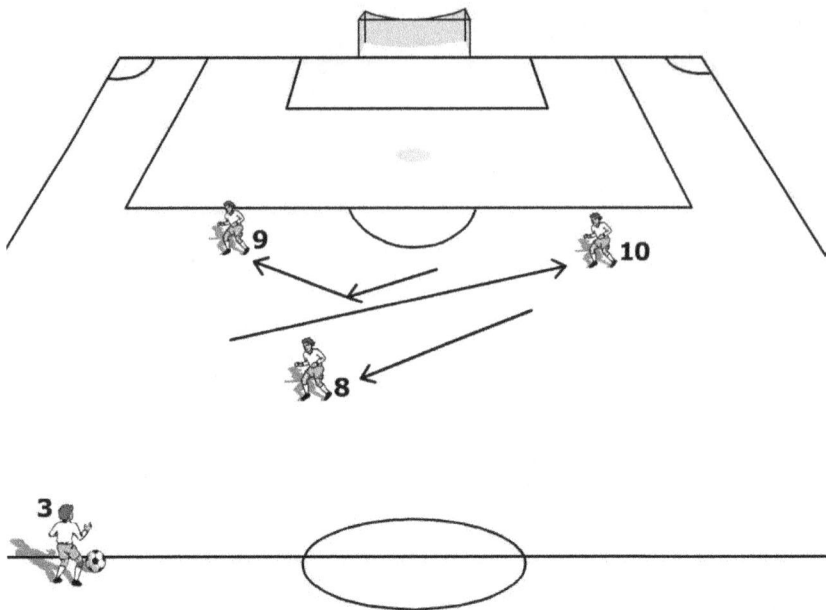

In this example, (8) checks to the ball for the short pass option, (9) starts to come short then checks away into the left channel and (10) comes all the way across for the long diagonal pass.

These movements are not the only ones they can make but I like the variation for the passer. He can make a pass short, a diagonal, or down the side.

If teams practice this, the player on the ball knows the front three will make certain runs, so it is almost like a set play within free play, and they know in advance where to pass.

Other players will be involved in the game of course and each of these may provide other options for the passer. Also, players will use their own imagination, as they should, but this is a starting point to get things moving in the right direction.

COACHING STRIKERS

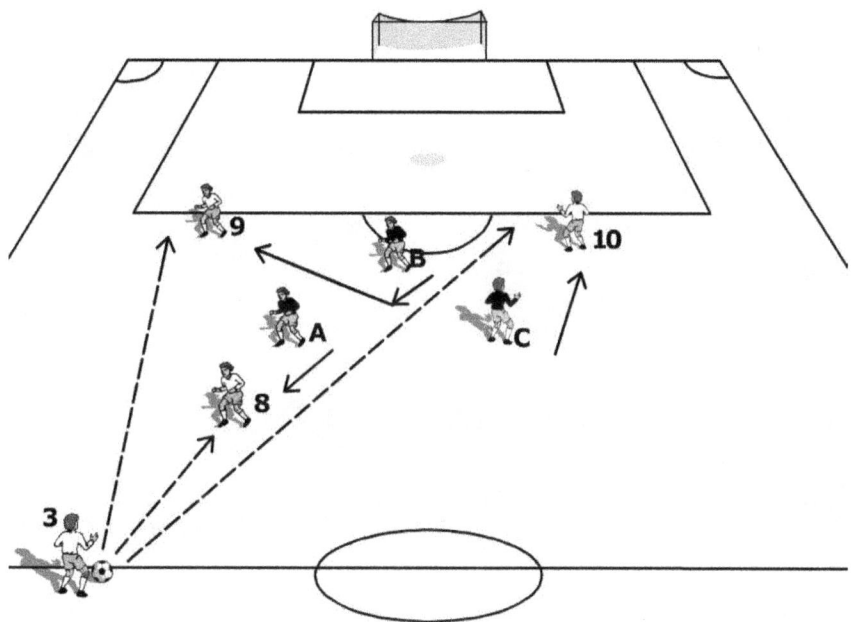

-133-

TRAINING SPECIFIC MOVEMENTS AND FORMATIONS

WORKING OPPOSITES WITH MOVEMENT OF STRIKERS
A VERY GOOD BUT ALSO A VERY SIMPLE EXERCISE TO PRACTICE THE OPPOSITE MOVE

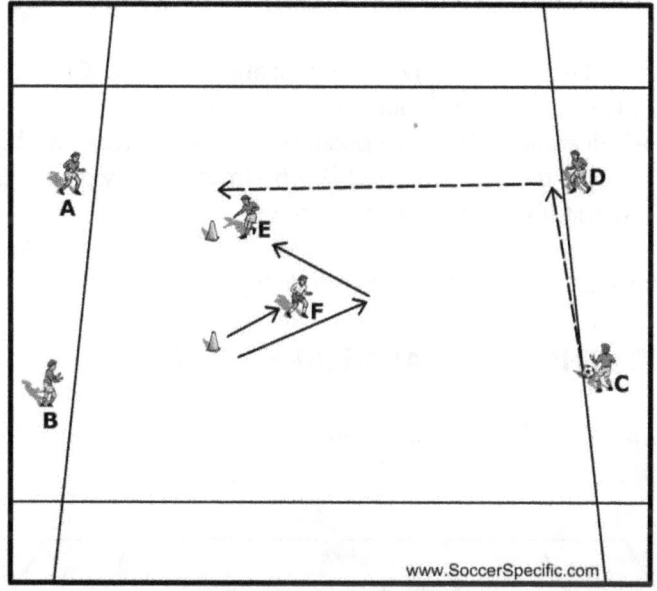

Striker (E) comes short and shows for the ball, asking for a pass. Defender (F) follows.

Midfielder (C) passes to (D), (D) then passes over the top into (E)'s path as he spins.

Defender must play passively. To continue the work once player (E) receives the ball he must beat (F) back to the touchline. Players (C) and (D) go to the middle and the next two take their place.

As the pass is going from (D) to (C) the striker shouts the code word and spins to receive the pass as player (C) is about to pass it. The shout must be early to (C) to make the pass at the exact same time (E) is spinning to receive it.

Develop: The player receiving the pass can get it "short or long", to keep the defender guessing. If short, combine with the passer to beat the defender.

This is the "Vialli Move".

Practice it also where (C) receives a pass from (E), has time on the ball, and can take two touches (liken to a game situation) and that player makes the next pass off the opposite move into the space behind the striker (E).

Alternatively, (E) has possession, comes short and passes to (C). As he passes, (E) shouts the code word and (C) can make a one touch pass in behind, knowing (E) will spin and turn back. If the code word isn't called, the ball can be passed to (E)'s feet or may be passed off to (D).

Options can be:
- The start position is (C) passes to (D), and (E) times his run off that pass, uses the code word and receives a pass in behind into space.
- (C) passes to (D) again as the start position. (E) times his run off that pass and doesn't use the code word so he gets it to feet. He can pass back and check back to the cone to start again.
- A different start position where (E) has the ball and passes to (C) and goes short; no code word so gets it to feet or the ball is passed to (D).
- Now (E) has the ball again as the start position and passes to (C) and goes short; he uses the code word as the pass goes to (C), who immediately passes the ball ONE TOUCH in behind and into space for the spin turn from (E).

Lots of different ideas can be used here. Introduce a goal to finish into.

WORKING WITH THE CENTRAL STRIKER ONLY

The start position of the session. The cones ensure the players check off at angles to the ball. We will focus on the movement of the central striker only.

Passing and moving at half pace getting a rhythm. (9) comes off at an angle to receive the ball. No defenders yet.

The striker must recognize when the man on the ball has TIME to play the ball forward. The striker moves towards the ball, dragging the man-marking defenders with him.

As the player checks toward the passer as if to receive a pass and is marked tightly by the defender, a sharp spin is made to receive a longer pass behind (into the space created by coming short) rather than the short one the striker seemed to be asking for.

A sharp turn/spin into the defender and across the shoulder is the best move rather than the arc run into space.

An arc run is easily tracked by the defender as there is time to see the ball and the player.

When the player has time on the ball to pass, expect lots of movement at pace e.g. short to go long. The passing player can pass down the side of the striker.

COACHING STRIKERS

OPPOSITE RUN SHORT TO GO LONG

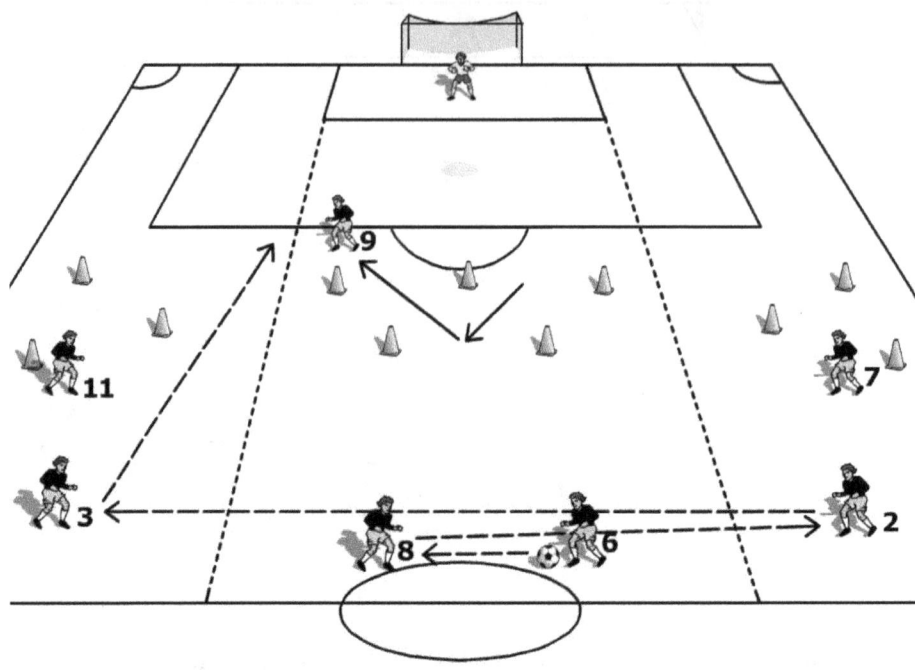

The passing players need to know the striker is playing opposites.

The opposite movement is if the striker shows to receive to feet, as above, he is going to spin away and receive in space in front of him in the form of a through ball. If he runs away, then expect a check back for a pass to feet.

To make the movement clearer the strikers can have a "Code Word" to call as a signal so the player on the ball knows what is happening.

They call it as early as possible. The Italian striker Vialli who played for Juventus and Chelsea was a master at this move. He would draw a defender towards the player on the ball in midfield and in a blink of an eye would spin and be away from them with the ball already into his path in front of him and bearing down on goal, the defender left stranded.

In a game the team could be prepared to play on the basis that they always make the pass off the first run unless they get a call from the striker using the code word to implement the opposite movement.

It isn't always possible in split second situations to recognize how much time a player has on the ball so it may be best just to work the movement off a call.

OPPOSITE RUN LONG TO COME SHORT

The passing players need to know the strikers are playing opposites. This time the striker is moving away to come back.

There is time on the ball for the passing player and the opposite movement comes into effect (working off the second run), but if there is no time the striker knows it will be played first time into the first run.

OPPOSITE RUN INSIDE TO GO OUTSIDE

Striker (9) runs inside to check back outside.

Here showing the end run of striker (9) as he cut away from the ball and away from the space to open it up for himself on the 2nd run. (3) can play a channel pass to (9) as shown here.

INTRODUCE A DEFENDER

Striker (9) draws the defender to the ball and creates space behind for himself.

Defender (A) follows and gets tight to him.

As the ball is traveling to (3), striker (9) calls the code word out which informs (3) he will check to the ball then check away, wanting the pass behind him and not to feet as the first run would suggest.

COACHING STRIKERS

INTRODUCE A BACK FOUR AND MIDFIELD TWO

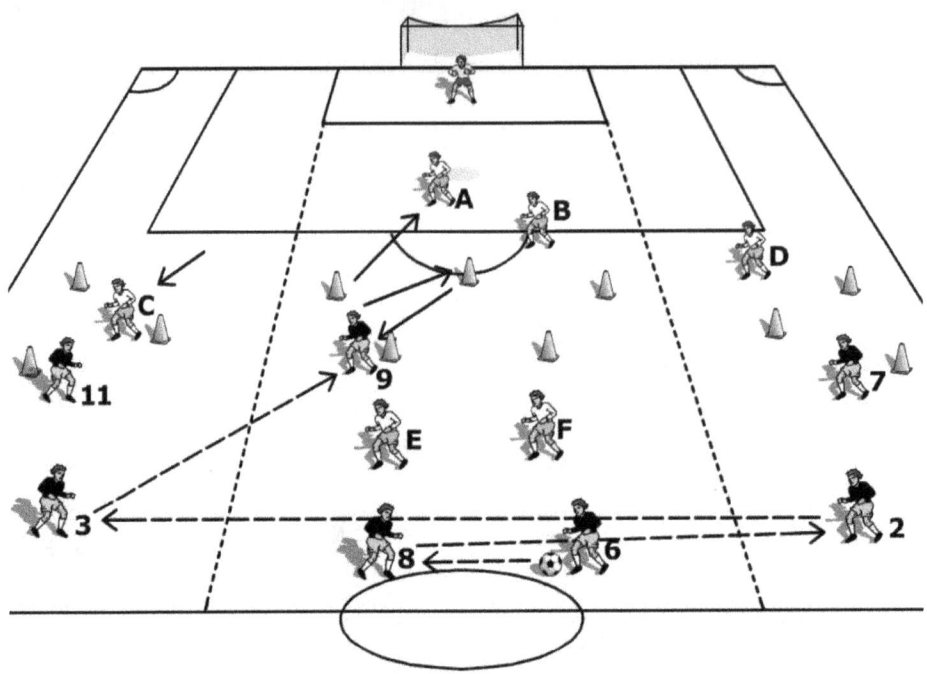

Here striker (9) runs off defender (A) who tracks his run.

Having called the code word, (3) knows he will check back to receive to feet, hopefully in space to receive and turn having lost (A) with the first movement (as above).

One striker playing against two center backs may look a big disadvantage but the striker can reduce this to a 1 v 1 by his movement. He can play against either of these players.

Above he isolates (A) 1 v 1 by moving in front of him and away from (B). (B) is now on the opposite side of where the ball is being played and is out of the main area, therefore it is a 1 v 1 against (A).

COACHING STRIKERS

Here the pass must be made on the outside of (A) and away from (B) so (B) will have to cover a lot of ground to get in position to cover.

(C) is drawn to (11) which creates a small space between (A) and (C) to play the ball into. Again the code word has been called to make this movement.

Let's say (3) is closed down very quickly and has only time for a one touch pass to striker (9). In this case, (9) must realize he hasn't time to do a double and opposite run so he should expect the first pass off the first run.

NOW DEVELOP THE WIDE STRIKERS (OR WINGERS / OUTSIDE MIDFIELD PLAYERS)

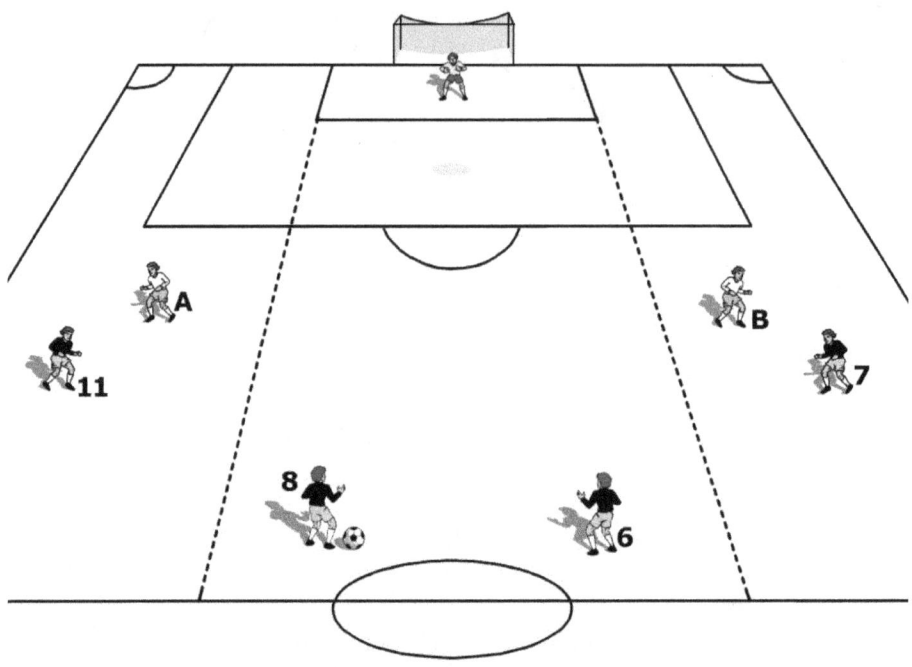

Only 7 players needed. This is a drill/function keeping the movements simple.

Two 1 v 1 situations teaching both sides how to cut inside and receive a pass inside the defender.

As the ball is passed between (6) and (8) the wide player (11) runs off defender (A).

So we are looking at the timing of the run and the timing of the pass. The run is in two parts, the first one to occupy the defender and the second one to get free of the defender.

(11) needs to be observing the body language also of the player on the ball so he knows when the pass will be delivered and he can then time his second movement off that.

You can have the players practicing these movements in your warm up, checking runs, breaking inside off the outside foot.

Keep practicing until it becomes embedded in their minds and it becomes a natural movement.

COACHING STRIKERS

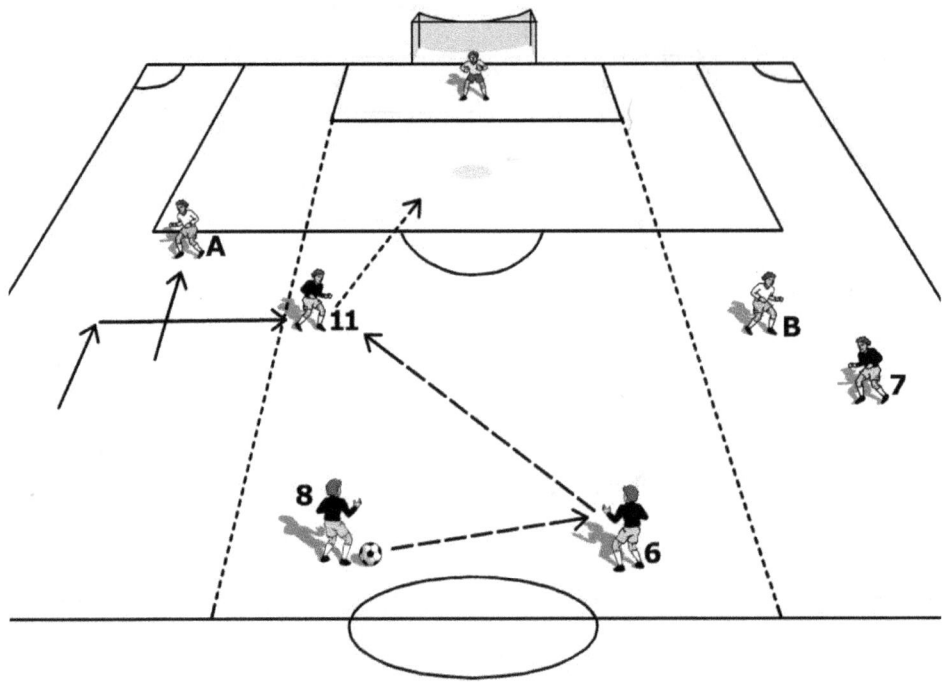

Here (11) makes his second run and cuts inside having run the defender off in the first run.

Again the key is the timing of each, the run and the pass.

If you have a right footer on the left and a left footer on the right then the player cutting inside will come onto his strong foot for the shot on goal.

Here the player breaks inside off his outside foot, the left foot in this case.

COACHING STRIKERS

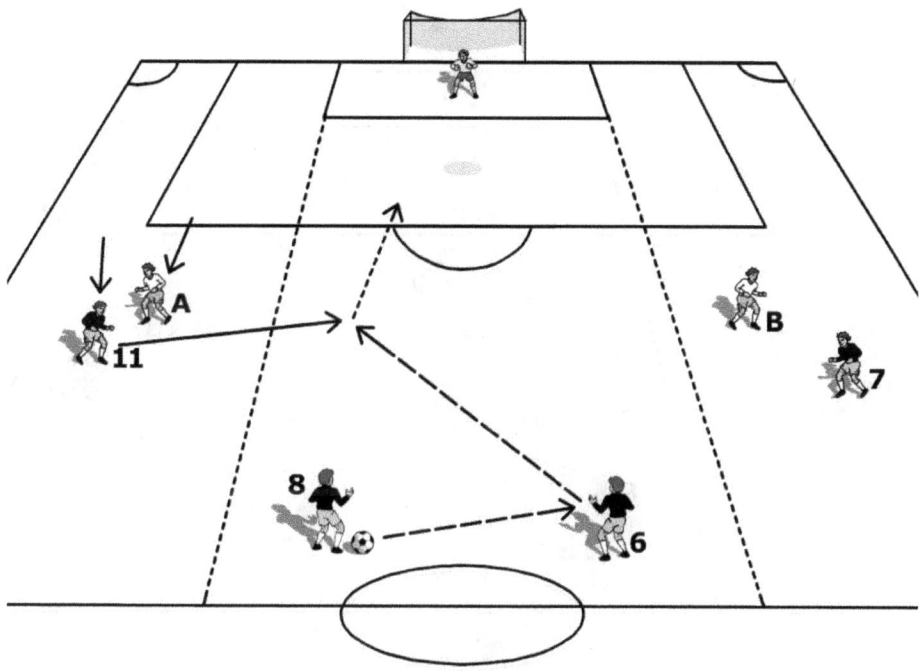

Here we see a different way to get free of the defender; this time coming towards the ball and bringing the defender with him.

Once the defender is tight, (11) cuts across his path and into the path of the pass in space in front of him. It is a very sharp cut, not a looping cut that is easier to defend against.

Here the player breaks inside off his outside foot again, but in this case it is the right foot. So they need to learn how to do this checking movement off BOTH FEET.

Now we have 10 players, bringing in a central striker and a defender and a defensive midfielder to develop the idea.

We are working with the midfield two and the wide players and the striker but not introducing the number 10 yet.

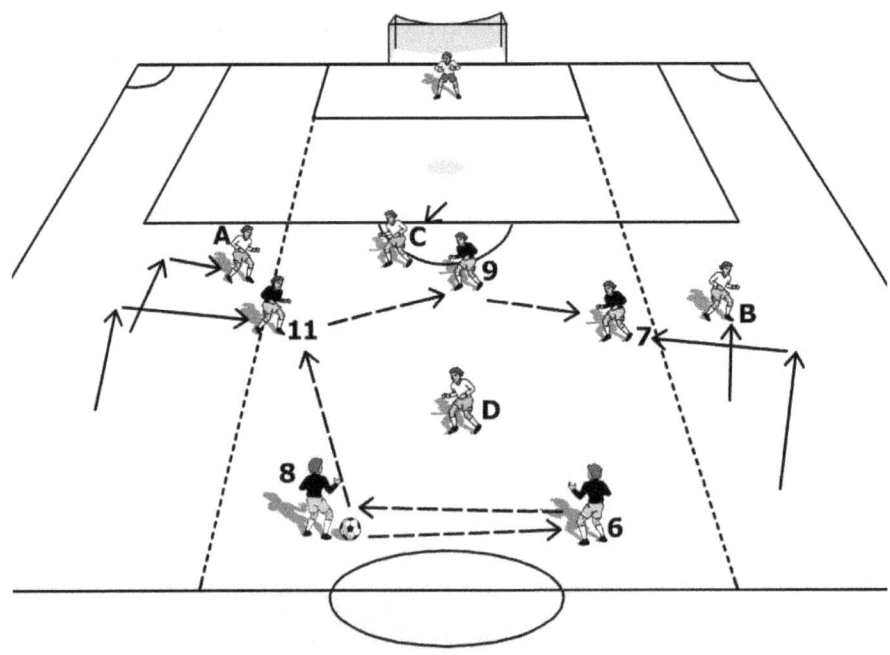

(11) cuts inside and links up with the central striker (9).

(7) comes in from the other side and develops the play further, having first run the defender off to create space for himself inside..

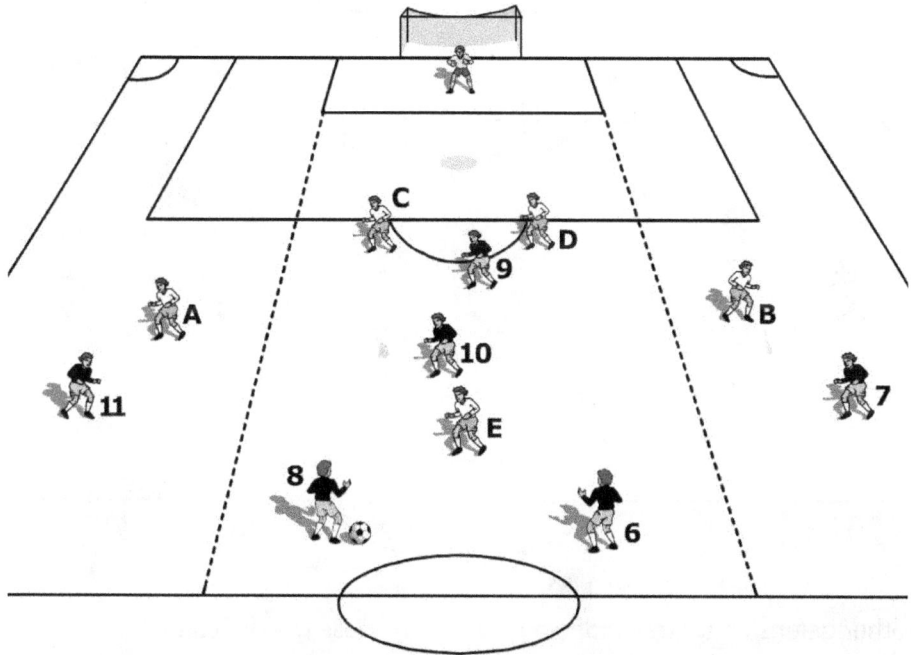

12 players. Add a defensive center back and an attacking number 10. We are building up the numbers as we go.

PHASE OF PLAY

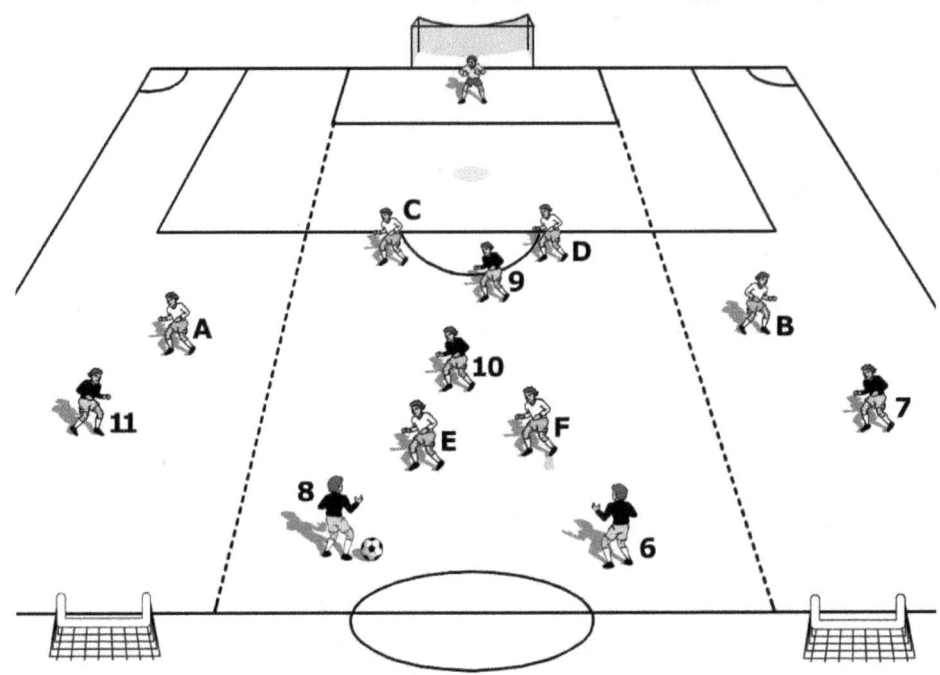

Add another defensive central midfield player to increase the difficulty.

Introduce target goals for the opponents and it now becomes a Phase of Play.

Now we have the 2-3-1 of the 4-2-3-1.

Showing how the two wide players can cut inside to support the front two; now in a 4-2 against a 4-2 (same as a lone striker situation but showing it can work in different formations).

One is going long and one is coming short, but both can be effective. In fact the one coming short can be the best one as it draws the fullback away from the space behind. So it is an opposite run.

The one going long means while you still lose him with the check inside he is at least in a deeper defensive position to counter.

Obviously the next phase would be to add the fullbacks and link them with the wide players, creating 2 v 1 situations on the outside.

It is important to teach the wide players these outside to inside movements because they can be effective in many systems of play, not just the 4-2-3-1.

The same movements will occur in a 4-2-3-1, 4-2-1-3, 4-3-3, 4-4-2, and 4-4-1-1, as well as in systems of play using three at the back such as 3-4-3 and 3-5-2.

SMALL SIDED GAME

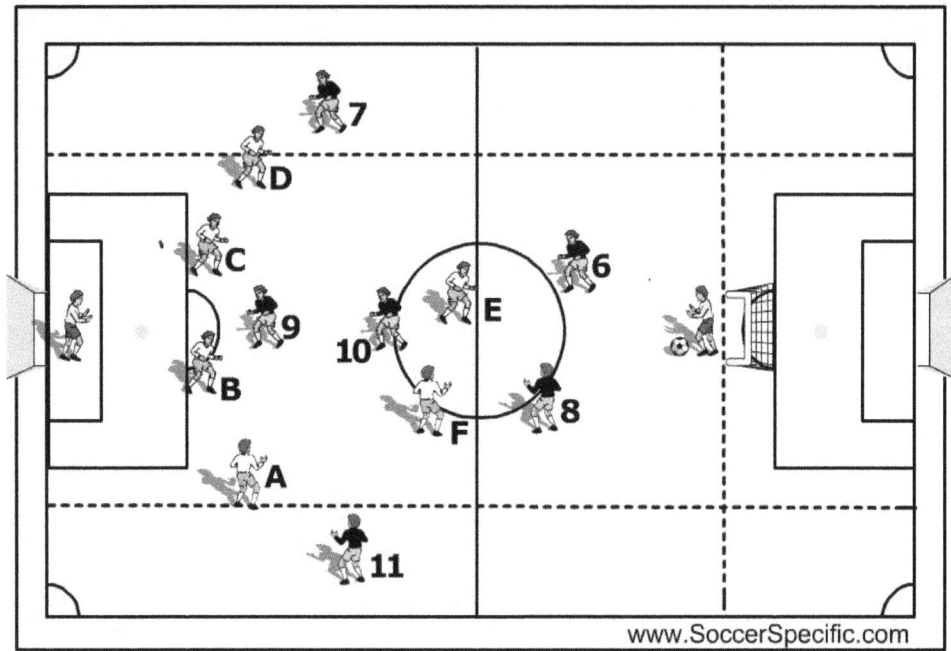

Introduce another full size goal and it becomes a small sided game continuing the 2-3-1 theme. Now fourteen players with the addition of another goalkeeper.

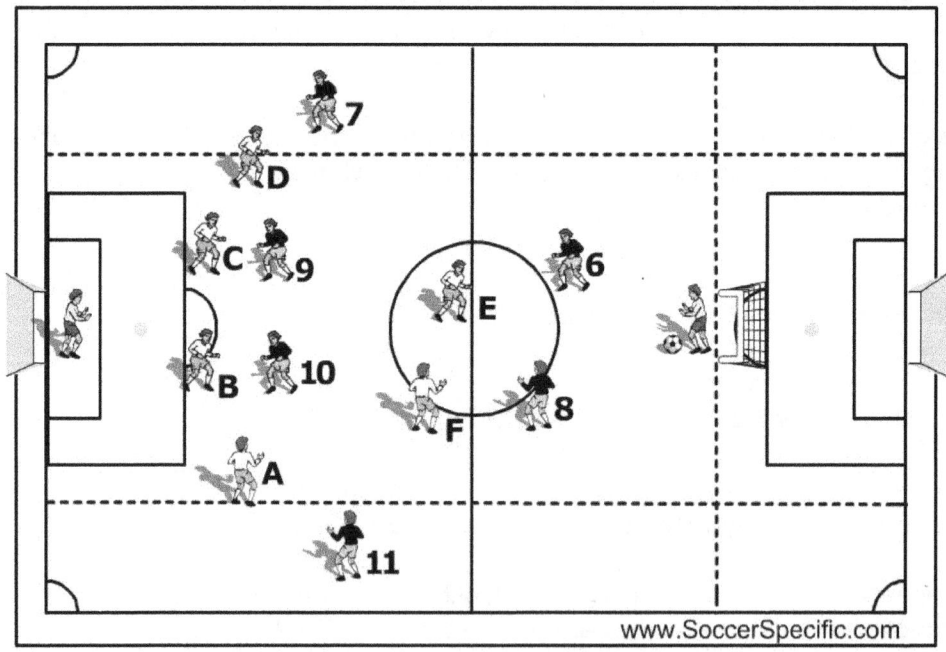

We can make a simple switch to a 4-2 from a 2-3-1 which represents the 4-4-2 formation if you decide to do this small sided game with two central strikers.

Eventually take it to an 11 v 11.

THE MOVEMENTS OF THE WIDE ATTACKERS TO GET FREE

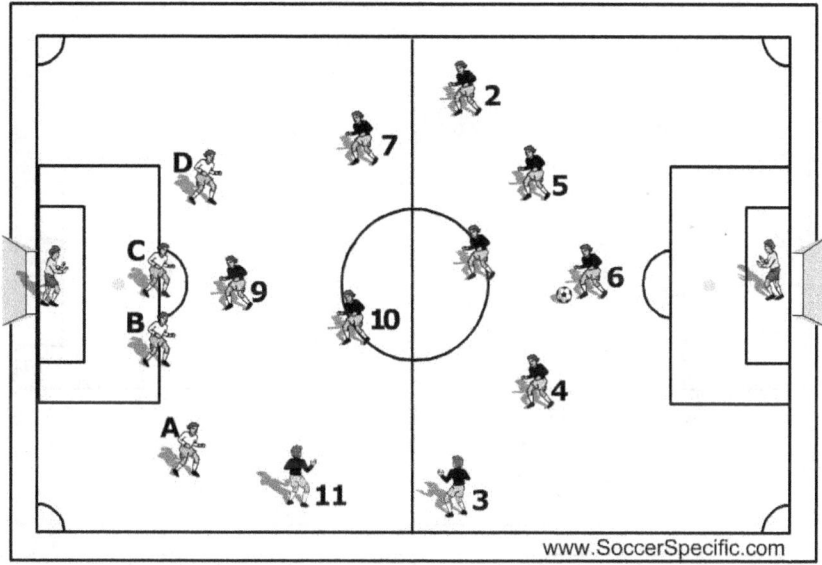

The normal attacking set up of the team. (11) is wide, looking to accept a pass from (6) and defender (A) is beginning to close him down.

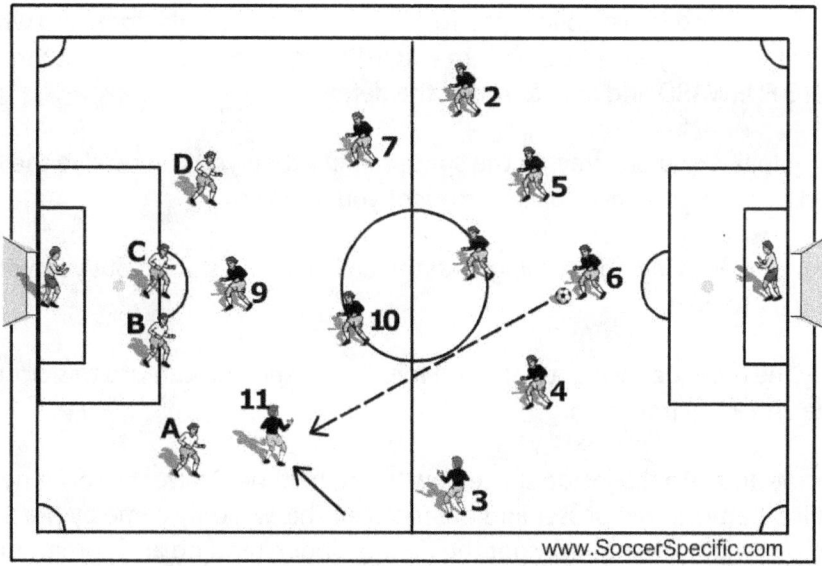

(11) goes in TOO EARLY and closes his OWN SPACE down.

By doing so he is marked by defender (A) and receives the ball with his BACK TO GOAL to feet and likely standing still.

This is ok because he still has possession and has his body between the defender and the ball to protect it, but he is facing backwards and away from the opponent's goal and not able to run at the defense. There are better situations he can get himself in to make it more difficult for the defender.

COACHING STRIKERS

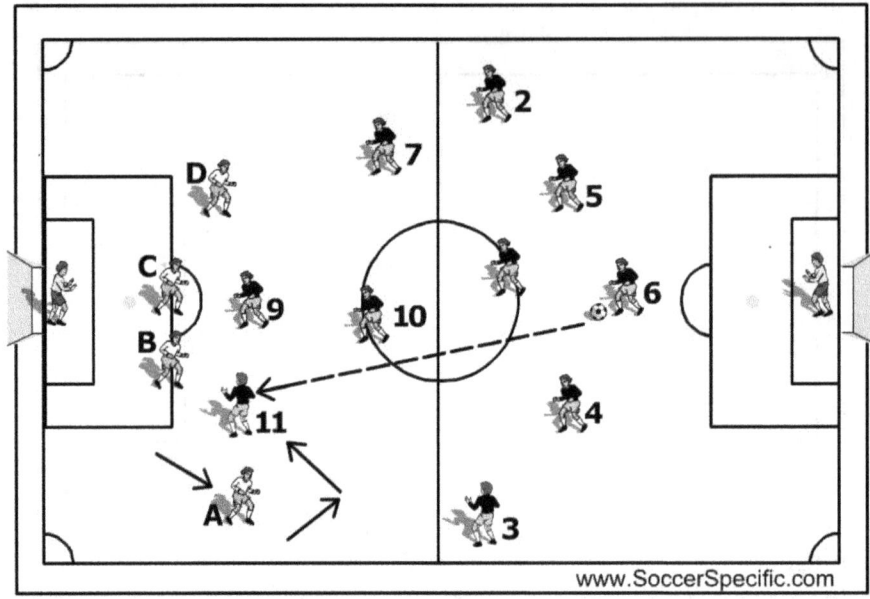

Run towards the ball but not too much inside because that is the space we want to keep free.

By doing so the defender may follow you to get tight. Once he gets tight, and with the right timing of the pass you cut across him and inside to receive the pass into the inside space FACING FORWARD and able to run at the defense.

If he does not follow you but stays in the space behind then you can receive the ball and face forward because you have space in front of you to do so.

This will be more receiving and turning with the ball, which is still ok, but you will still have the defender (A) to beat.

So hopefully the defender will get tight and follow you and you can use this closeness to check inside and away from him.

The pass inside and into the inside space now has to be timed correctly so we need great understanding between the passer and the receiver. This will only come by practicing this in training over and over until they get the timing, understanding and communication right.

Coaching Points:
- Timing and accuracy of the pass (into SPACE INSIDE)
- Timing of the run
- Angle of the run

Timing of the pass: If it is too early then it may be intercepted; if it is too late then the player will receive it facing backwards as previously shown.

Timing of the run: If it is too early then again the player will receive it facing backwards as previously shown; if too late then the defender may get to the ball first.

Angle of the Run: Must be away from the defender and here I show two ways to do it as it is TWO RUNS, not just one. The first one to affect the defender and create space, the second to exploit the space created.

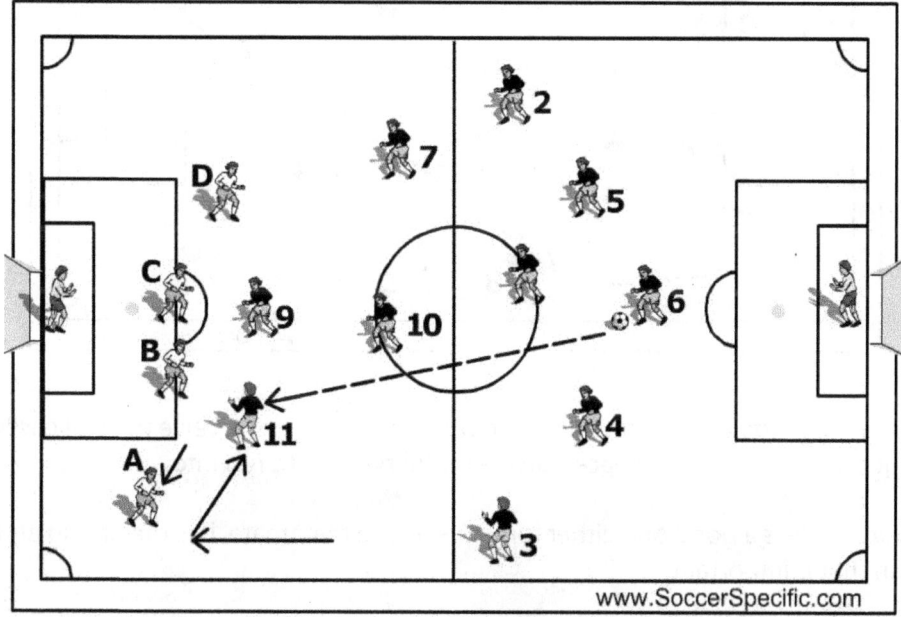

If you have time to do it, try to run the defender away from the space you want to move into first.

If you make the first run into the space YOU WANT then you take the defender INTO IT with you.

Therefore you close your own space down for yourself and then may have to receive the pass facing backwards and to feet rather than into space facing forward. This is still ok as we have possession but there are better solutions.

As shown here, you take the defender away and then check back and inside to receive the pass inside and therefore you are in a great position to be free of (A) and running at pace at (B) with the ball.

COACHING STRIKERS

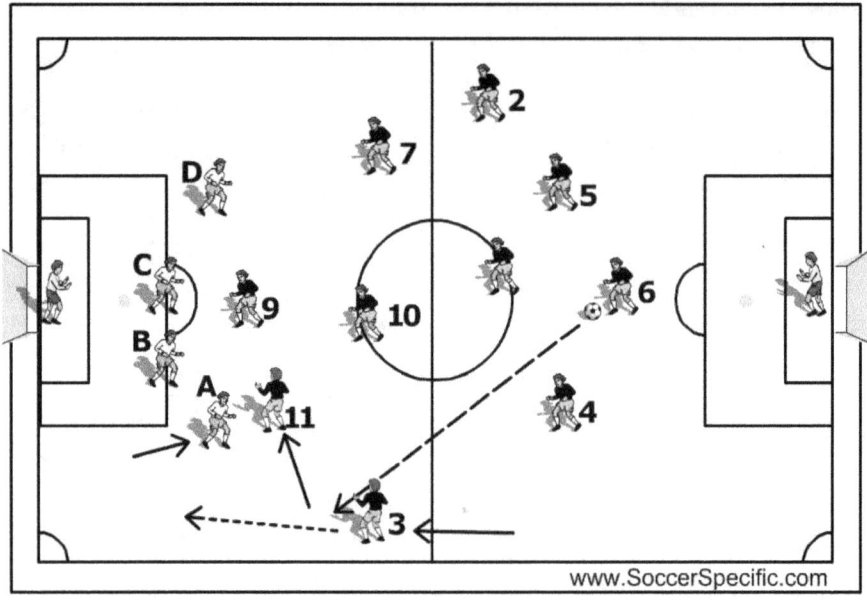

Even if you run inside and the defender is tight and you cannot receive the ball easily, this is still a good run as it creates space outside for fullback (3) to run into.

So, the run inside is a good one either for yourself or a teammate. It is the timing and angle of the run that is important.

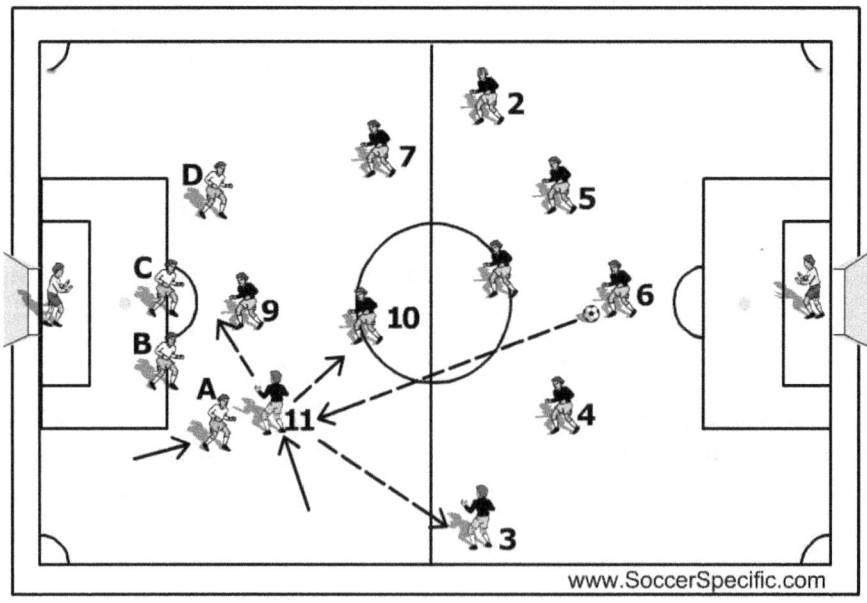

Here you have received the ball facing backwards so your own MOMENTUM has stopped but you can still bring other players into play.

Here I show three options of a potential pass to maintain possession.

COACHING STRIKERS

MESSI OF BARCELONA

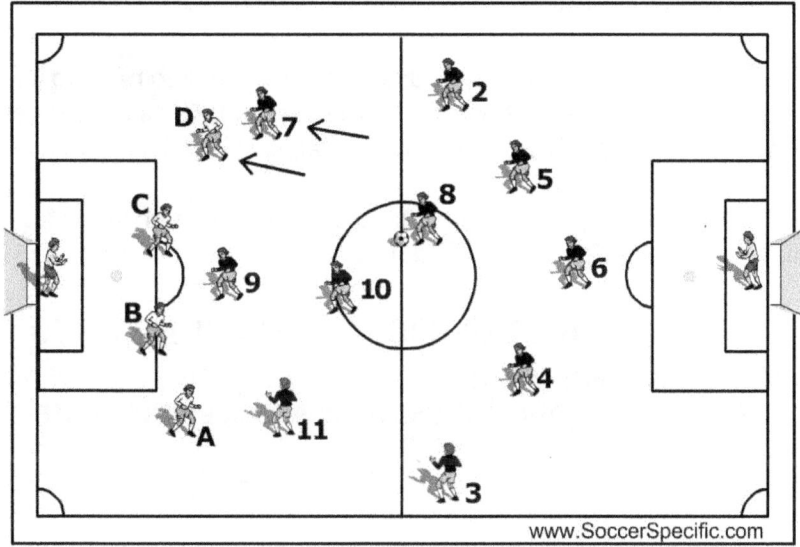

Watching Lionel Messi of Barcelona as they play in the build up; the timing of his movement is exceptional.

I am sure this does not just happen naturally. He has practiced this hundreds of times in training. It is a fact that the best players in the world are also the hardest working players.

Here Messi (7) sprints forward, attacking defender (D). At the same time he is observing the body language of (8) to see when he is about to release the pass.

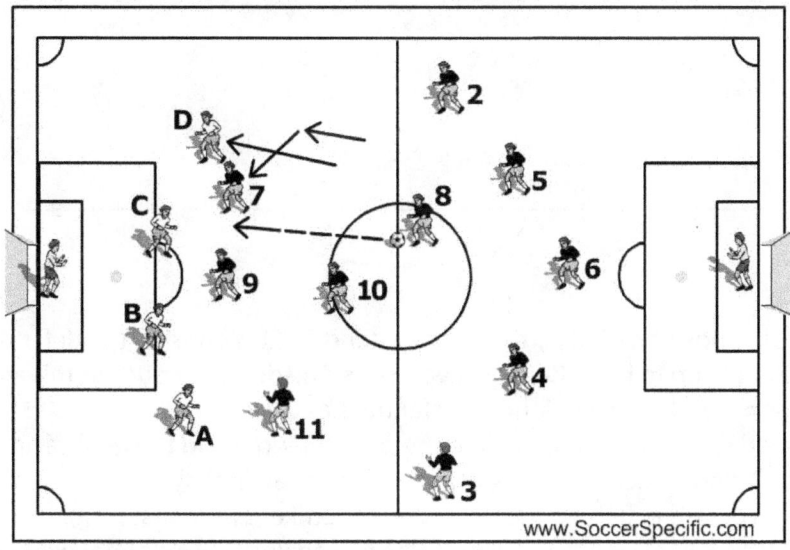

Fullback (D) is recovering back and tracking Messi's run, trying to stop the ball in behind.

At the correct moment Messi cuts inside to accept the pass INTO HIS PATH and running at full pace to attack the center back (C). (D) is now effectively out of the play.

If all is in sync, that is, the timing and angle of the pass and the timing and angle of the run, then Messi does not have to break his stride to receive the pass in front of him and he is now at full pace.

Striker (9) checks away from the immediate space to allow Messi to run into it and hopefully he can take a defender out of it too, in this case (C). (C) has to decide in a split second to either track (9) or position to defend 1 v 1 against Messi.

If he defends 1 v 1 then perhaps (9) can be free to play a give and go with Messi. Messi is of course coming inside onto his favored left foot, so he could also get a strike on goal.

USUAL POSITIONING OF STRIKERS WITH THEIR BACKS TO THE DEFENDER AND TO THE GOAL
(YOU SEE THIS ALL THE TIME, TAKE A CLOSE LOOK AND SEE FOR YOURSELF)

This is the typical position of the strikers. They stand STILL alongside the defender and do not open the angle up to help them receive a pass. The disadvantages to this are:
- Striker has his back to the defender. Defender has control.
- Striker's body position is square on to the ball, defender and the goal, facing back.
- Striker can't see the defender clearly nor see the goal directly.
- If the ball is played in behind the defender, the striker has to first turn, then run forward and probably is second best to the ball against the defender who has a yard or two headstart and is probably side on already so only needs to do half a turn.
- It is easy for the defender to mark the striker as he can see the ball and the striker at the same time and be in control of the situation.

COACHING STRIKERS

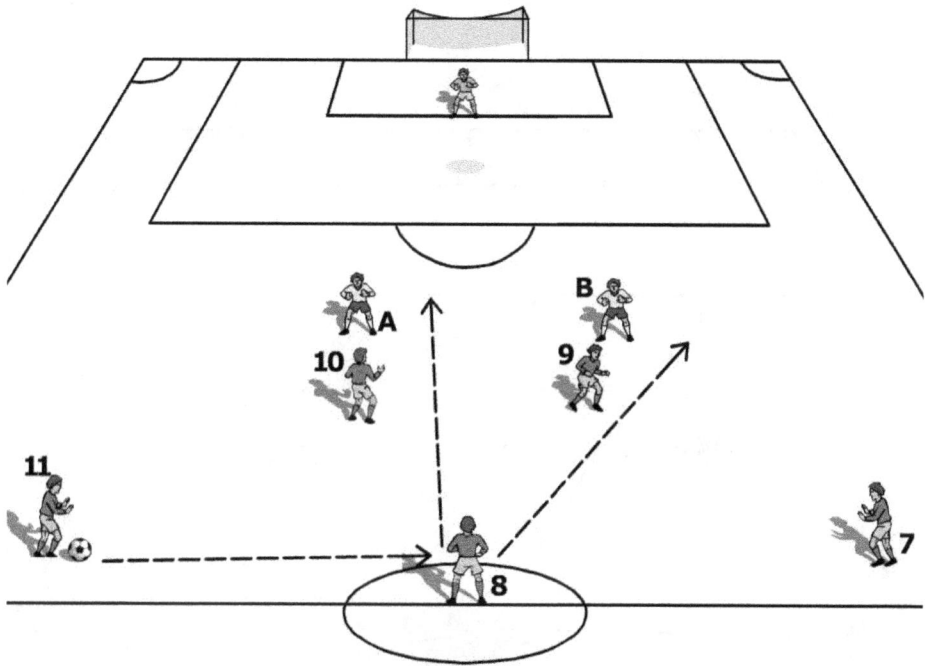

The ball is played straight and behind the defender (A) who is likely to be first to the ball as the striker (10) has to turn and run after the ball and in behind the defender.

If the ball is played wide past striker (9), defender (B) should be first to it based on the starting position of (9), which is back to goal and back to the direction of the ball and where it is traveling to. He would have to turn and chase it, losing vital seconds.

It is all about the starting position of the striker and his body stance in terms of open or closed, open being half or fully turned in the direction the ball is going, closed being with his back to where the ball is going.

Too often strikers start from a closed body stance.

INDIVIDUAL STRIKER MOVEMENT OFF THE SHOULDER

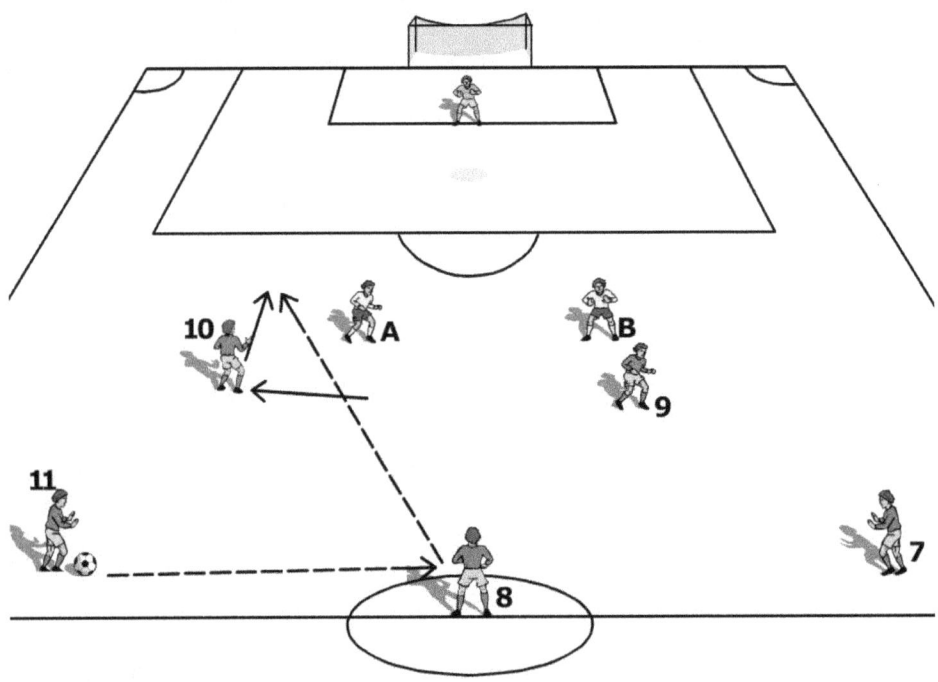

Striker moves "OFF THE SHOULDER" of the defender. Just a few yards can open up space and attacking opportunities.

In this case, moving off the shoulder of the defender means there is a space in behind that the player on the ball can deliver to that was previously difficult for him to see. If the defender does not adjust his position, this is a great chance for a decisive penetrating pass and attack on goal.

Key points:
- Striker is now facing forward, and off at an angle, not having to turn and run forward (saves time and puts the defender at a disadvantage).
- Striker can now see the ball, the goal and the defender at the same time.
- Striker can even take his position off the sweeper (in terms of being offside) if the opposition employs one, so he is almost in advance but also wide of the marking defender. This position (off the shoulder) is very difficult to defend against.
- Striker, if not facing forward, is at least in a side-on position so he can see forward and not have his back to the defender.

Striker moves "OFF THE SHOULDER" of the defender.

The defender comes with the striker and closes him down. Now the timing of the pass and timing of the run come into play. Striker then checks back inside into the space the defender has vacated and attacks inside and across in front of him. Striker (9) can run off the other center back (B) to create the space inside also. The player on the ball plays it inside the center back.

The striker (10) should try to time it so that the decisive cut is made just as the defender (A) plants his right foot down so his momentum is taking him away from the second run. This can provide a valuable yard or two of space for the striker who can receive in stride facing the goal.

COACHING STRIKERS

Striker moves "OFF THE SHOULDER" of the defender.

Same as the previous diagram where the defender closes the striker down but this time the striker makes a run outside and behind the defender rather than inside and across him. Timing of this is important for being onside.

Again, timing the movement when the defender is in an off-balanced stance makes it more difficult for him to check back in one movement and cover the striker's run.

STRIKERS RECEIVING THE BALL TO FEET WITH THEIR BACKS TO GOAL AND INTRODUCING QUICK PLAY IN AND AROUND THE BOX

All start positions should be with the idea of getting the ball into the strikers' feet to receive it with their back to goal and then developing the play from there.

Emphasize the striker getting across the defender if the defender tries to get in front of him to intercept the pass, using his body to block him off.

This can be a big problem for a striker if he is not aware of where the defender is.

Warm up:

In fours, receiving and turning or passing back and playing forward. First thought is "Can I turn and beat the defender and pass to the target?". If not, the passing player gets the ball back and plays it forward to the target, so the striker then acts as a rebound player.

Strikers must be strong to keep the ball at their feet with their back into the defender.

The striker can do this side-on to the defender also, protecting the ball with his body using the opposite foot to maintain possession.

Once the ball is at the other side the defending players become attackers and have to do the same in the other direction.

Teach receiving both with the inside and the outside of the feet. Strikers can drop their shoulders one way and move the other as a feint to fool the defender.

If there is no space behind for the passer to pass into them, the strikers need to get the ball to feet and be able to work from there.

Coaching Points:
- Using the body to hold the defender off, so the striker initially backs into the defender
- Communication between the passer and receiver as to where the receiver wants the ball (using verbal or visual cues)
- A good first touch (perhaps turning with the ball on the first touch)
- Receiving and turning, beating the defender 1 v 1 to shoot on goal, using the defender's body as a pivot
- If the striker can't turn he tries to work a combination with the 2nd striker and act as a rebound player
- Lay the ball off to a midfield player to develop the secondary phase of play from there.
- Get a finish on goal

RECEIVING TO FEET WITH YOUR BACK TO GOAL

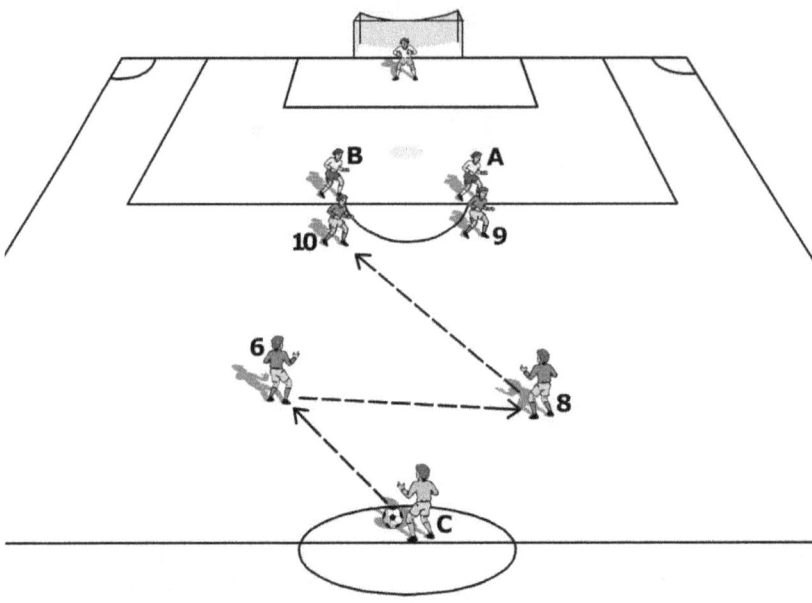

Use a full goal and a keeper and two defenders. You can cone the area you are specifically working in if you like.

If the defenders win the ball, they get it to the server (in this case the coach) and start again.

Coaching Points:
- Using the body to hold the defender off, so the striker initially backs into the defender trying to spin him
- Communication between the passer and receiver as to where the receiver wants the ball
- The angle of the pass can determine where the defender stands. In this case the defender marks inside the player and goal side (so pass to the attacker's right foot away from the defender)
- A good first touch (perhaps turning with the ball on the first touch)
- Receiving and turning, beating the defender 1 v 1 to shoot on goal, using the defender's body as a pivot
- If the striker can't turn then try to work a combination with the 2nd striker
- Lay the ball off to a midfield player to develop the secondary phase of play from there
- Strikers must also be looking over their shoulders as the play is developing and assessing where the defender is marking and can even show the passer where they want the ball by pointing. This is good awareness on the part of the strikers.

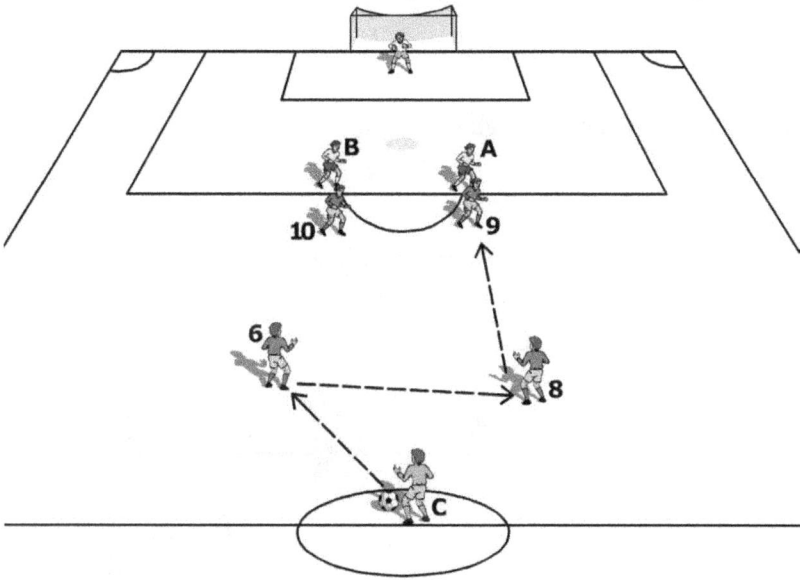

Now the pass is straighter and the angle means the defender (A) perhaps marks slightly outside the striker (9) so (9) cannot receive down the channel side and attack there.

The pass could be to the striker's right foot so his body is between the ball and the defender.

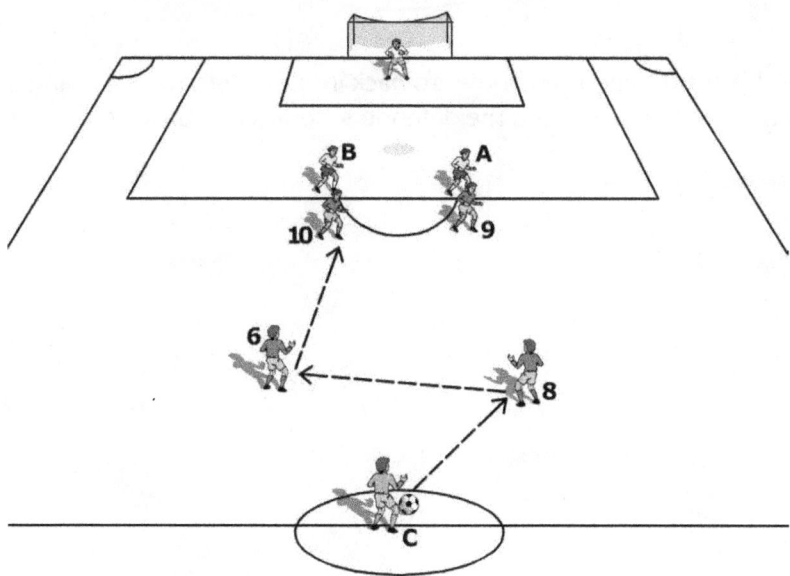

Defender (B) marks channel side and so the passer may play the ball into the striker's left foot and away from the defender.

VARIOUS "START POSITIONS" FOR THE STRIKER AS THE BUILD UP IS HAPPENING

HERE TIGHT TO THE DEFENDER

Strikers (9) and (10) are using their bodies to back into the defenders, leaning into them to get them off balance and also using the defenders' bodies as a pivot to spin and turn with the ball.

COMING SHORT FROM BEHIND THE DEFENDER

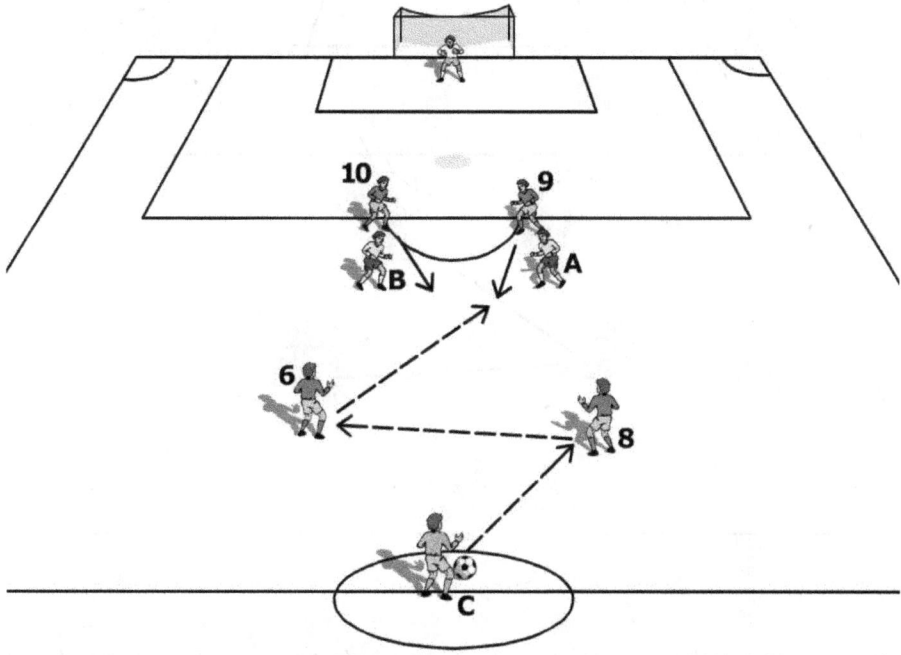

Strikers (9) and (10) start behind the defenders, always aware that they have to be careful of being offside when the ball is passed forward. It is all about the timing and angle of the run and the timing and angle of the pass.

If the defender looks at the striker he cannot see the ball and vice versa. Either way it is to the striker's advantage.

Even half a yard gained by this could result in maintaining possession or not, so it is a move well worth practicing and learning.

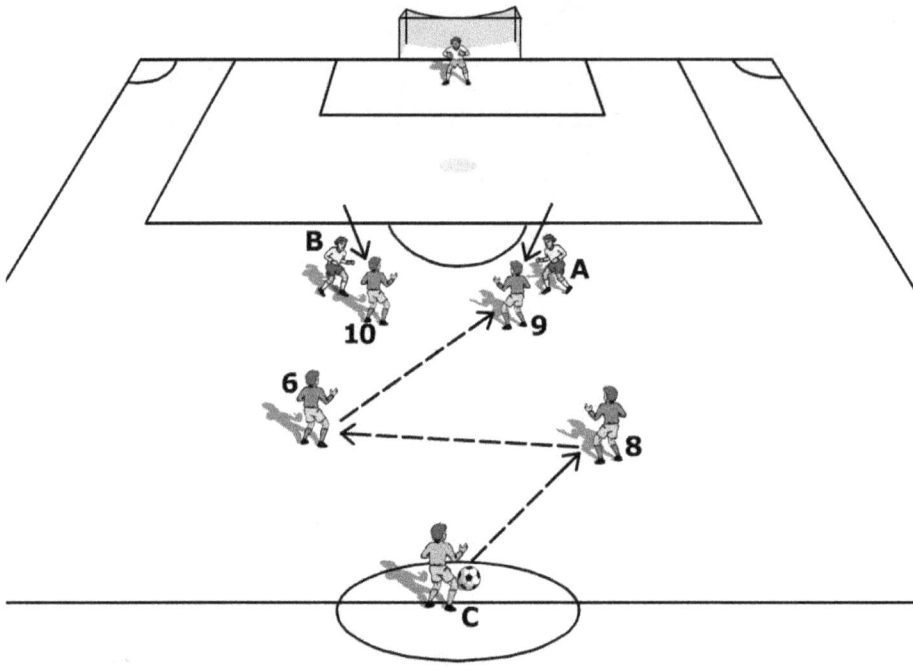

Strikers (9) and (10) may be able to make their moves fast enough from behind and catch the defenders flat footed as the ball is traveling from (6) to (8) and so are not offside when receiving it.

They may be able to confuse the defenders (A) and (B) enough so that they can get turned and face them, with and without the ball, as in the diagram. They are now in control of the situation and the defenders are at a disadvantage.

Strikers can come back either side of the defender depending on the best way to do it at that moment in time and perhaps based on the defenders' start positions.

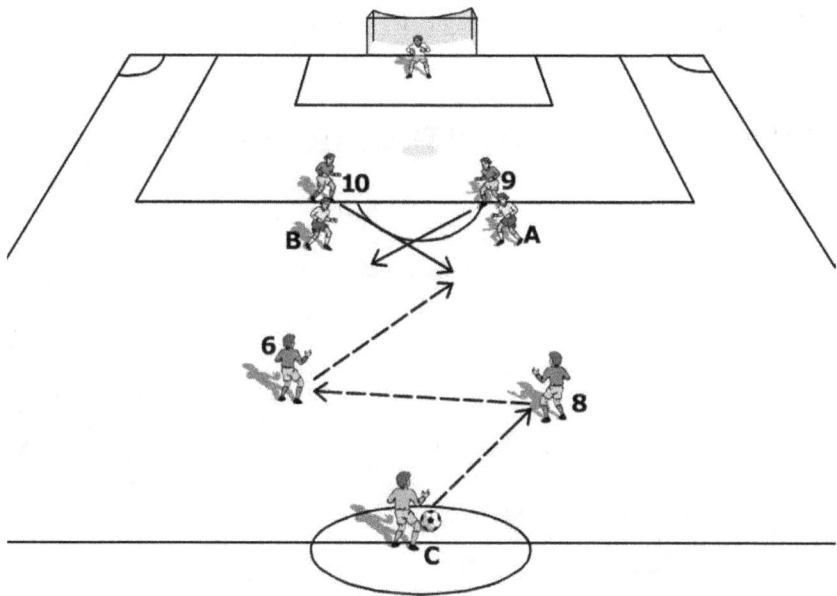

Coming from behind again but this time switching positions to hopefully further confuse the defenders.

CHECKING AWAY TO CHECK BACK

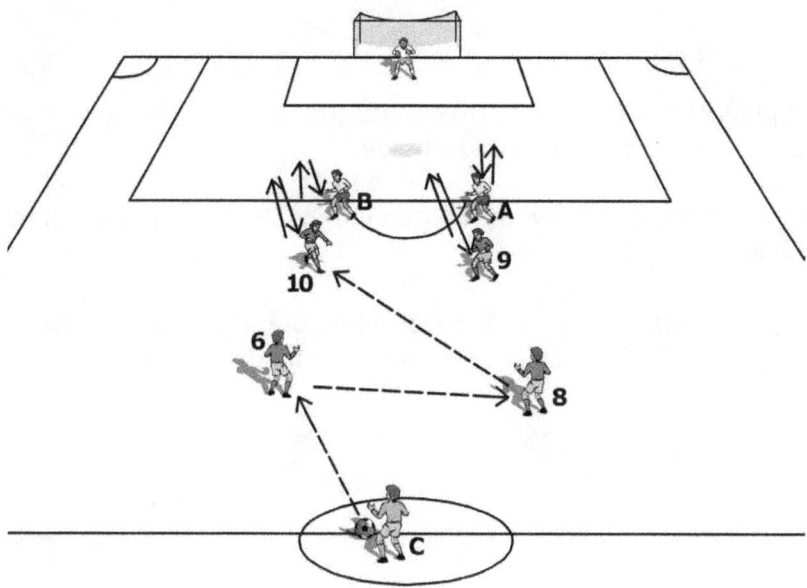

An opposite run, checking away and trying to take the defenders away from the space in front of them to check back to it to receive. Again, if they get half a yard with this movement it was worth the effort.

Players can have a "code word" to determine when this happens.

As the play is developing the striker can call the code word so the passer knows he is going to do the opposite run.

COMBINATION PLAYS BETWEEN THE STRIKERS

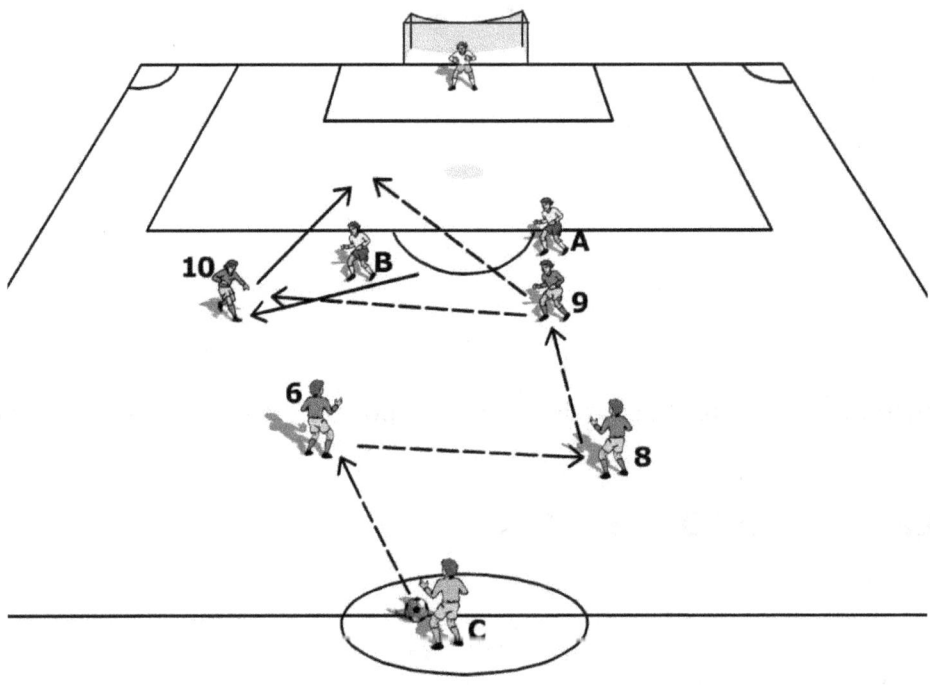

Combination plays now between the strikers. (10) checks off the shoulder of (B) to face forward, and now (B) is at a distinct disadvantage.

(8) passes to (9) to feet and (9) plays the ball around the side to (10) in one of two ways, depending on how the defender sets up.

If the defender drops off, (10) can get it to feet. If (B) closes (10) down, the space is behind (B) and (9) plays the ball there for (10) to run onto and finish on goal.

COMBINING WITH THE MIDFIELD PLAYERS

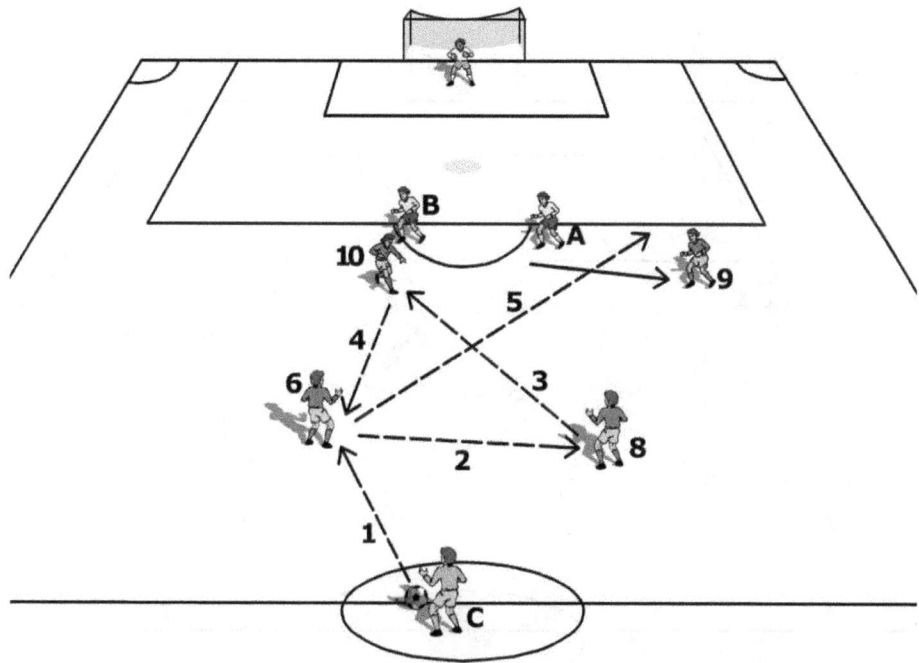

Rather more interaction here but all the same a good example of strikers and midfield players combining to get free to shoot on goal.

Striker (10) acts as a rebound player and holds the ball up well, keeping it away from defender (B) and lays the ball off the midfielder (6).

As this is occurring striker (9) is moving off the shoulder of defender (A) to be ready for a diagonal pass in behind.

(9) has gotten faced up with this defender now so is in a much stronger position than previously with his back to goal.

This is about the timing of the pass and the timing of the run as well as the angle of the pass and angle of the run.

How (6) passes the ball and where (9) goes to receive (to feet, or to space) can depend on the reaction of the defender and how that player positions.

Various scenarios can occur now. If the defender checks outside and marks (9) tightly then there is space inside. If the defender stays put then (6) can look to play the ball in behind and over the defender's shoulder, either inside or outside.

If the defender drops off to cover that ball and not get caught then the striker has time and space to receive to feet and be faced up again against the defender.

SOME STRIKER MOVEMENTS TO GET FREE OF AND POSSIBLY FACED UP AGAINST THE DEFENDER

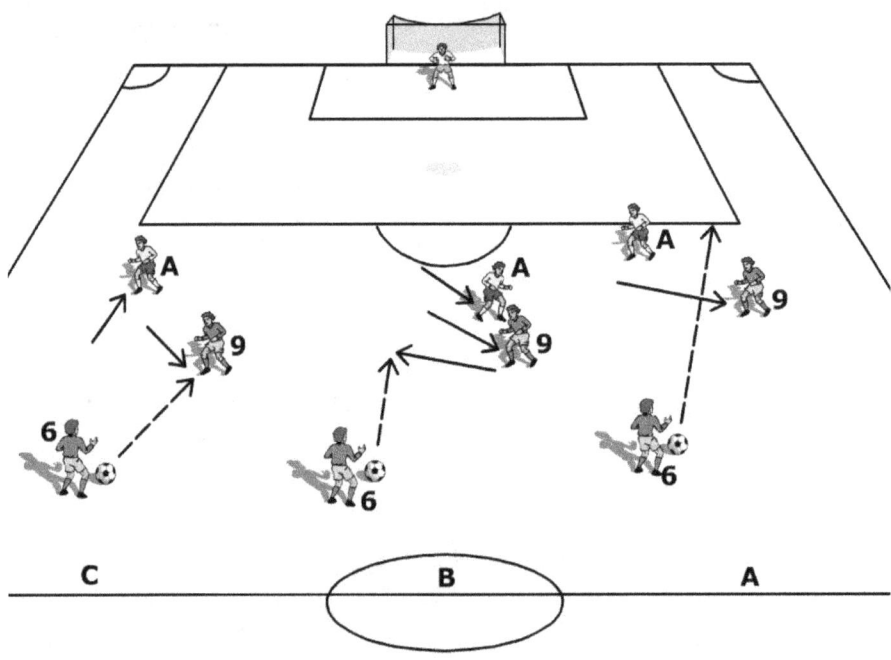

Here I show three ideas on striker movement, all based on the striker (9) coming off the shoulder of the defender (A) and getting faced up against him.

All movements and resulting decisions can be based on how the defender sets himself up:
A) If the defender stays in the same place, then the ball over the shoulder and into space behind becomes a good option. The defender is facing the passer, the ball is played behind him and he has to turn and chase it down. With his movement, the striker is already facing forward and ready to go.

B) The defender moves with the striker and marks tightly, thus opening up space inside for the striker to check back across and in front to receive the pass.

C) To protect the space behind and not get caught, the defender drops back into the space the ball is likely to go. This puts off (6) from passing it there, but it also releases more space for (9) to receive the pass to feet and face forward.

So any of these three moves can result in a positive situation for the striker

PHASE PLAY: (A 3 v 1 IN MIDFIELD)

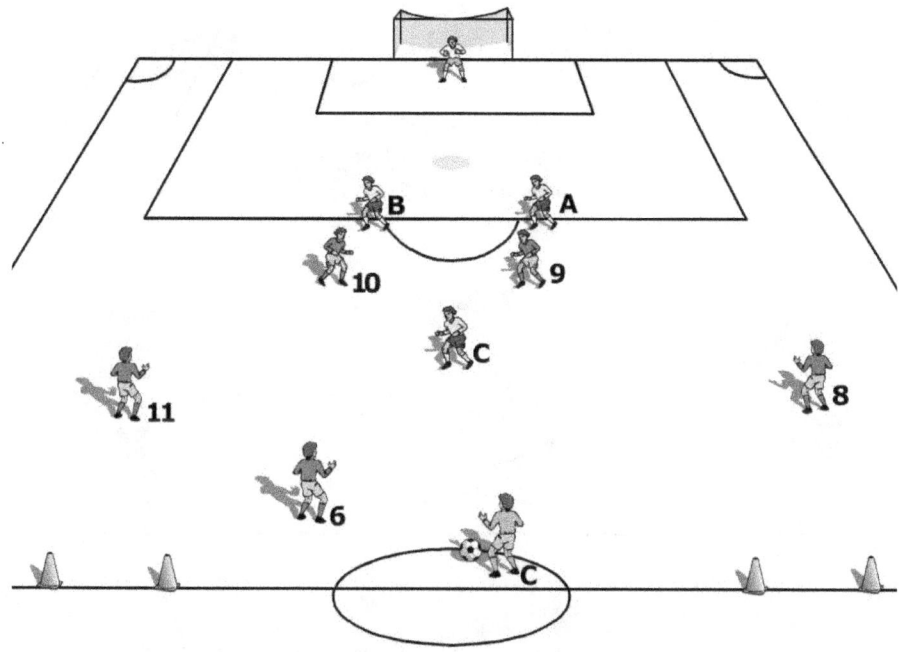

As we are focusing on the striker receiving to feet, the start position should always be as above, so the coach can pass to a midfielder and the first thought of that player should be "Can I pass to a striker's feet?". But only if it is on to do so! Perhaps playing the ball wide initially opens up a better situation to attack.

Adding target goals for the defenders to play to now on winning possession and having a 3 v 1 in midfield.

All previous points made still apply to this set up.

COACHING STRIKERS

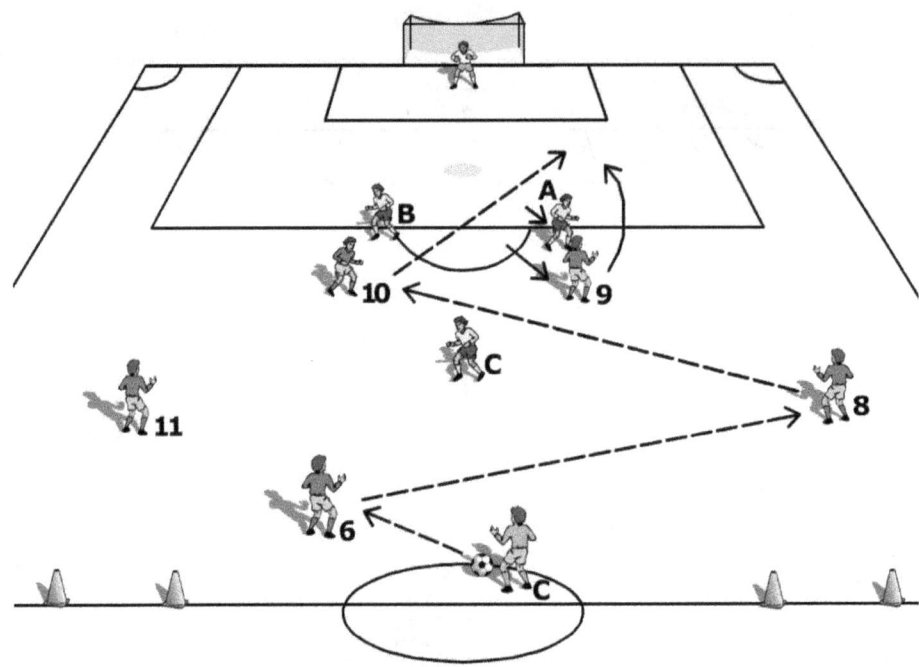

Here is another example of a combination play> the ball is played into the space behind (9) who goes to the ball and takes the defender with him (creating space behind the defender) letting the ball run across his body and behind to striker (10).

(10) can check to receive to feet and is able to get side-on and play a first time pass in behind defender (A). (9) has spun (it could be the Del Piero spin where the player spins away from the defender) and gotten in behind defender (A) for a shot on goal.

If defender (B) is positioned in the space inside to intercept this pass then (10) could receive with the outside foot and spin away and outside from (B) and turn and shoot (Del Piero spin WITH the ball for example), or lay the ball off to a free midfield player, likely (11) here, and continue the attacking movements.

COACHING STRIKERS

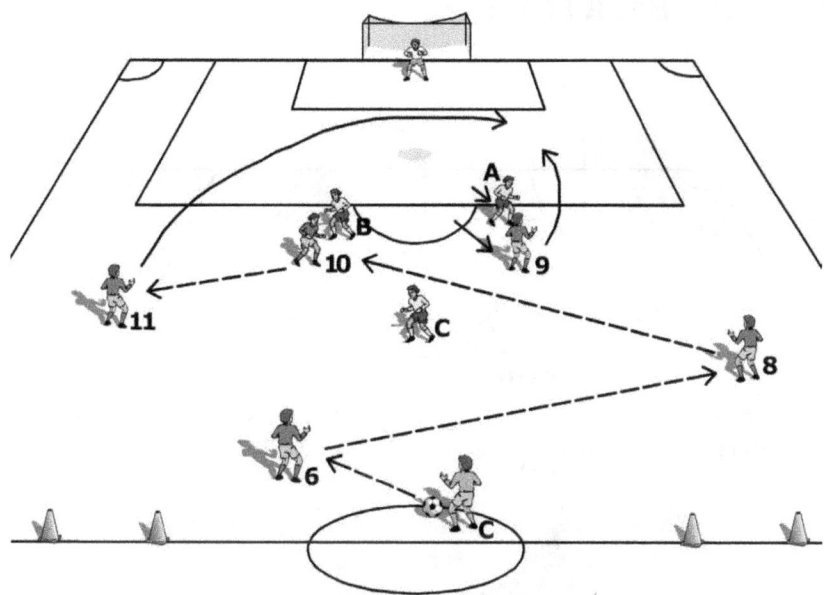

Instead of playing striker (9) in, the defender (B) blocks the pass and striker (10) receives to feet and lays the ball off in the other direction and wide to (11). (11) then plays the ball back into the striker (9) who has taken the defender (A) away from the space and spun back into it behind to receive the cross.

The ball could have gone to (6) too for the same result.

DEVELOP: A 4 v 2 OVERLOAD IN MIDFIELD

Add more players making it a 4 v 2 in midfield. Using previous points discussed.

COACHING STRIKERS

DEVELOP: ADD A BACK FOUR

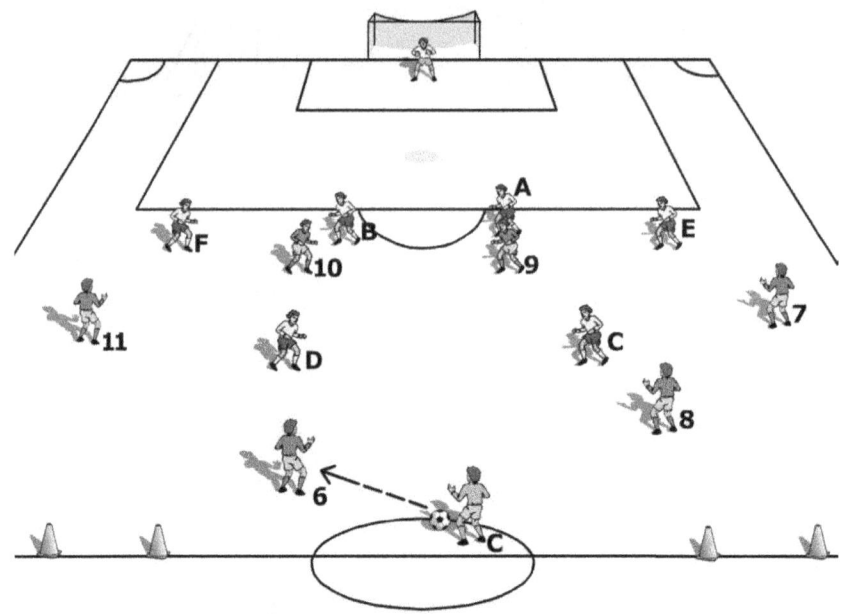

Add a defensive back four and now a real challenge is on for the attacking team.

All previous ideas apply.

A 3RD MAN RUN WORKING FROM A REBOUND PASS FROM THE STRIKER IN THE BUILD UP

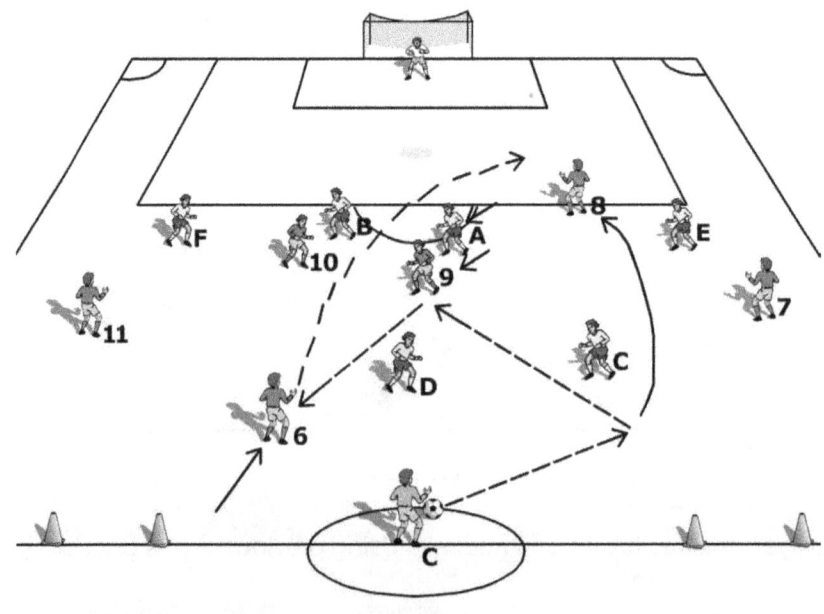

(9) comes short to receive to feet from midfielder (8) and can't turn, but is strong on the ball using his body against the defender to keep it, and acts as a rebound player. (6) moves to support the back pass from (9) and (8) makes the 3rd man run beyond and behind his marker for a great through ball from (6).

(9) and (10) can spin as the ball travels behind them to (8) and get into the box to receive a cross; or if (8) is close enough he can go for goal with a shot and the two strikers can get in there for potential rebounds off the keeper.

There are lots of ideas you can develop with this type of situation involving all the players.

AN 11 v 11 GAME SITUATION

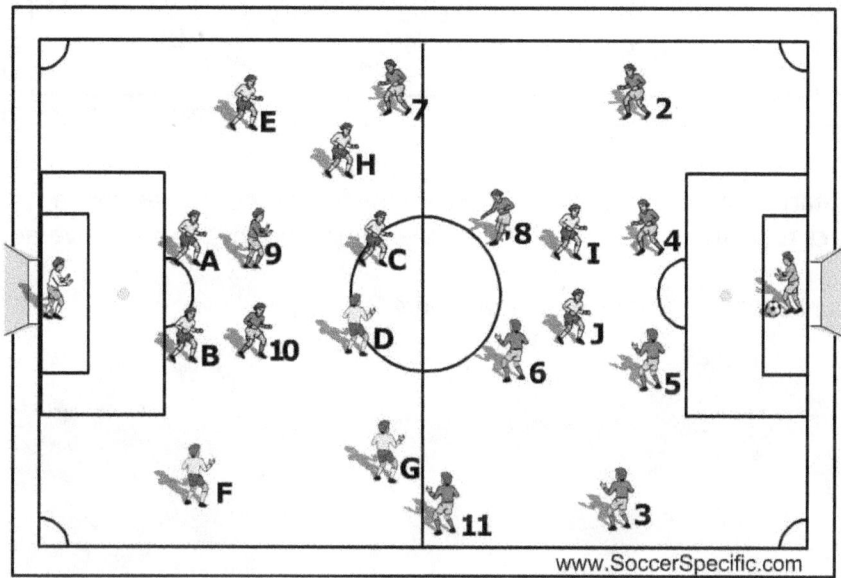

Focus on getting the ball quickly into the feet of one of the strikers with his back to goal and develop the play from there. That can be the start position of the session.

Coaching Points:
- Center forward receiving to feet and backing strongly into the defender, using the defender's body as a pivot to spin against
- Turning or setting up as a rebound player and/or combining with others
- Communication between passer and receiver as to where they want the ball to go
- The angle of the pass can determine where the defender marks, and hence where the pass may be made to help the striker (away from the defender)
- Timing and angle of the run / movement, timing and angle of the pass have to be in sync
- A positive and good first touch to maintain possession
- Can I turn and beat the defender 1 v 1?
- Linking with the other striker or with midfield players
- Support play for teammates either behind / facing the striker or beyond them and closer to the goal (a 3rd man run for example)
- A goal scoring opportunity created

COACHING STRIKERS

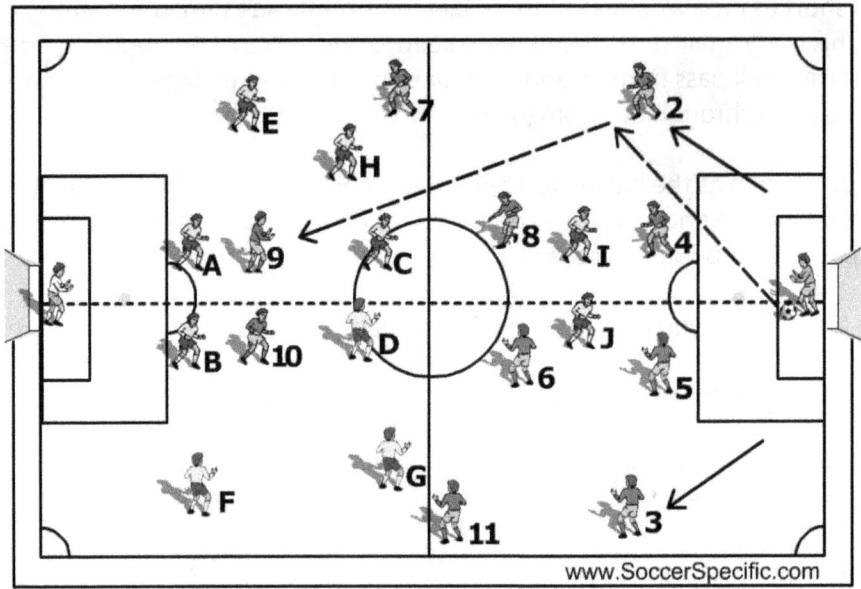

This is the start position we should aim for with the first or second pass into a striker's feet with his back to goal and then we play from there ensuring the theme is covered.

All secondary but related play comes from there.

COACHING STRIKERS

HOW TO GET INTO A "SIDEWAYS ON / OR FACING FORWARD" POSITION : THREE GREAT MOVEMENTS FOR STRIKERS TO LEARN

Warm up:
Angled support and sideways on positioning. Two team set up

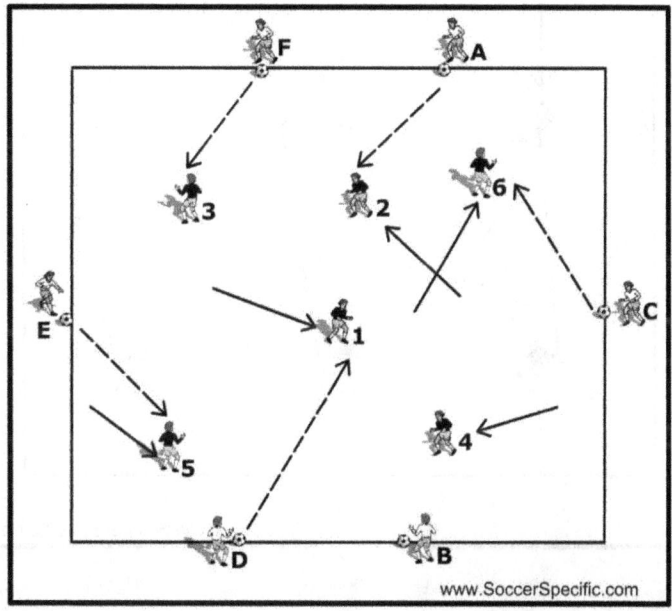

One team inside, one team outside. A ball is with each outside player to begin. Pass to an inside player who receives and turns and finds another free outside player with a pass.

Then look to receive from another outside player. The outside player receives and moves the ball side to side until another inside player is free to receive a pass.

This ensures all the players are working both inside and outside the grid.

Players support at angles to receive, opening up the field of play.

Change the practice to all balls starting with the inside players. These players now look to pass and receive a give and go from an outside player.

Rotate the players so both teams have the chance to play in the middle of the grid. Move both teams to the middle; divide the grid into two with each team passing to their own team within their own grid area, keeping teams separate to begin.

Mix the play up: let it run through the legs and turn (weight of pass), chip the ball into space, use the inside and outside of the foot to receive and turn, play a double pass, look twice before you receive etc.

Competitive: Have the receiving players count the number of times they receive and pass the ball in a set time period. Only count the passes that are accurate. This speeds up the decision making process.

COACHING STRIKERS

PASSING AND RUNNING ANGLES OF SUPPORT

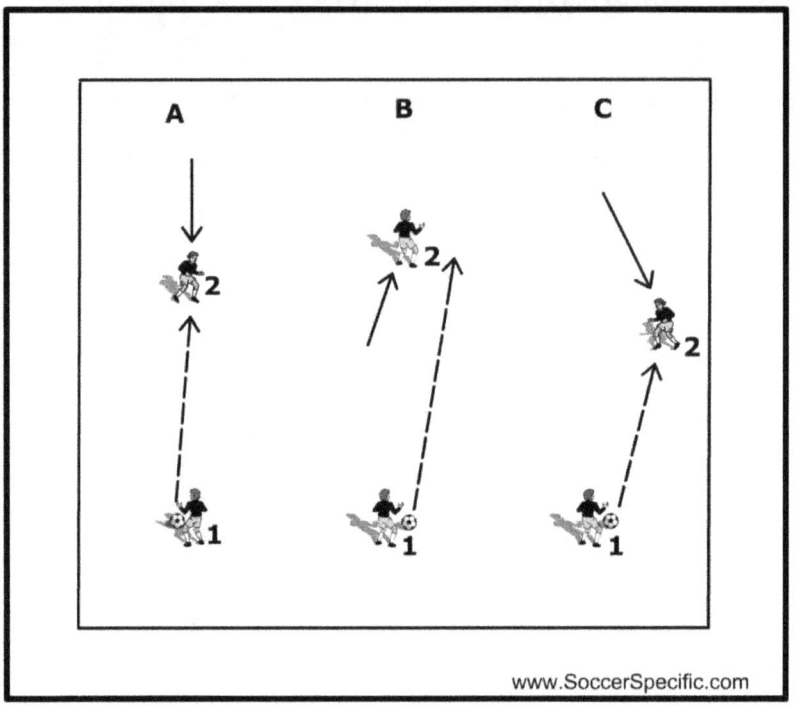

A: Straight run / Straight pass / No options
B: Straight run / Straight pass / No vision
C: Angled check / Angled pass / Options and vision

Here we show the differences between runs and passes in straight lines or at angles and the effectiveness or non-effectiveness of each.

Opening up the body and getting side-on to receive means the player can see both the defender behind him and the ball in front and subsequently is aware of the options available.

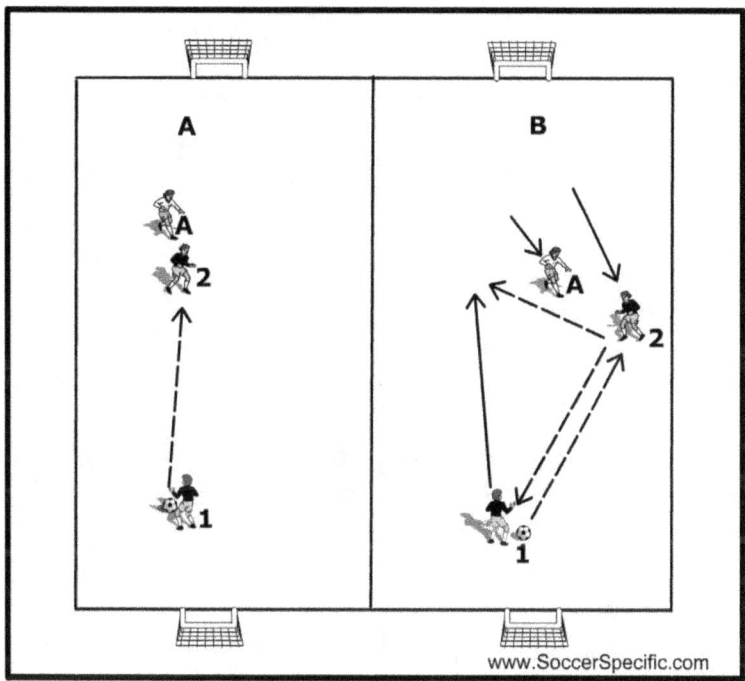

Two 30 by 10 yards areas.

Stay in the same corridor for this introductory part of the clinic.

Examples:
A: No options, no vision. With straight lines it is more difficult to affect the defender and beat him.
B: Check to the side at an angle. The defender follows and is tight but space is created to the side and in front to run onto.

(1) can pass to feet or into space. The pass should be to the opposite foot away from the defender to give the receiver time and space.

The striker can check away to come back to work the defender's position also.

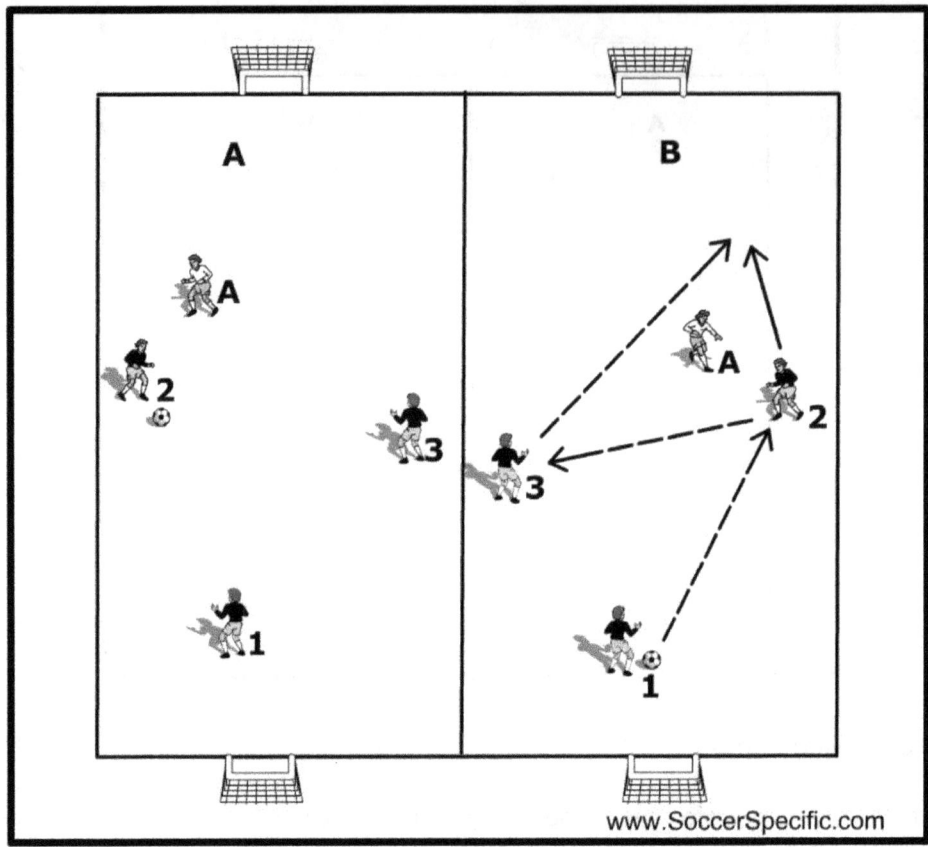

Stay in the same corridor for this introductory part of the progression. Defenders start passive to begin.

Players look to get side-on to be able to see the defender behind and the ball in front. (3) must try to get behind the defender if possible to receive a pass and score.

This is all about ANGLED SUPPORT and not supporting or passing in straight lines.

The striker is always trying to get AT LEAST side-on; but preferably facing forward.

Ideas:
- Check to the ball but at an angle,
- Check away then back towards the ball,
- Check away and receive the pass in behind and off the shoulder of the defender,
- Check to and play a give and go with the support player as in (B).
- Defender drops off to stop the pass in behind; so check to feet to receive

INDIVIDUAL STRIKER MOVEMENTS

The three ideas for movement of the striker, working opposites on the first two.

A) Short to go long, (opposite run)
B) Long to come short, opposite run)
C) Off the shoulder of the defender. Player A makes a diagonal run away to invite a ball "off / over the shoulder" of the marking defender.

On movement (A) the striker takes the defender towards the ball to create space behind, either for themselves or a teammate. On (B) the striker takes the defender away to create space in front and short to check back into for themselves or a teammate. With movement (C), the striker runs away and invites a ball off or over the shoulder of the defender.

The ball may be delivered off (outside) the right shoulder of the defender so it goes wider, or (inside) the left shoulder of the defender so the striker cuts inside the defender either in front or behind, or moves towards the ball and receives to feet.

OFF THE SHOULDER : THREE FURTHER MOVEMENTS TO CONSIDER

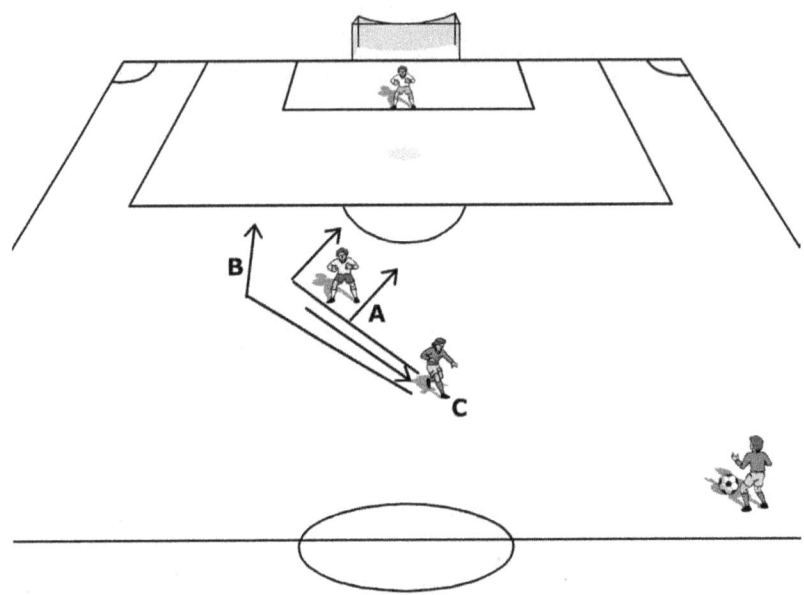

So, the striker (10) in this position has three options, each of which helps him to end up in a position where he is facing FORWARD:

A) Away from the defender then back across either in front or behind for the delivery inside. If the defender checks away with the striker, then the striker checks back inside to the right (the defender's left) always facing forward. If not checked by the defender then the striker attacks behind for the diagonal pass inside the defender's start position (on the ground or in the air).

B) Moving and staying off the shoulder for the delivery outside the defender to attack. The player on the ball plays a diagonal pass over the inside shoulder of the defender into the path of the striker facing forward. With this move, the striker opens up the angle for the pass and gets in line with the defender so as not to be offside but again facing forward, ready to attack.

C) Going short to the ball to receive the delivery to feet after first moving not towards but away from the defending player and the ball, and ending up facing forward. In this case the defender "should" drop off so the striker can't make a run behind him, but this is the cue for the striker to check to the ball from a wider angle and more open body stance so he can receive the ball at his feet, facing forward with space to run at the defender. The first movement helps to create this space.

The defender starts in the same position as the striker though it isn't shown here.

I believe this is a good way of simplifying movements by the strikers in this position and giving them a framework to play from. They may develop their own variations of these three moves but it is a good planning tool to use in training so the players making the delivery at least have an idea what the striker may attempt in terms of his movement based on the position of the defender.

THE THREE MOVEMENTS
INTRODUCE FUNCTIONAL TRAINING MOVEMENTS ALSO:
FOR EXAMPLE THE DEL PIERO; CRESPO; AND THE VIALLI

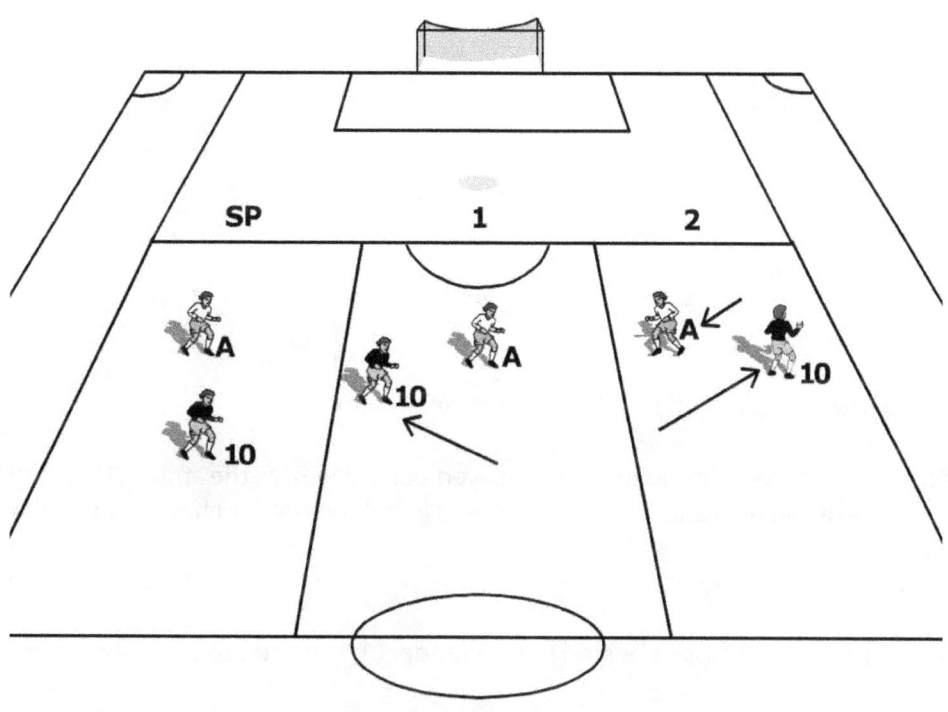

Start Position: The player (10) is positioned with his back to defending player (A) and the goal (likely to be a more central to goal position than shown here).
Movement 1: Off the shoulder of defender (A), offering a pass in behind (A). Try to position along the same line as (A).
Movement 2: Defender (A) moves across and closes down striker (10). As (A) plants his right foot, striker (10) cuts back across (A) into the space.

Movement 3:
Striker (10) now positions "off the shoulder" of defender (A).

Defender (A) is now vulnerable to the ball played behind him, as the striker (10) is facing forward towards the goal and if the ball is played in behind then (A) has to run and recover.

So, (10) is in the best position.

To prevent a ball being passed behind him, defender (A) drops off to cover the space behind.

This means striker (10) can move towards the ball and receive to feet facing side-on or face-up to the defender and the goal.

COACHING STRIKERS

MOVEMENT ONE

Movement 1: Here is the movement broken down. The first run by (10) is away to the side of defender (A) to open up the angle of the pass and to create vulnerability in (A)'s defensive positioning (this is the Crespo).

STAYING ONSIDE:
Striker (10) must try to position as high as possible off the shoulder of defender (A), without being offside, thus improving his time and space situation, meaning closer to the target pass in terms of his start position and thus giving less time for the defender to react.

COACHING STRIKERS

THIS IS THE END PRODUCT OF MOVEMENT ONE

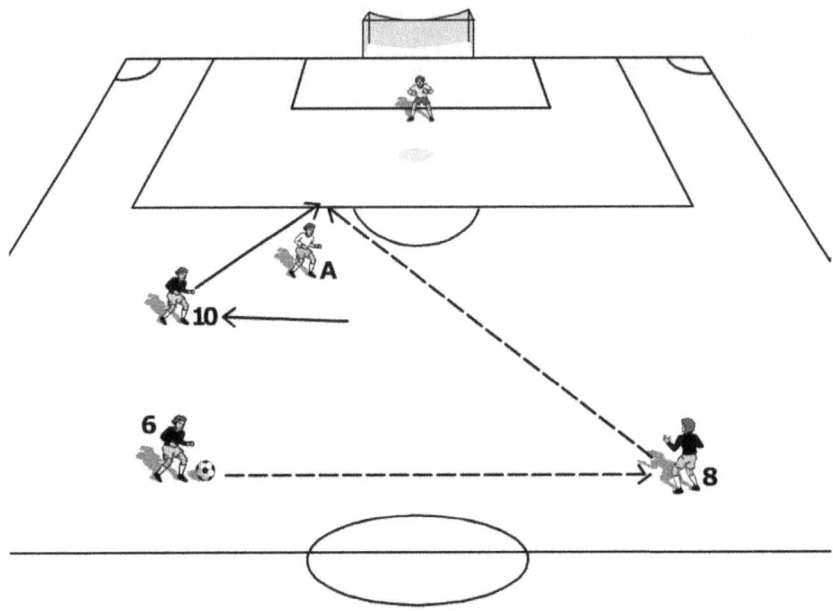

(A) stays in the same position and in that instant of the first "off the shoulder" movement of (10), the ball is delivered behind (A), either inside on the ground (if there is space to do so between the center backs) or over them in the air and inside the shoulder of the defender (the most likely scenario as space on the ground will be very tight).

The defender is at a distinct disadvantage as he is facing forward towards the ball and the striker and away from the goal and has to first turn and then track the striker's run, whereas the striker is facing towards the goal and has a straight forward run.

MOVEMENT TWO

Movement 2:
Here with the "off the shoulder" movement of (10), defender (A) decides to stay tight with (10) and closes his space down by moving towards him.

This now opens up important space INSIDE of defender (A) for the pass from (8) for (10) who is now facing forward and towards the goal.

As (A) plants his right foot, (10) checks inside. (10)'s timing is crucial to give himself the yard or two of space he needs to gain the advantage.

The body language of (8) delivering the pass will also dictate when (10) checks to receive inside.

(8) should also assess the body and foot position of (A) to determine when to deliver the ball.

COACHING STRIKERS

THIS IS THE END PRODUCT OF MOVEMENT TWO

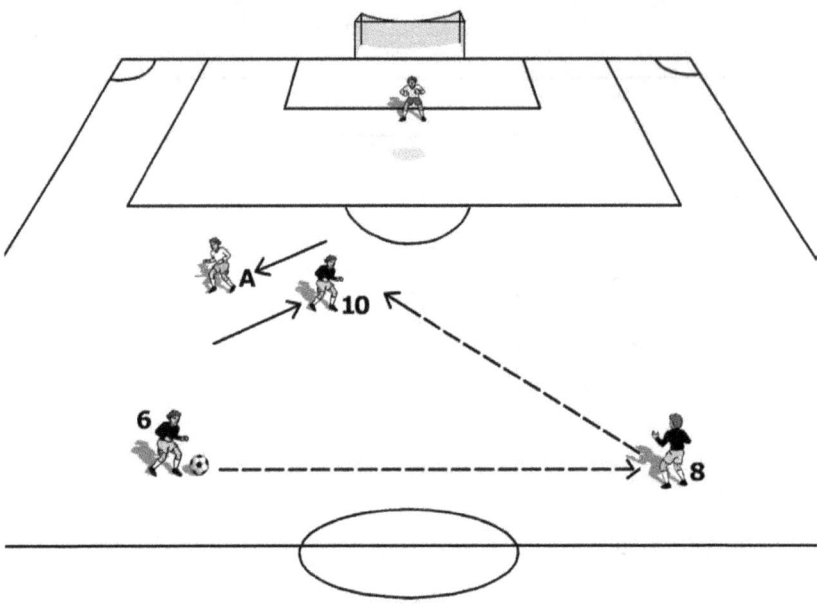

Here is the end product. (10) receives the ball in front of him, running forward and in on goal, and defender (A) has been left for dead and out of position with little chance to recover.

A great tactical situation for (10).

DEVELOPMENT 1:
(10) can also check to the ball and then check away, drawing the defender to the ball and then checking behind him, as an opposite run (this is the Vialli).

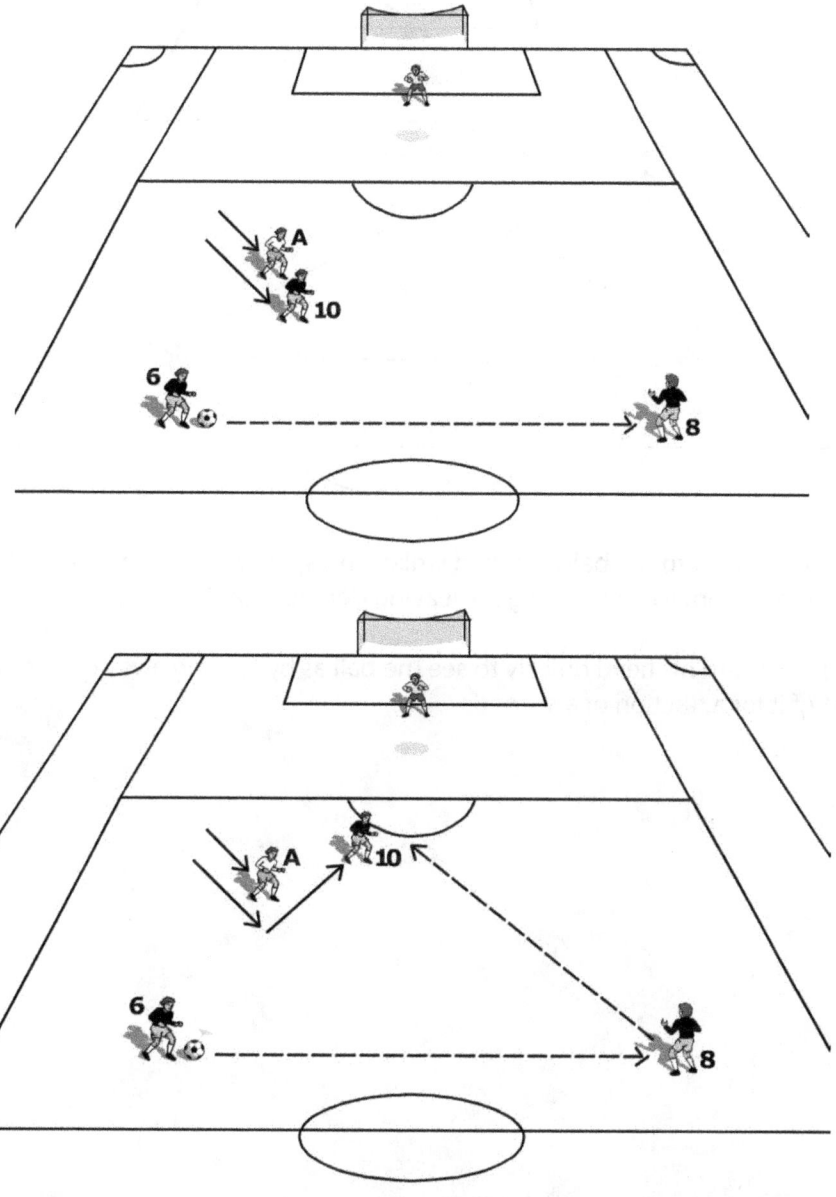

(10) can also check back and behind (A) rather than in front as above, depending on how close the defender (A) gets to him or depending on the angle of defending he takes up.

DEVELOPMENT 2:
(10) can also do the Del Piero spin here, away and behind the defender.

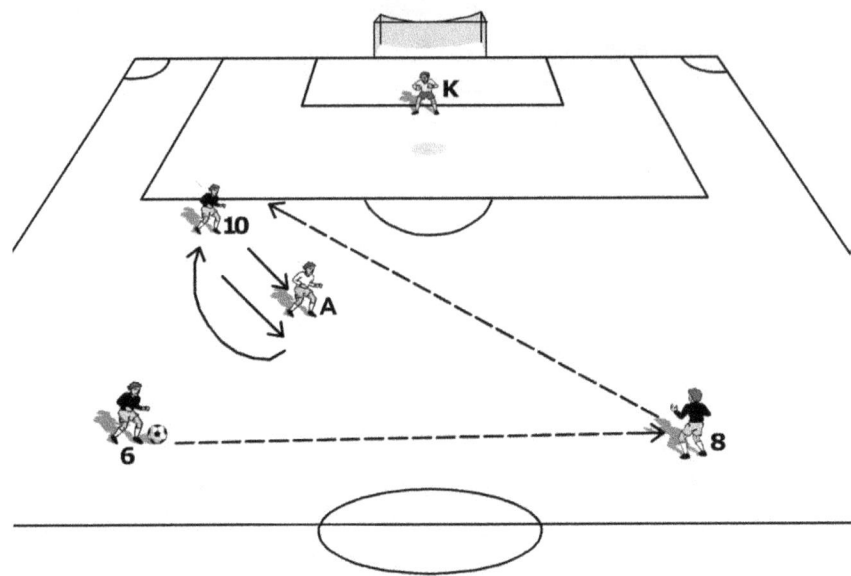

Defender (A) is drawn to the ball and then striker (10) spins away and behind (A) to receive the ball in front of him to attack the goal, leaving defender (A) in limbo.

Player (10) must turn his head quickly to see the ball as by turning away on the spin, he loses sight of it for a fraction of a second.

MOVEMENT THREE (PROTECTING THE SPACE BEHIND)

Movement 3:
The first move of (1) is off the shoulder and to the side of defender (A).

Defender (A) is now vulnerable to the ball played behind him, as the striker (10) is facing forward towards the goal and if the ball is played in behind then (A) has to turn, run and recover.

So, (10) is in the best position.

To prevent a ball being passed behind him, defender (A) drops off to cover the space behind.

This determines the 2nd move of striker (10). This means striker (10) can move towards the ball and receive at his feet either facing side-on or even face-up to the defender and the goal.

COACHING STRIKERS

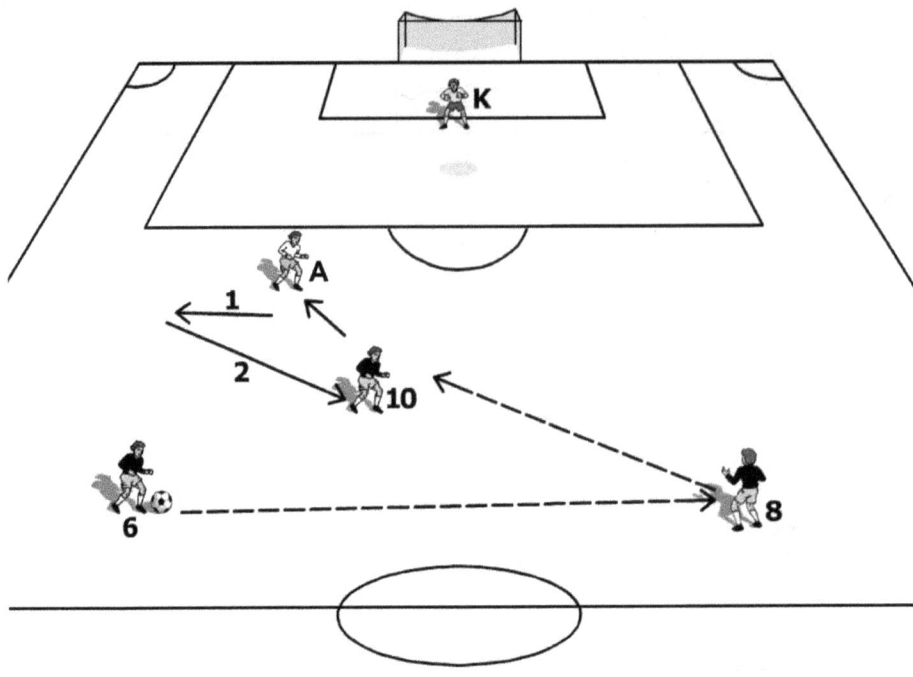

While this is a better scenario for defender (A) than in movements 1 and 2, as (10) still has to beat him, it is also still a much better situation for (10) than if (10) did not position off the shoulder and therefore received with his back to the defender and the goal (AS SO MANY STRIKERS DO). In that situation the defender is still in charge of the situation, even though (10) may have the ball at his feet.

Striker (10) can now attack defender (A) in a 1 v 1 situation and he is able to run at the defender at pace or alternatively combine with other players around him.

THIS IS THE END PRODUCT / POSITIONING OF MOVEMENT THREE

(10) has created TIME and SPACE for himself against defender (A) by the two moves made, off the shoulder and then moving towards the ball and receiving to feet.

It may be only 1 or 2 yards of space created, or it may even be several yards depending on how defender (A) positions, but at least (10) is facing FORWARD and ready to run at (A) with the ball at his feet.

The moral of the story is strikers must be constantly on the move, not standing waiting for a pass and then receiving with their backs to goal because their initial movements were poor or even non-existent.

I see this too many times where strikers do not realize they have to work the defenders (move them around off the ball) to get themselves in good positions for when the ball eventually arrives.

SIDEWAYS ON SOCCER USING CORRIDORS

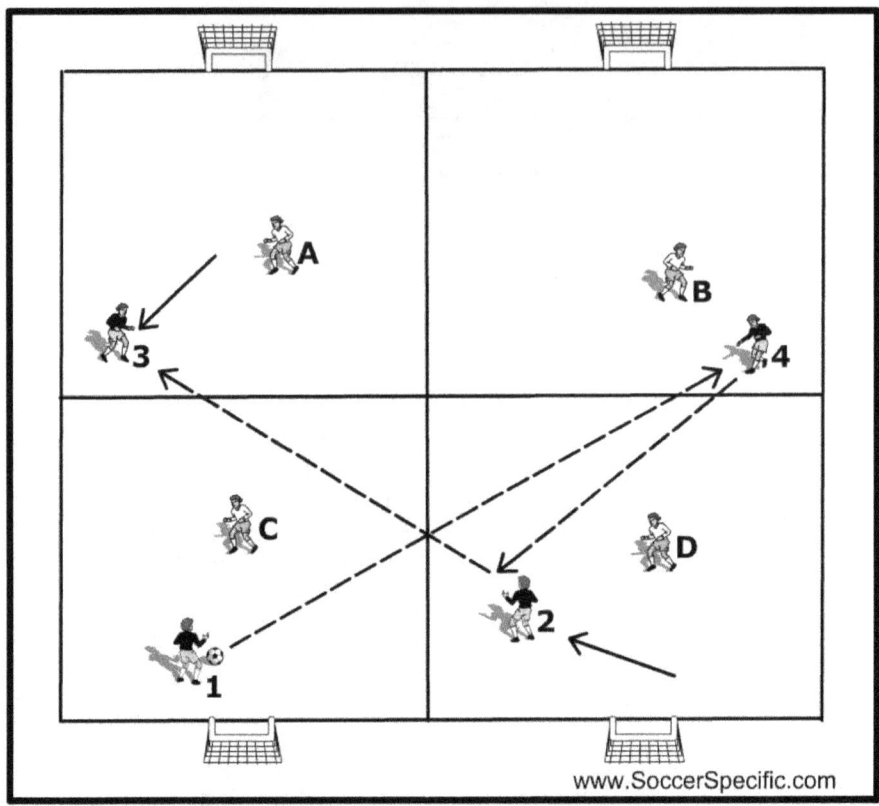

We have the two groups play together. To start, player (1) passes into player (4). Defender (B) cannot close (4) down until he has had his first touch. It is important to keep the start position passive from a defensive perspective.

Rules:
a) A player can't pass forward in his own corridor or zone.
b) A player can pass forward to the other corridor.
c) A player can pass back in his own corridor.

4 v 4 game. Players have to pass diagonally forward because of the condition set. This develops the checking and passing habits of players. Players stay in their same corridors or zones. Theme is to have them check off at an angle and sideways on so they can see the opponent, their teammates and the goal behind them.

Strikers work together and link up trying to create angles of support between each other, one short, one long etc.

Develop: Increase the number of corridors and players.

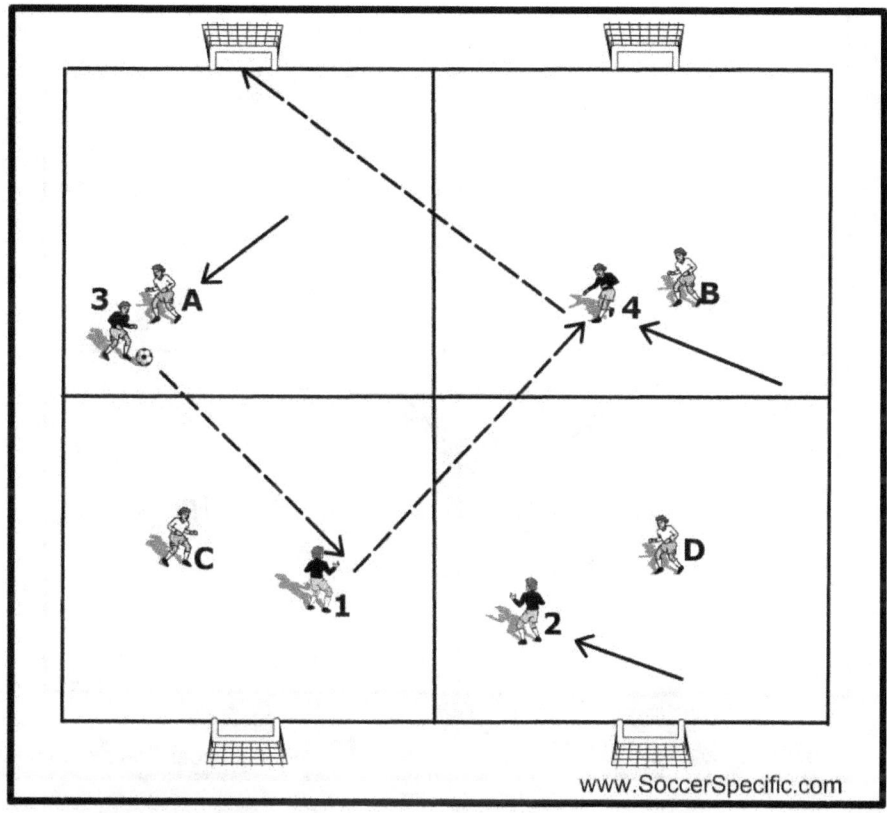

Continuing the movement, (3) is side-on to receive and can see opponent (A) and across to teammate (4) and plays a one touch pass into (4)'s path.

(4) moves into the space where the ball is passed, loses the defender (B) and scores with a one touch finish.

Defender (A) closes down (3) and stops the shot at goal for (3). But the side-on stance of (3) allows him to see (4) and affects the pass to (4).

If defender (A) had not closed down the shot at goal for (A) then (3)'s best option was to shoot.

Players have to decide what is the best option, a shot or a pass. It may be determined by the positioning of the immediate defender.

Back players can attack also.

COACHING STRIKERS

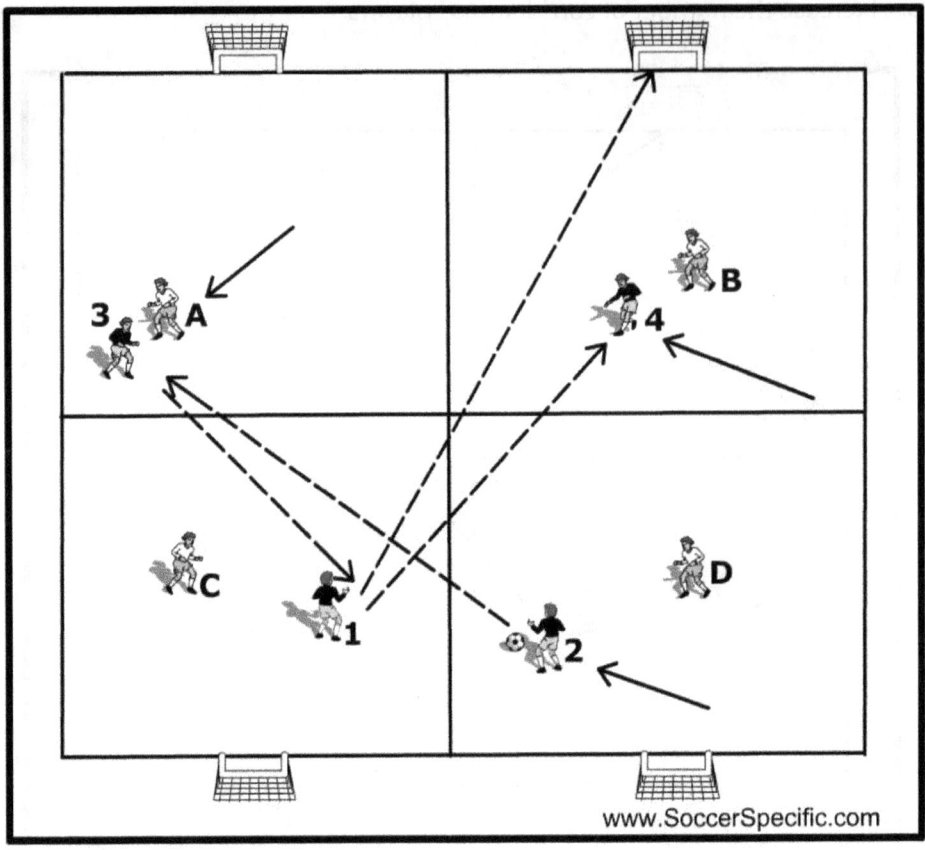

More passing ideas.

Focus is on scoring where they can. Check the defender's position to see if a shot is on or if a pass is the better option. Read the space between the striker and the defender when you pass the ball in.

Passing away from the striker into space in front or to the side rather than into feet helps the striker move and receive and get away from the defender. The striker can make the movement first and motion to the passer where he wants it by pointing.

Here (3) checks off short and wide to receive a pass and passer (2) passes the ball away from the defender on the inside of the striker so the striker has his body between the ball and the defender but is also side-on to see in front of him.

Here (1) has a forward pass to (4) or a chance to shoot at goal. (4) could take (B) away to open up the space for a shot also.

THREE CORRIDORS TO PLAY IN

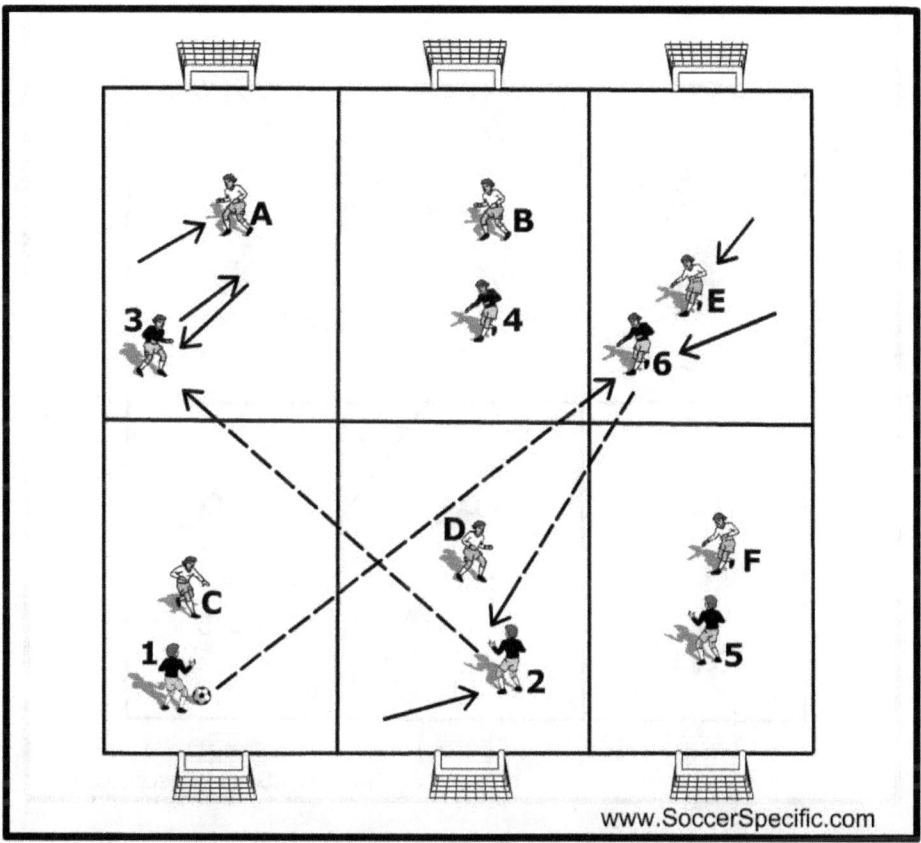

Make sure strikers do not come so short that they close their own space down and get too close to the passer or next support player.

To create more space for themselves they can check away, take the defender with them and further away from the ball then check back quickly and side-on to receive.

Here (3) does this to defender (A) and checks back to receive to feet in space to turn and shoot.

To ensure this does not happen you can put a dividing line in each corridor at the half way point so the players have to stay in their own half of the corridor.

Detail: Players can pass to the foot furthest away from the defender so the receiver can get his body between the defender and the ball to protect it. But if he gets space to run forward, the passer can pass in front of the nearest foot for the receiver to run onto.

FRONT PLAYERS CAN CHANGE CORRIDORS

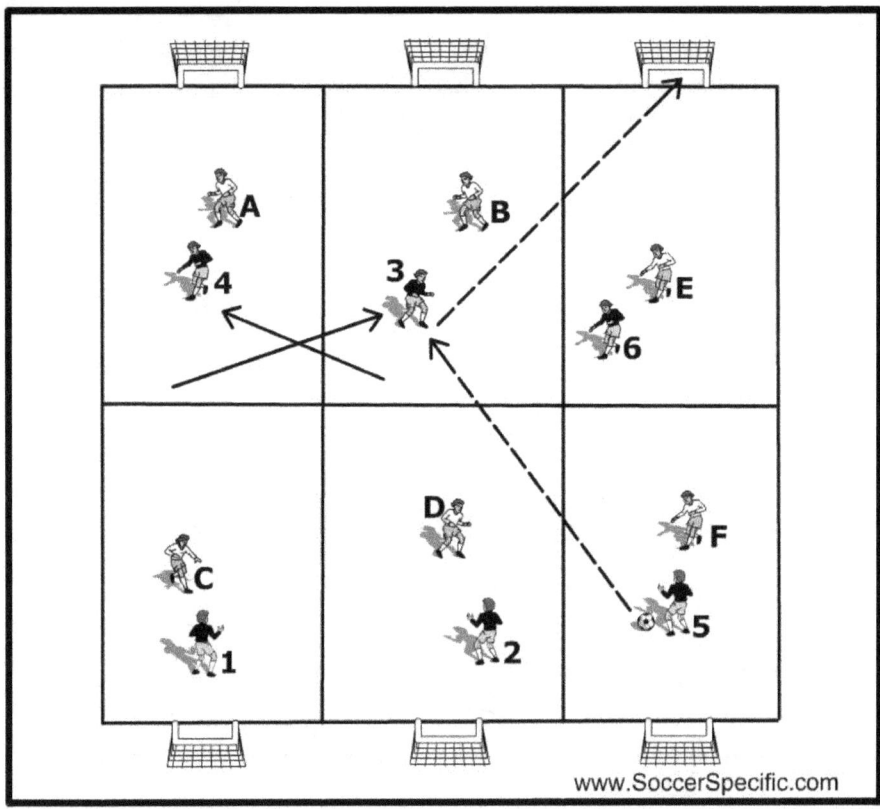

Develop: Front players can change corridors but the same passing rules apply; no straight passing in your own corridor.

This opens up even more opportunities for diagonal passes into side-on receivers and diagonal and short and long movements, especially when it is attacking players (strikers) making the movements.

They may work long and short between each other or you can liken it here to working a three striker system of play.

DEFENDERS MUST FOLLOW THEIR STRIKERS

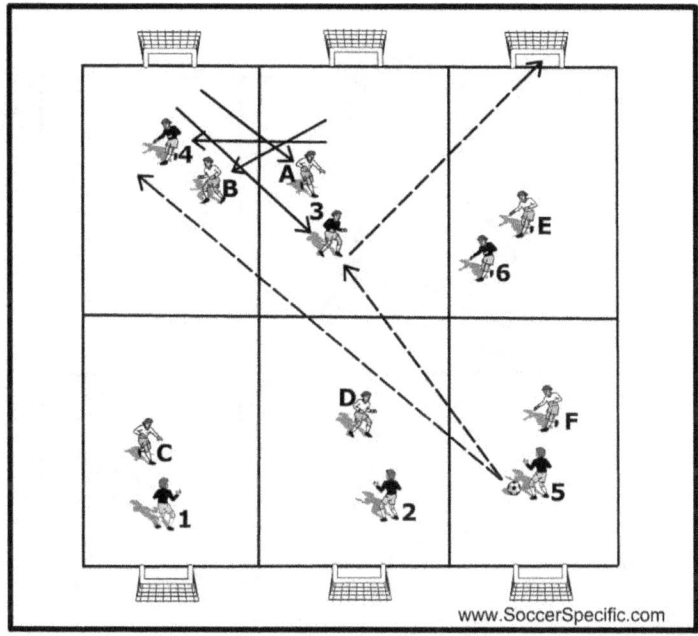

Develop: Now have the defenders stay with the strikers so they man-mark them. This creates all sorts of options for the strikers when they make their movements. (5) can play to the feet of (3) or into the channel and space to (4).

If they both lose their markers they are in. Each player's movement creates space for the other one to run into.

Many teams play a man-marking system so this allows these movements to be successful.

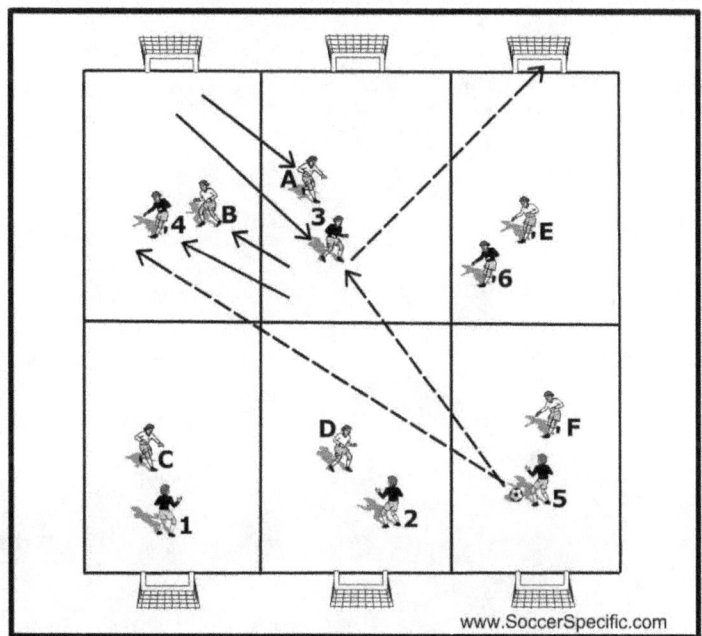

COACHING STRIKERS

INTRODUCE KEEPERS AND FULL SIZE GOALS TO THE GAME

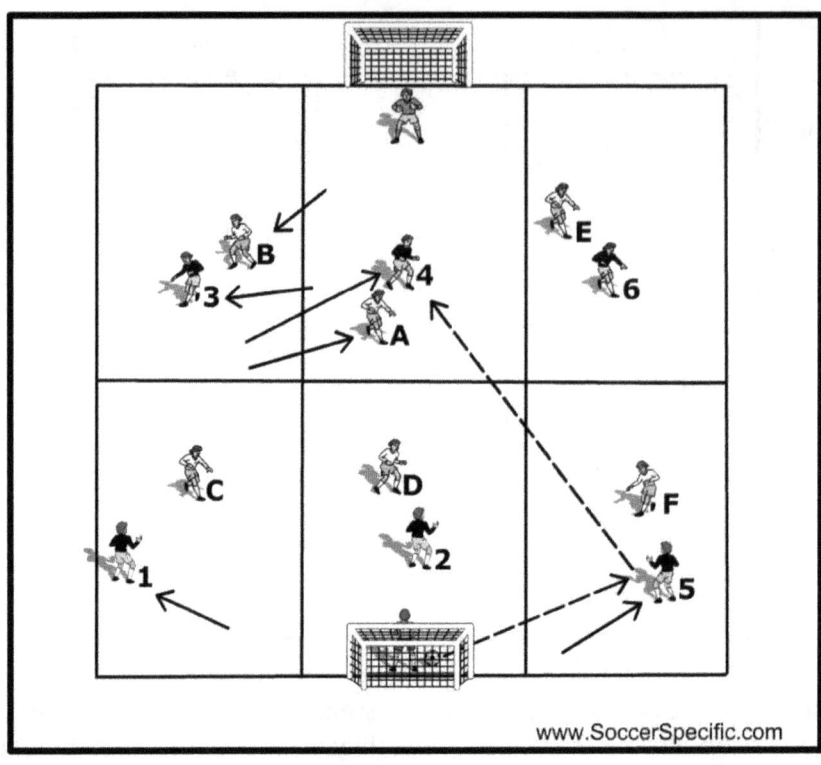

Now we have a finishing game incorporating movement of the strikers.

(3) goes wide and defender (B), per the rules of the game, must go with him. This opens up the space centrally for (4) to run into for a pass from (5) and a shot on goal.

Eventually let them all go free to see if players continue to make switching movements with each other.

INTRODUCING MIDFIELD PLAYERS USING THREE UNITS OF PLAYERS

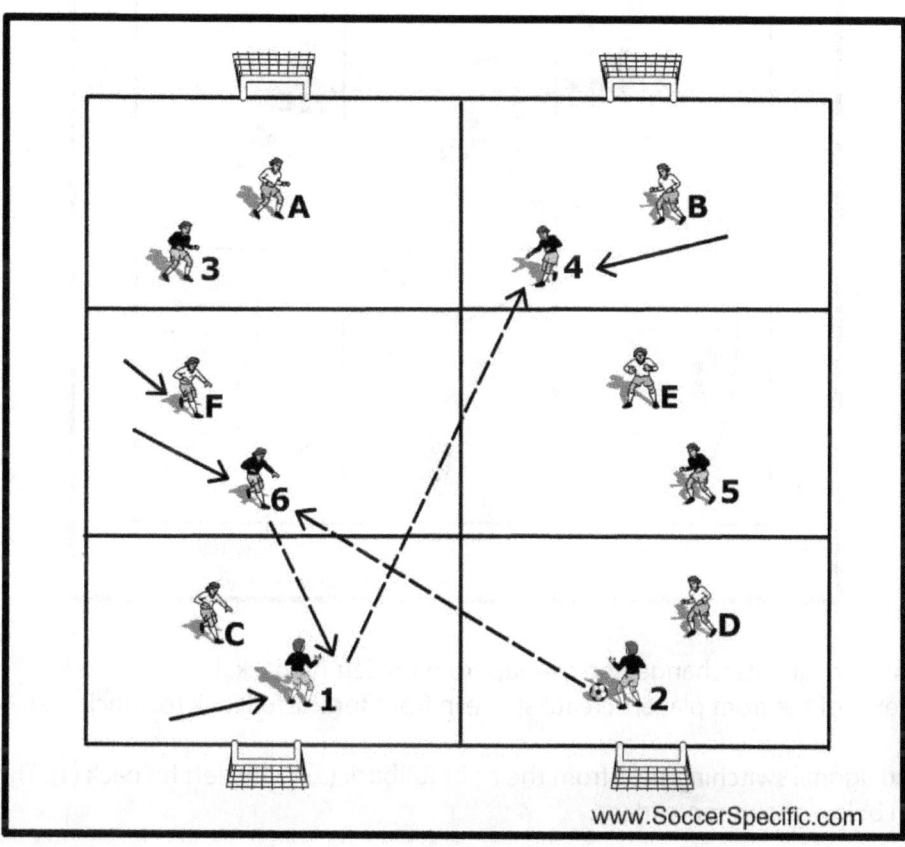

Same rules apply, only diagonal balls passed forward.

You can zone it off in thirds if you like to keep the shape clear and have the players staying in their thirds to begin.

Develop: Players can interchange zones up and down the field but not across and they still have the same passing rules.

Develop: Players can go into any zones but the forward passes must still be diagonal.

COACHING STRIKERS

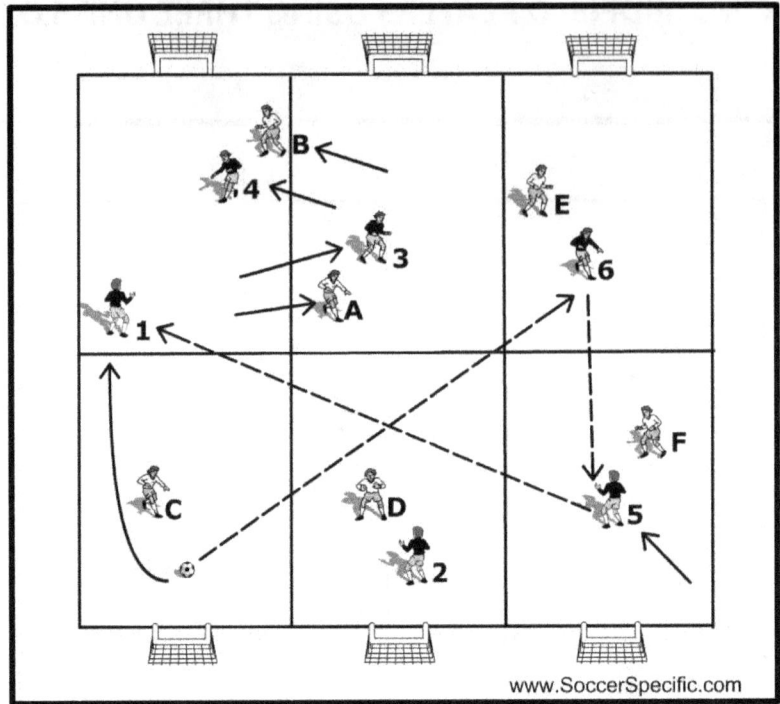

An example of an interchange and overlap from the left fullback.
Movements of the front players create space in front for the fullback to attack into.

A good diagonal switching pass from the right fullback (5) to the left fullback (1). The diagram below shows more ideas.

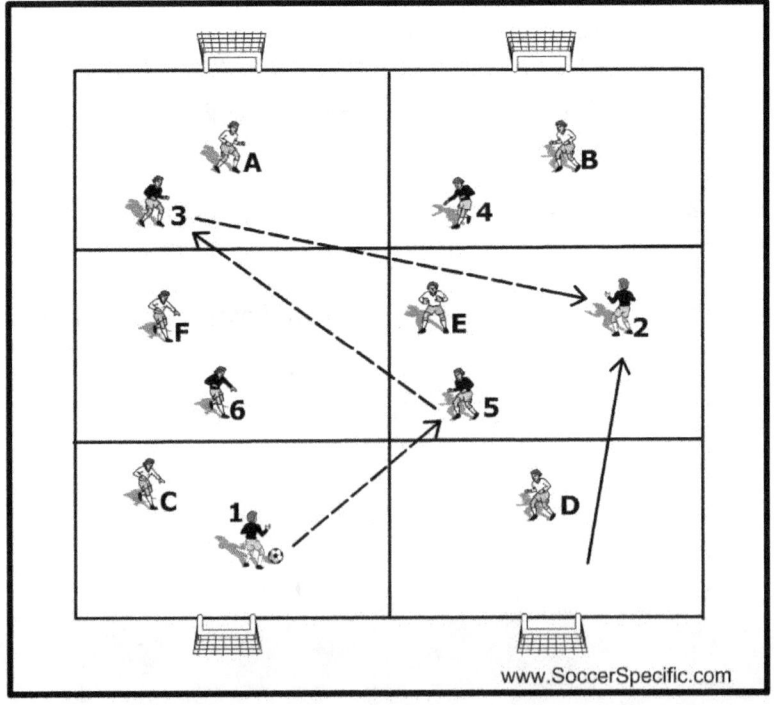

FOUR CORRIDORS TO PLAY IN

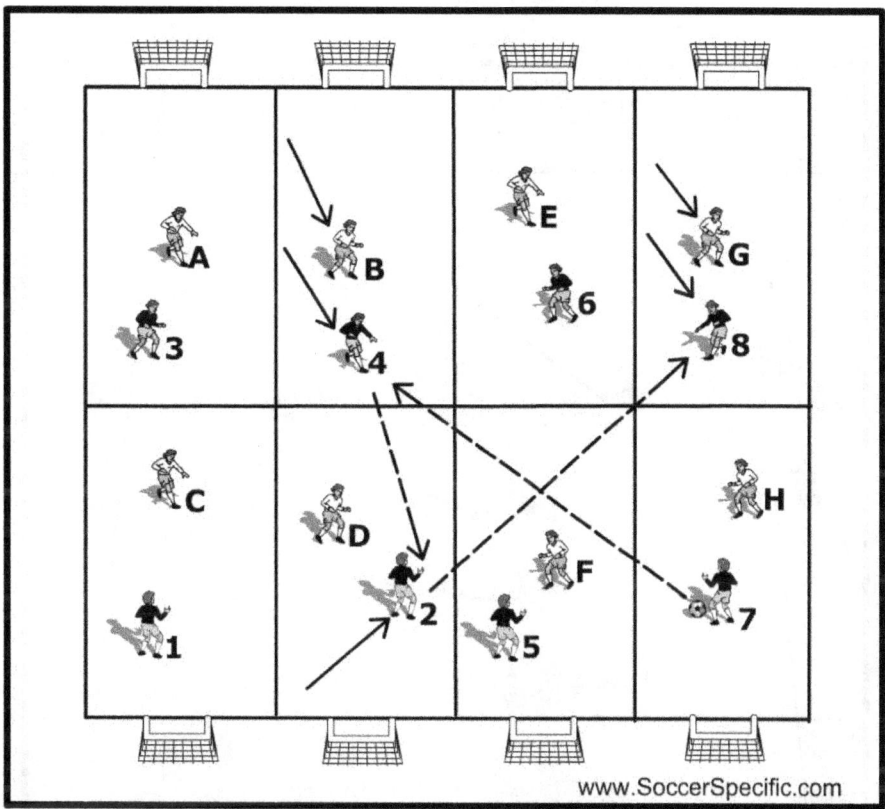

Four corridors to play in.

Now we have diagonal passes forward into another corridor; and straight or diagonal backwards into their own corridor.

Develop 1:
a) Players stay in their own corridors to begin.
b) Change the number of touches on the ball to speed up the process. Unlimited touches initially, then three touches then two touches then one touch where it is possible to do so.

Develop 2:
Players can change between corridors.

Now players have lots of passing options when we let it go free.

All the progressions can be used at any level. The simpler ideas at the start for younger teams, the more sophisticated ideas later for older teams.

Develop 3: Players can pass the ball straight forward only if the players in front of them interchange, so it is now angles of runs rather than angles of passes.

A VARIETY OF INDIVIDUAL STRIKER RUNS DEVELOPING MOVEMENT AND FINISHING TECHNIQUES

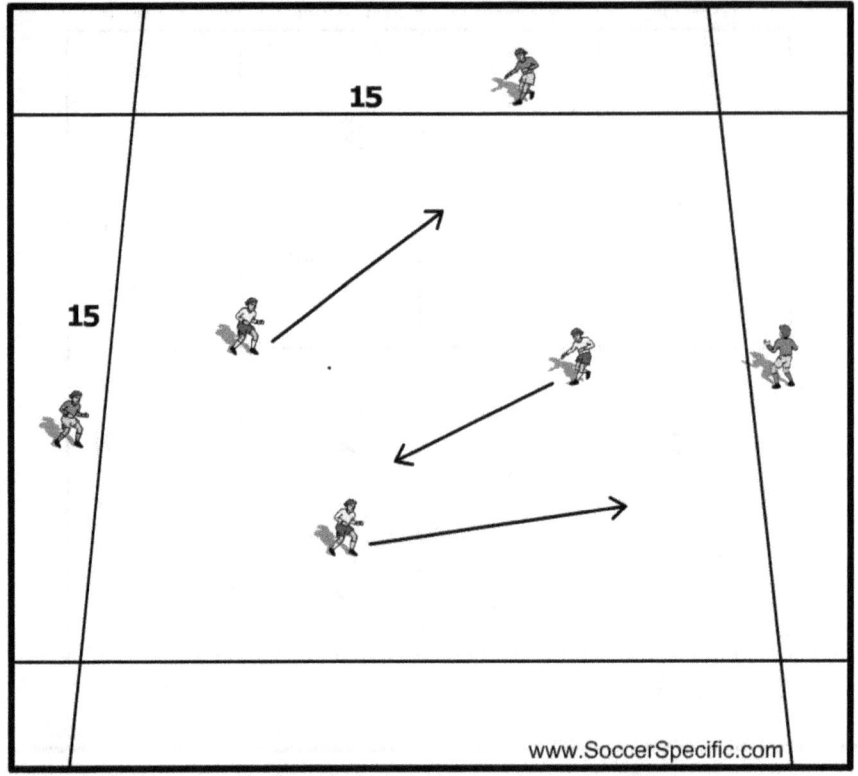

As at the start of the book here we have the warm up for the strikers. Players jog inside a 15 by 15 yard area. They must suddenly change direction and speed.

Players must move as fast as possible over five yards.

COACHING STRIKERS

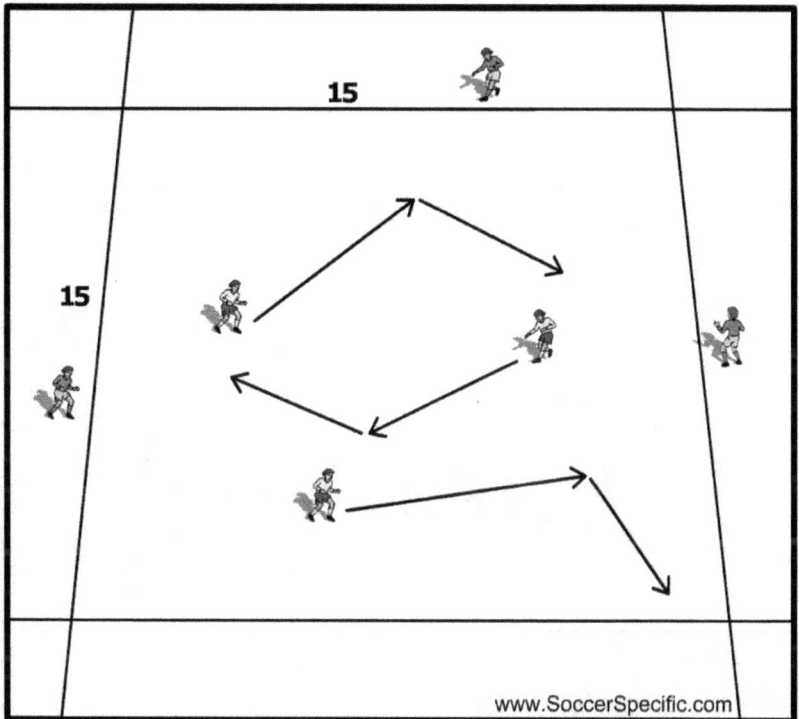

Now the players are making two movements because defenders can read the move more easily if only the one run is made.

Progression 1: Now three directional changes, each run about 5 yards long and as fast as possible.

Take a rest between each sequence and switch with the outside players. Have an awareness of where the other players are so you have a spatial awareness of the area you are working in.

When changing direction, PLANT the foot firmly and explode away.

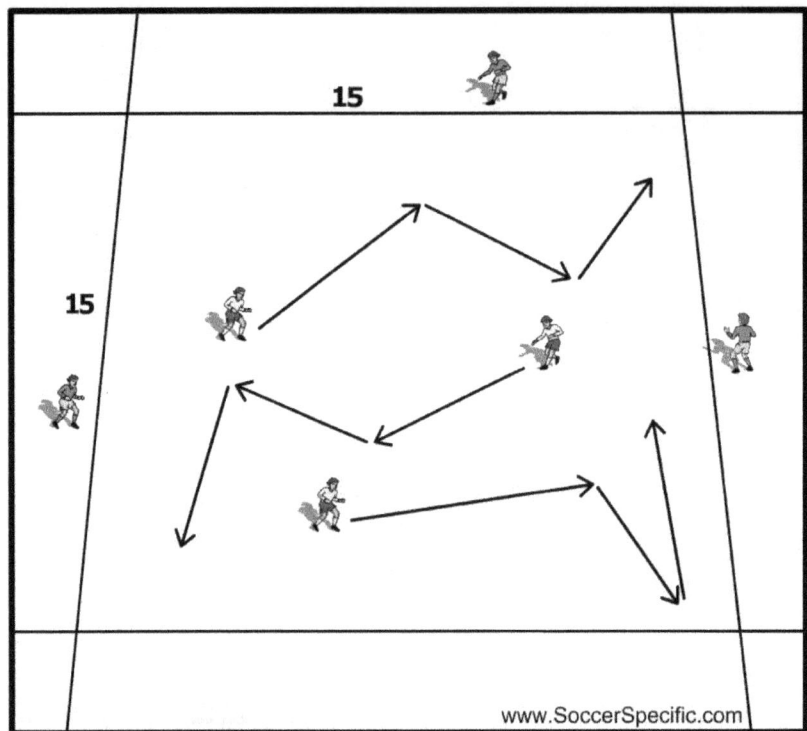

Progression 2: Have the players make different movements, for example the "Del Piero Spin" in the next diagram.

COACHING STRIKERS

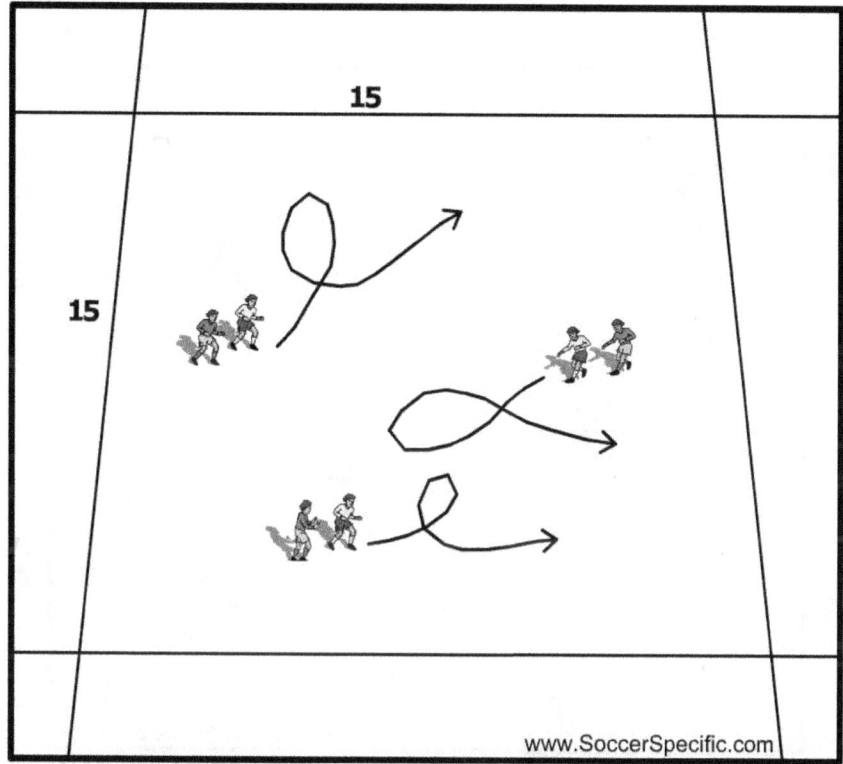

Progression 3: Now in two's with an attacker and a defender. The same idea but now the attacker has to get away from the defender.

The defender does not know when or where the striker will move or what moves he will do. This is a very good practice for defenders too.

The coach can dictate one, two or three movements. Put 3 flags at the half way mark and across the field as shown below. Players follow their pass. The passing must be sharp and accurate.

First Movement
Use the flags for timing of the run so you are not offside. Start with two players at cone 1. The striker checks off the flag and inside as if it were a defender, creating space for himself outside. This is a long, strong, and looping EARLY run (the Crespo).

Their movement is as the ball travels from (1) to (2). There are three movements in this: the first one early as the ball travels from (1) to (2), then a looping run as the ball travels for (2) into space for (3) to run onto.

Strikers must turn their heads as quickly as possible to see the ball, making the time that they can't see the ball (as they are running across the intended path of the pass) as short as possible.

Player (2) passes into space for the striker (3) to run onto. The pass must be played with pace and backspin to control it.

COACHING STRIKERS

First Movement

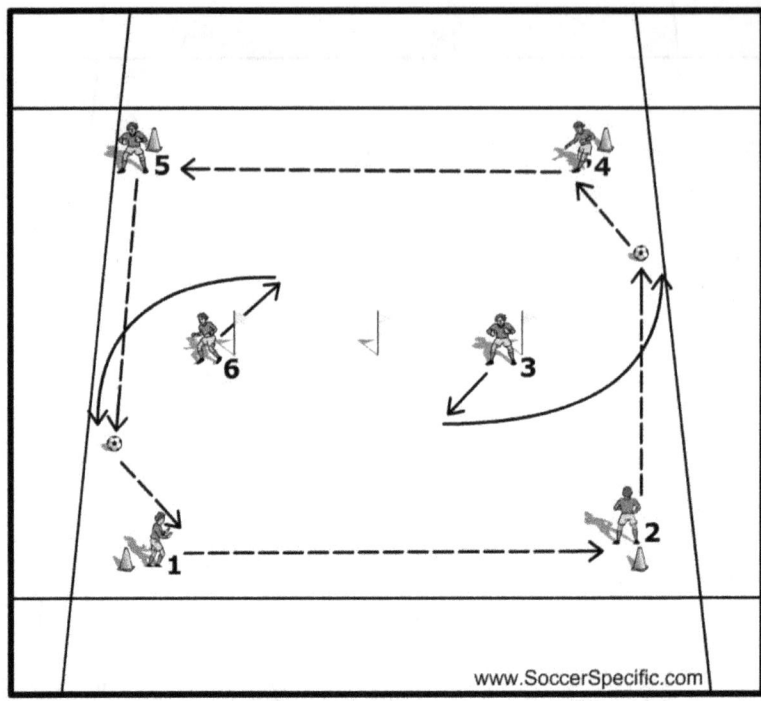

Second Movement

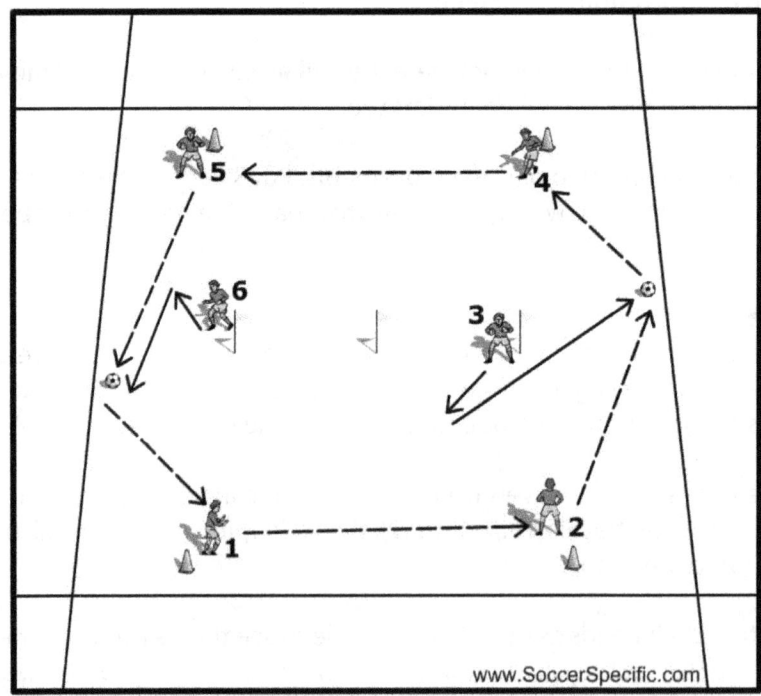

This is the opposite of the last one in the timing of the run. This time the run is LATE and is a SPIN / CHECK (Vialli) rather than a loop. It is late, fast and the spin is OUTSIDE.

So, the striker must not go too early, the ball has to be passed alongside the striker (outside the run), and the striker must keep his eyes on the ball as it is delivered and have a side-on body position to receive. This is a shorter and sharper run than the last one.

Third Movement

This is late, quick and a spin INSIDE.
The striker must check to the spin inside, and make the run inside the flag for the pass outside.

Third Movement

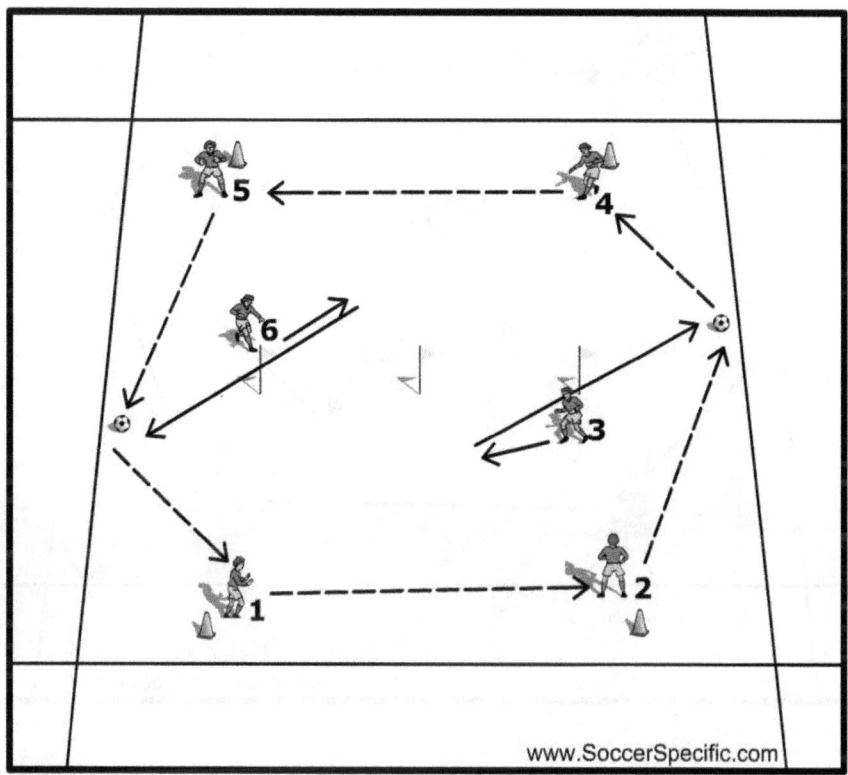

Run outside to the pass.

Fourth Movement

Now start at the middle flag. Check inside as the ball travels from (1) to (2) to create space in front. As the ball arrives at (2) the striker is moving slowly across the field. He makes ONE step towards the ball then runs in behind.

Fourth Movement

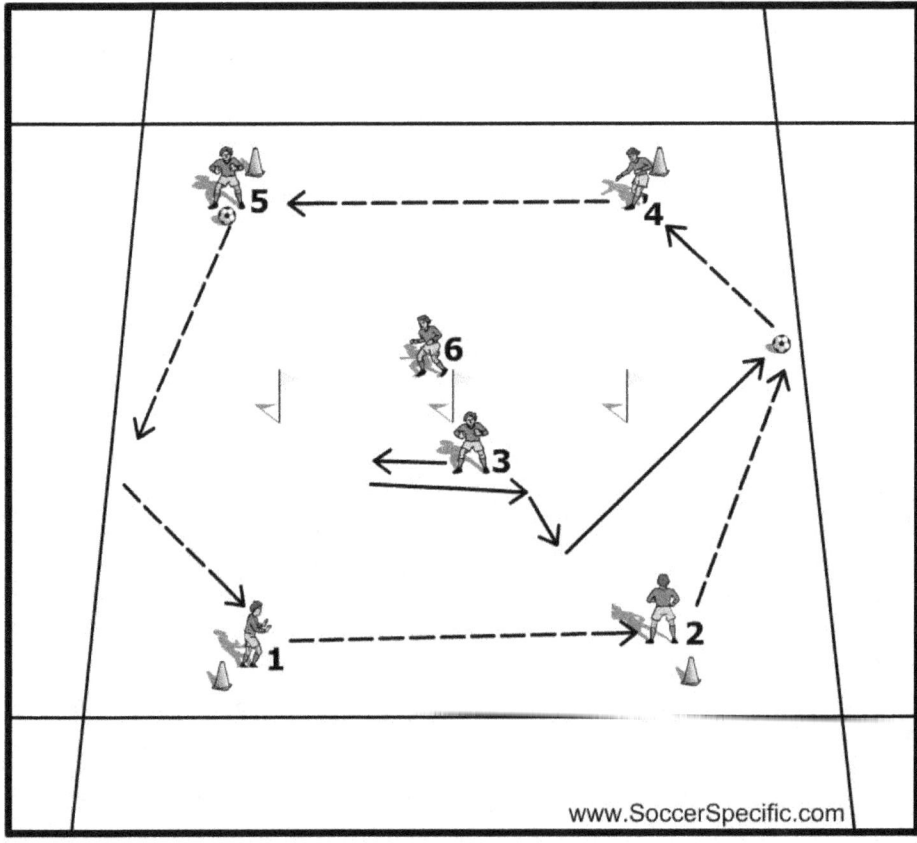

This STEP should get the defender on his front foot going towards the ball and that is the moment to make the run in behind (another Vialli Move).

It might only gain a yard on the defender but that yard may be all that is needed to get away. So, check away then back (taking the defender's eyes from the ball to the player), step to and towards the ball, then run in behind.

Fifth Movement

The Del Piero Spin: This movement is about the timing of the run and the timing of the pass. The head must turn around quickly to view the ball as soon as possible after turning away from the sight of it. The hips must open up quickly.

Fifth Movement

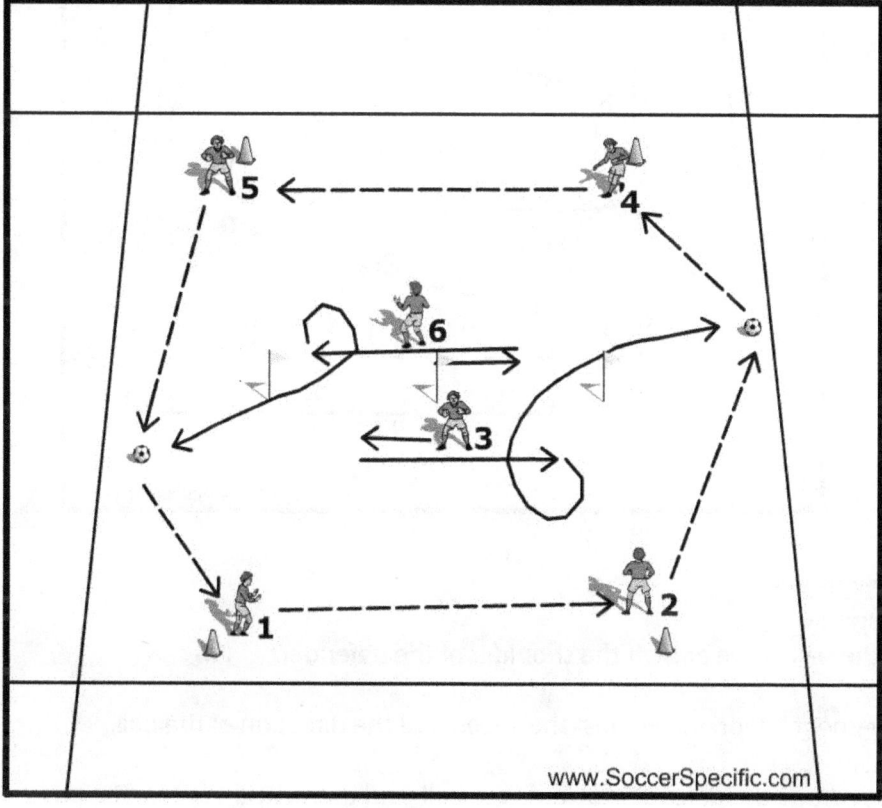

Sixth Movement

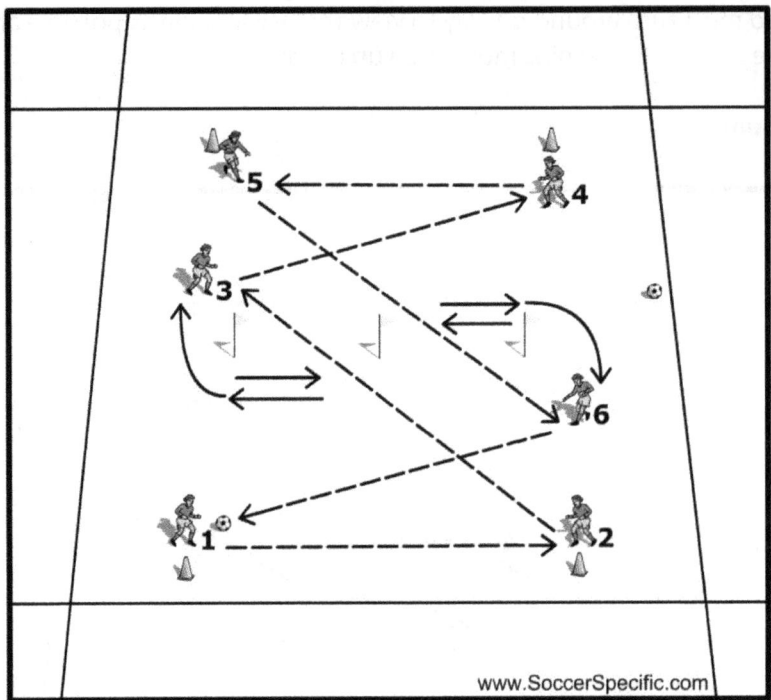

Sixth Movement:
The "Crespo":
Inviting the ball inside and off the shoulder of the defender.

This movement is working against the speed and the direction of the ball.

The striker draws the defender towards the ball, and then checks away. The passer plays a diagonal pass inside the defender (designated by the flag in this case) into the path and inside of the striker.

Develop:
Use the three movements idea here to show different moves based on the flag representing the defender.

So player (3) moves;
a) Off the shoulder with the pass inside the defender and into space in front of striker (3);
b) Off the shoulder then back across and inside the defender for the pass; so in, out then in again; and the ball is into space in front of the striker (3).
c) Off the shoulder then come to receive to feet and then pass the ball across to (4); so in, then out, then in and the ball is to feet.

Argentine legend Hernan Crespo was the master of these runs.

FINISHING

Introduce goals and keepers.

The strikers now can use different movements previously practiced in this session to create space for themselves and the ensuing pass and finish on goal.

Two flags only now. Have three strikers on each flag. Use the flags as center backs so they can judge offside.

Each striker gets two shots on goal; the 2nd shot is a different service from the coach. The delivery of the pass is crucial to the success of the finish on goal.

1st Shot
The strikers have to look at the keeper to see their position before receiving the pass and decide how to execute the shot on goal to score.

A striker may have 2 or 3 touches on the ball here, so there is more time to think on the 1st shot.

2nd Shot
The service of the 2nd ball makes the striker adjust his position for the 2nd shot because there is not as much time to think about it and decide.

This is a more difficult shot because of the time factor (an instant decision is required here) and is likely to be a one touch finish.

Finish with pace and placement.

The Timing of the Run:
Look for a trigger or a cue as to when to make the run.

In this case as the midfield player receives the pass, turns and has his head up, that is the cue to start the run.

Do not go before the midfielder is ready to pass.

I am showing these diagrams with only one striker for ease of presentation, there are obviously 3 on each flag during the actual session.

COACHING STRIKERS

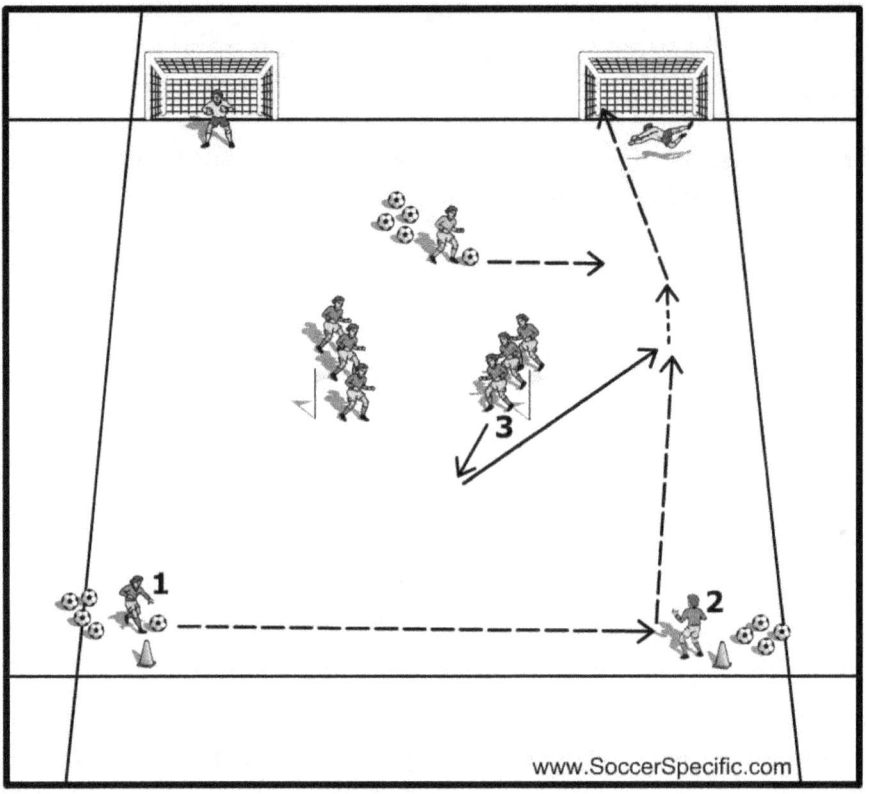

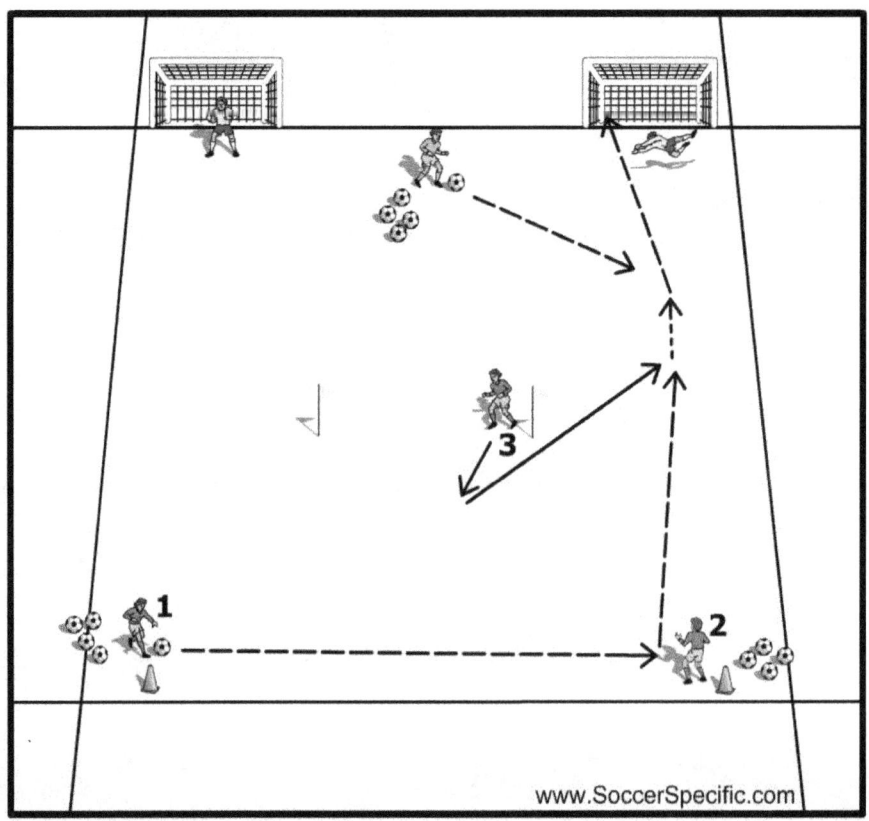

Now it is a diagonal pass. It has to be a quick delivery to get there, as it is a longer pass. Ask the players to put back spin on the ball to hold it up at the end of the pass to help the striker running onto it to receive.

The striker here needs a great 1st touch on the move and AT SPEED to set up a good finish. Try one touch to control and one touch to shoot.

The timing of the run is important, so again use the flags as defenders and do not run offside.

Players need to:
- Know where the back defenders are positioned
- Know where the space is to go into
- Have faith in the player on the ball to deliver it where the striker wants it, and know when he will deliver the ball to help his timing.

DIAGONAL PASS

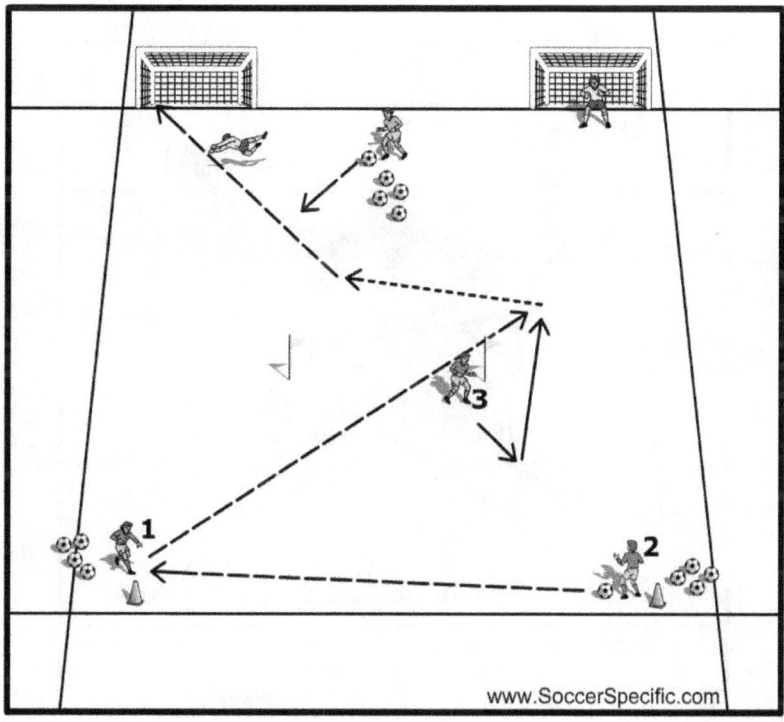

Same idea but now they can score in either goal.

Here the striker breaks forwards and shoots at the other goal.

STRIKERS ATTACKING IN PAIRS

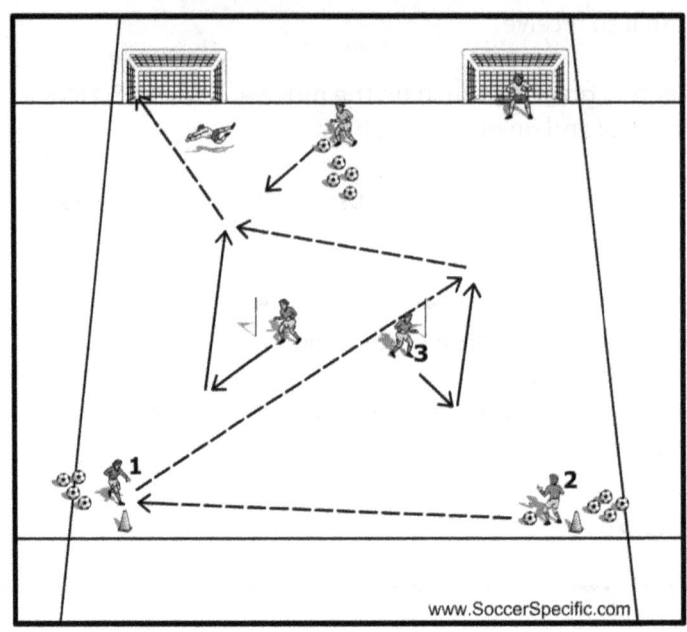

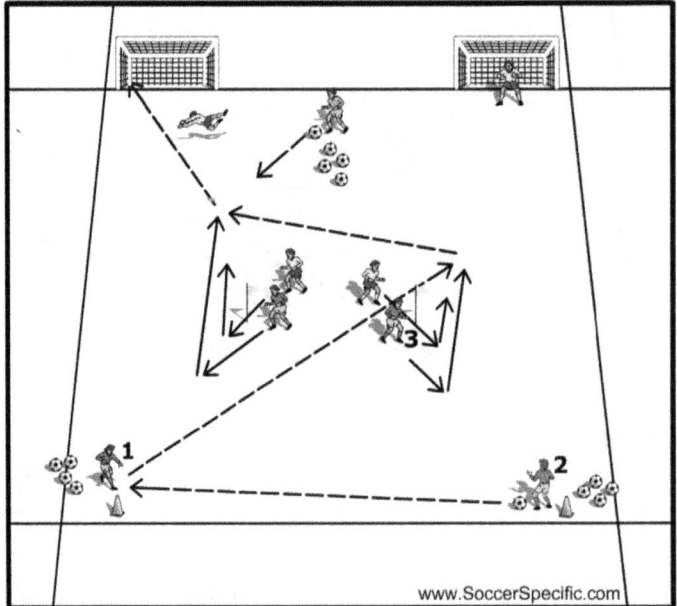

Now they attack in pairs and the 1st striker can pass it to the 2nd striker on the other side to finish.

Now we are getting strikers linking up. Just pass it down one side for ease of understanding for the players.

Both players can make their movements to affect the imaginary defenders (designated still by the flags).

The timing of the runs of both strikers now is vitally important to make this work and for them to not be offside during the buildup of the play.

Progression 1: Have defenders track the runs of the strikers to show how they are affected by them. Have defenders play passively to ensure success initially. It can often be easier to see how the striker movement is implemented by adding defenders instead of just using flags that are stationary.

Progression 2: We can also do Combination / Crossover runs between the two strikers as a development and the pass can be a diagonal one or a straight run down the side.

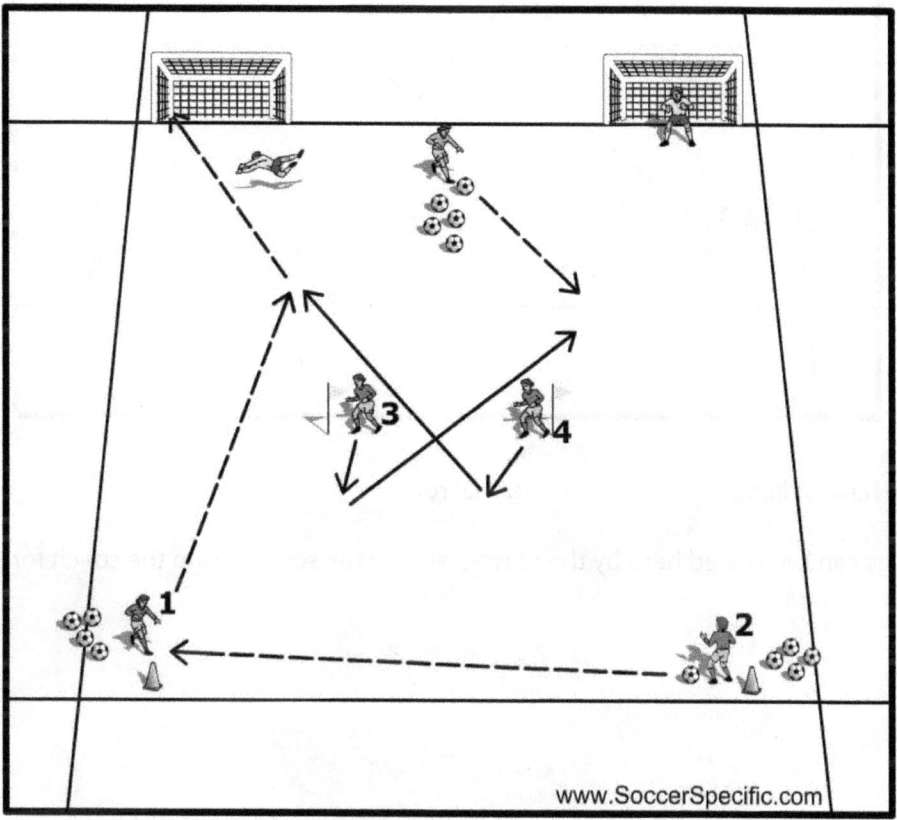

Here we have a straight pass from a diagonal run and the 2nd ball goes to the other striker.

Vary the service so sometimes both balls go to the same striker. Both players have to be alert and on their toes.

COACHING STRIKERS

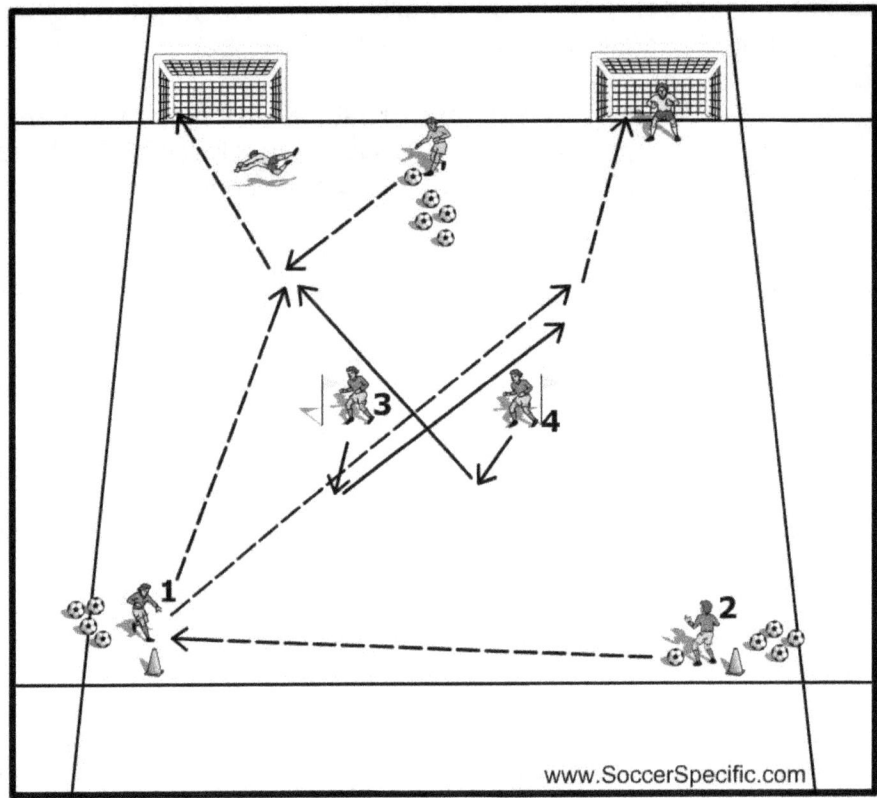

Here we have a diagonal pass and a diagonal run.

Variations can be created here by the players and by the service from the coach for the 2nd ball.

A 3 v 3 GAME CREATING TURNING OPTIONS

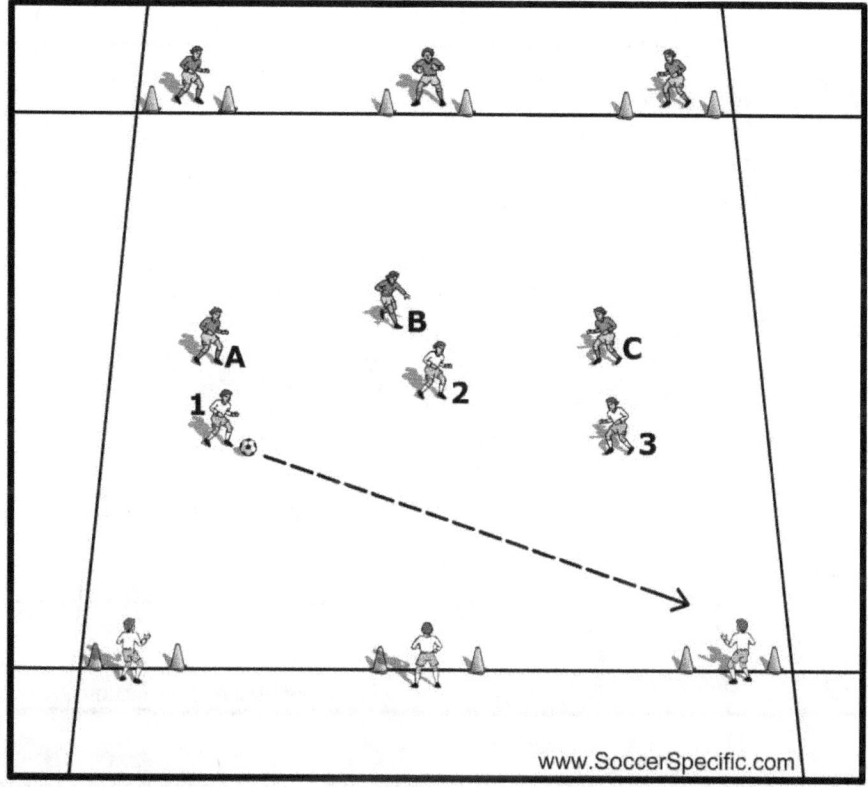

The team who scores stays on and must quickly defend the 3 new players coming in (one from each goal that the opposition defends).

Instant transition with the same ball that the opponents scored with. The other three players must get off the field ASAP.

Infield players can pass back to the support players in the goals to then implement a move they have practiced.

COACHING STRIKERS

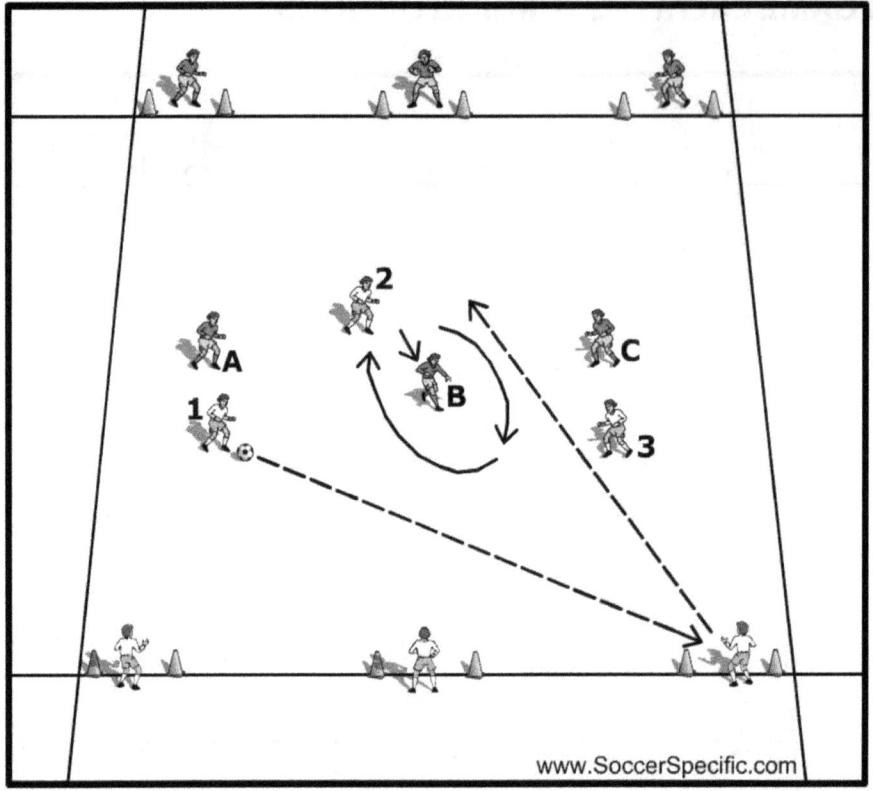

Here player (2) draws defender (B) towards the ball and creates space behind to run into.

(2) then makes a sharp turn and gets away from (B) and the ball is passed into the space behind (B) for (2) to run onto and score. You can liken this to a center forward against a center back and it is an opposite move.

This could be the perfect time and place for the Del Piero Spin.

Can all three attacking players get into a position to be side-on or face forward when they receive the ball.

There can even be an interchange between the strikers to create space for the pass.

OBJECTIVE: AN AWARENESS OF WHERE THE SPACE IS TO EXPLOIT USING THE SHADOW STRIKER

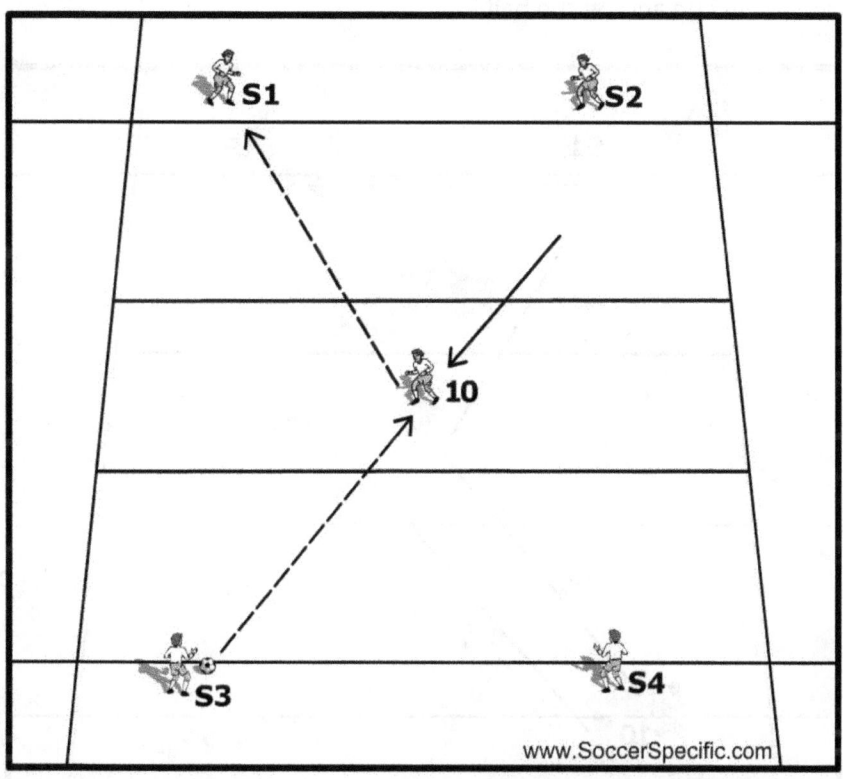

Server S3 feeds the shadow striker (10).

(10) turns and feeds S1 at the far end.

S1 feeds S2, striker switches with another S (S3 or S4) and the cycle continues.

Technical Coaching Points:
- Support angle / distance of (10)
- Receiving skills of (10)
- Passes into and from (10)
- Awareness of (10)

Progression:
a) S's change sides before receiving a pass from (10).
b) Introduce another striker.

Liken the thirds to the attacking third, middle third and defensive third so the shadow striker is dropping back from the attacking third to the middle third to receive the ball.

You could liken this to a midfield player dropping short to receive from the back players also.

COACHING STRIKERS

This is a great all round clinic for many skills, including: Passing quality and the weight and angle of the pass, Movement off the ball, Creating and finding space, supporting positions (particularly angled support), decision making without pressure to begin, transition, and ultimately awareness on and off the ball.

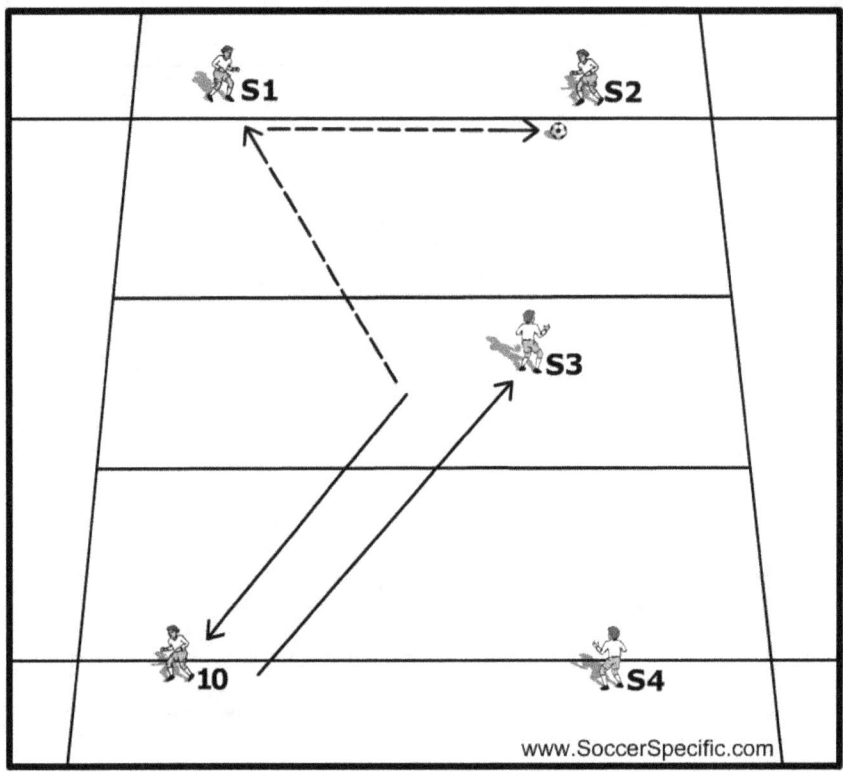

Here (10) has passed to S1 who plays the ball to S2 to change the angle of the pass to the next shadow striker S3.

As (10) lays the pass off he chooses a player to switch with. This player, in this case S3, then goes to receive from S2 and the cycle continues.

All the players get the chance to make the necessary runs as the shadow striker in the middle and into the middle third.

Liken here S1 as the second striker in front who has received a pass from (10).

Once this pass has been undertaken, S1 and S2 become essentially midfield support players going the other way, and (10) and S4 are target second strikers.

Who the middle player passes the ball to can determine which player the middle player switches with to ensure there is an angled support.

Here the ball will eventually finish up at S2 so the logical player to switch with is S3 as shown to maintain the angled support. If the switch was to be with S4 then that player needs to ensure he does not support a pass from S3 in a straight line so should work an angle to receive, making a run to the center of the field, not straight at S2.

POINT STRIKER / SHADOW STRIKER

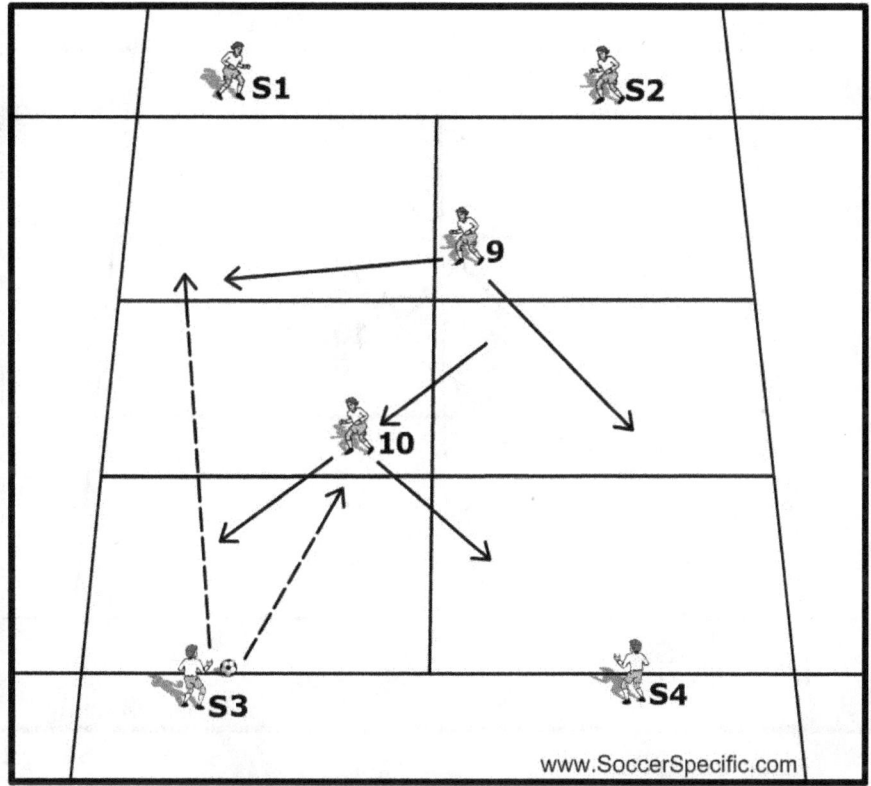

Central area marked off into thirds. Six players (4 servers, 2 players); S's serve to each other then into one or the other player. Initially pass to the shadow striker first.

Both (9) and (10) must touch the ball before it is transferred to the other side.

(9) and (10) must be aware of each other's positions. They must never be in the same third of the field to ensure one goes short and one long.

Working on receiving skills and release skills.

Avoid supporting in a straight line, working angles off each other to support.

Progression 1: Play the ball into the second striker or point striker who then lays it off for the shadow striker. The difference is when the ball goes to the shadow striker first, he has to receive and turn and pass, whereas if it is passed into the point striker then it is all passing the way you are facing.

Progression 2: One S player can move into the area as a supporting midfield player and receive passes off (9) or (10).

COACHING STRIKERS

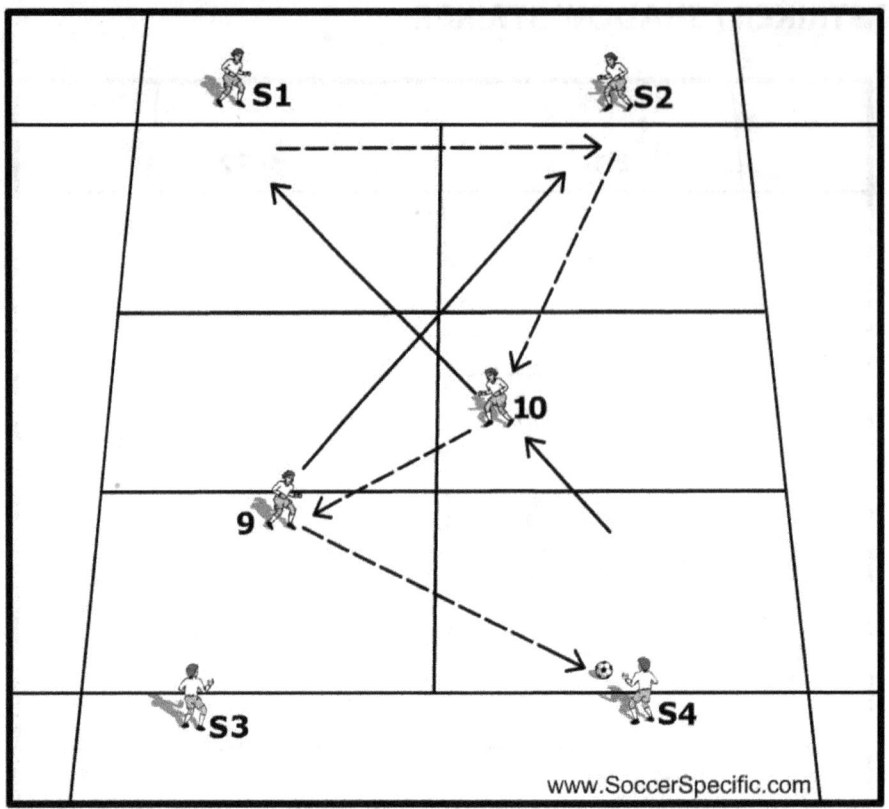

The play starts at S1.

All players have the opportunity to play in both roles, the point striker and the shadow striker.

When (10) and (9) have combined and passed the ball to S3 or S4 they switch with S1 and S2 who become the two strikers going the other way.

One player has to go short into the midfield third to be the shadow striker and one stays up top in the attacking third as the point striker.

Have them both make diagonal runs to get into position because this will make them more difficult to pick up in a game.

COACHING STRIKERS

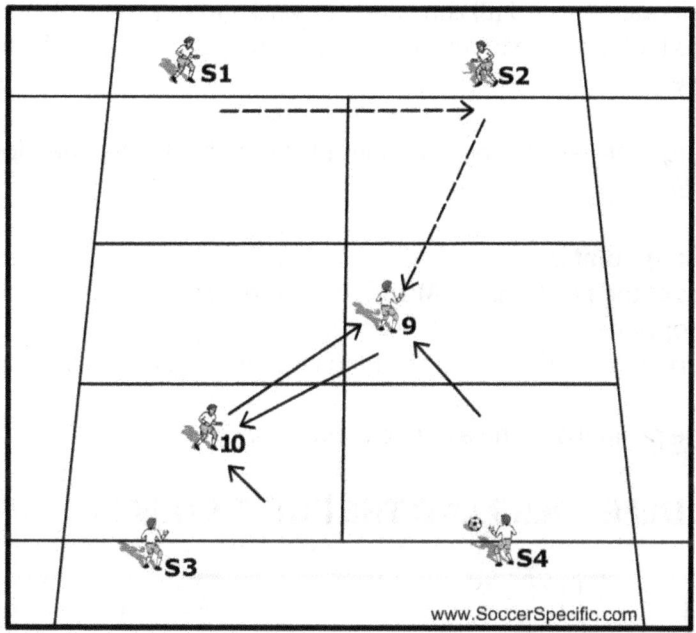

Here the timing of the runs is too early so the two strikers switch positions to make the timing right. In a game this will make it more difficult for defenders to mark them.

INTRODUCE DEFENDERS

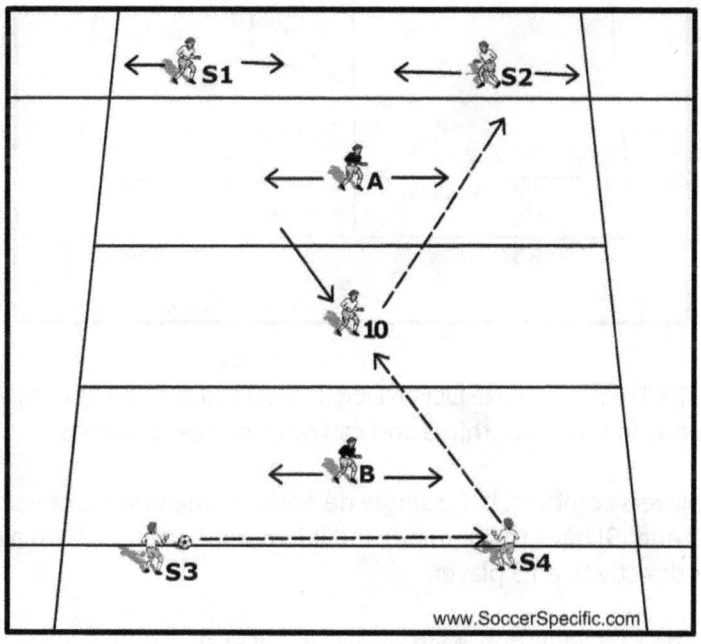

(A) and (B) work along the lines to try to intercept the passes made by (10). Here S1 and S2 can move along the line to open up the angle to receive from (10). The defenders (A) and (B) must stay and defend in their own third initially.

Progression: Defenders (A) and (B) can come forward and oppose (10) after (10)'s first touch. This means (10) has time to receive and turn and pass successfully, so the pressure is essentially passive.

(10) feeds an S target player and then changes places with S3 or S4, therefore alternating the shadow striker.

Technical Coaching Points:
- An awareness of the positions of (A) and (B) before receiving the ball.
- Passing past opponents
- Attacking opponents with the ball; running with the ball, wall passes

All players change positions as the exercise continues.

INTRODUCE DEFENDERS AND THE POINT STRIKER

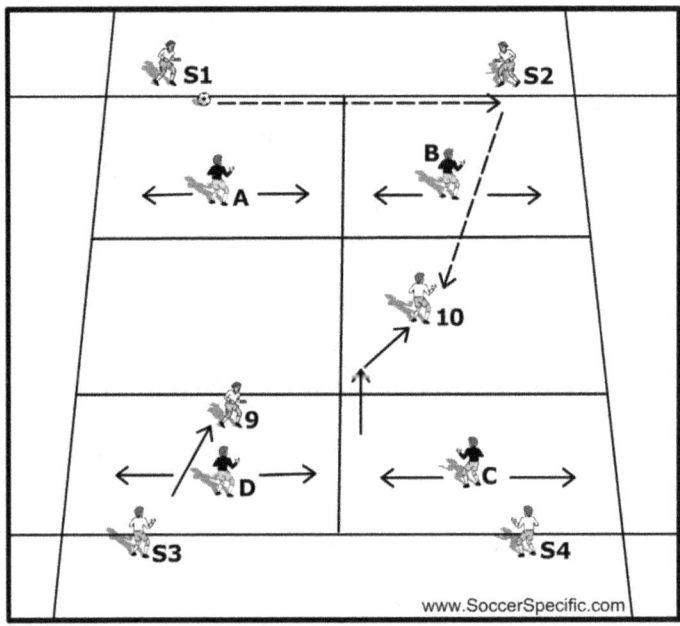

Progression 1: TRY THIS WITH ONE DEFENDER IN EACH SIDE FIRST TO GAIN SUCCESS. Defenders must stay in their own thirds and can only intercept the pass.

Try to have the players combine. If the single defender in the first progression closes down (9) (knowing (10) and (9) have to combine) and it becomes artificial, then allow (10) to receive and pass directly to an S player.

Progression 2: Add two defenders each side. This will ensure one defender tries to get into the passing lane to stop this and may in fact release (9) for a pass.

S players on the outside must move along the line to open up the possibility of the pass from (9) or (10).

In this case (A) and (B) can intercept the pass to (9) or (10).

(10) must maneuver a position into the middle third and so get free to receive, but also into a position between or either side of (A) and (B) to open up the angle for the pass from S2.

(9) stays in the attacking third and so can be challenged by (C) or (D).

The idea is for (10) to drop deep to become the shadow striker and get free from the marking of (C) or (D) as neither can encroach into the middle third.

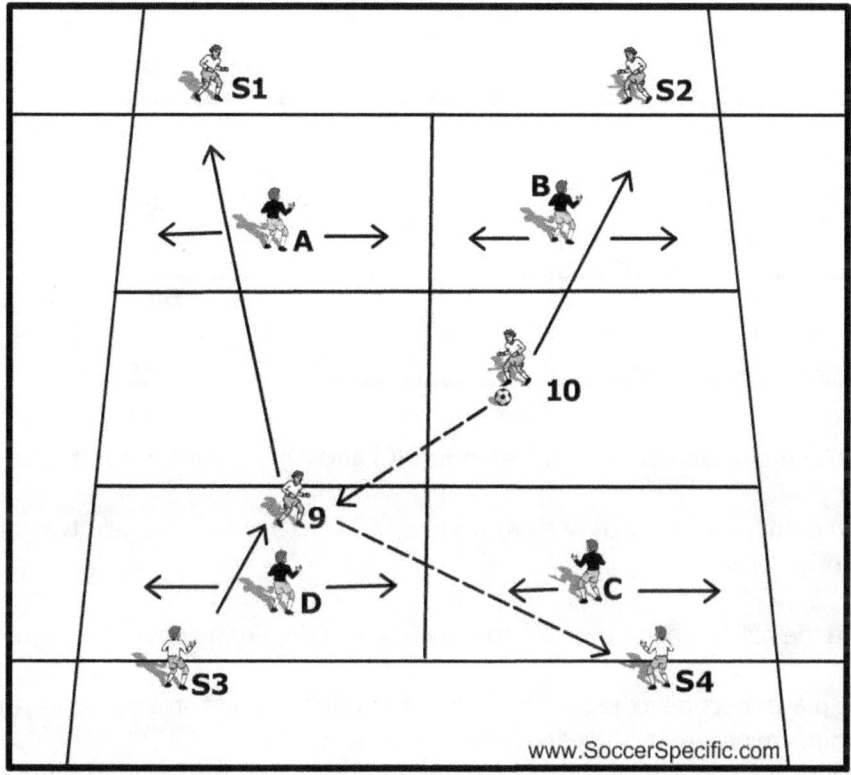

Here (9) and (10) combine and pass to S4 then switch with S1 and S2.

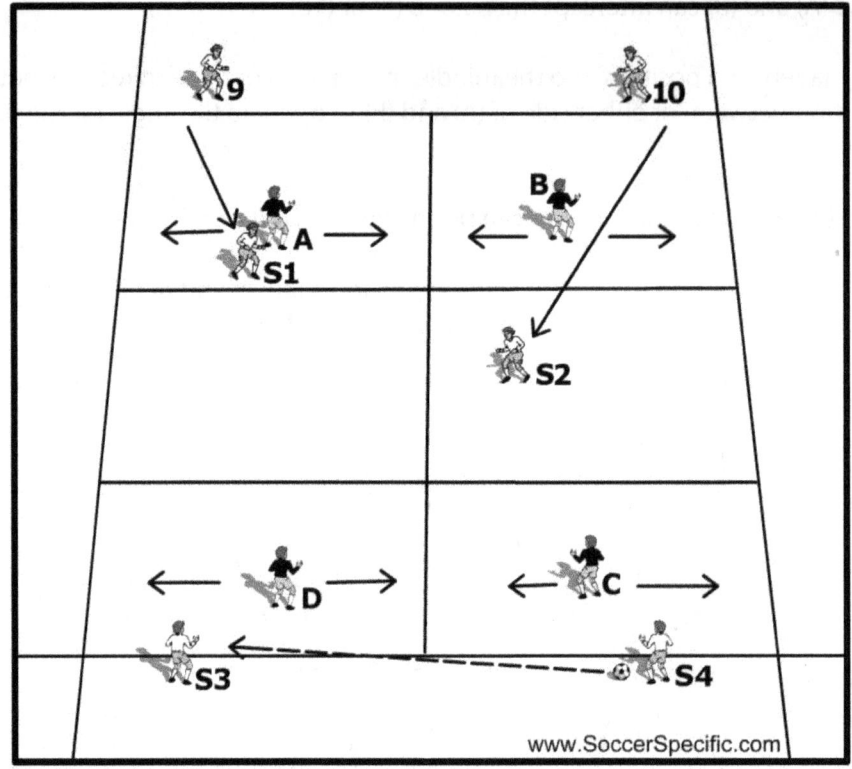

(10) and (9) combine and pass to S4. Defenders (C) and (D) try to intercept the pass.

(10) and (9) then have to switch back with S1 and S2 who become the next two strikers going the other way.

By the time the ball has been transferred from S4 to S3 the timing should be right.

Again, one player becomes the shadow striker and one the point striker, staying in different thirds to ensure there is depth between them.

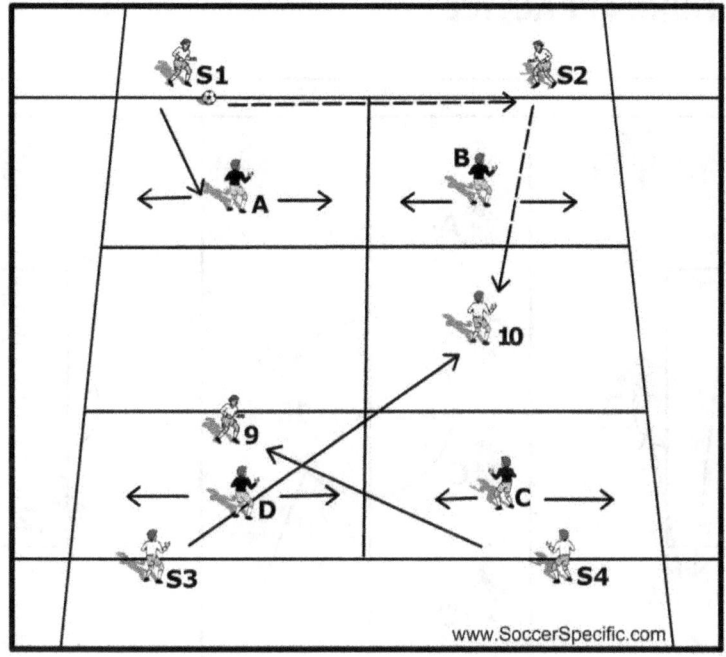

Here they both make diagonal runs to receive the pass. The pass could go to player (9) or player (10) first.

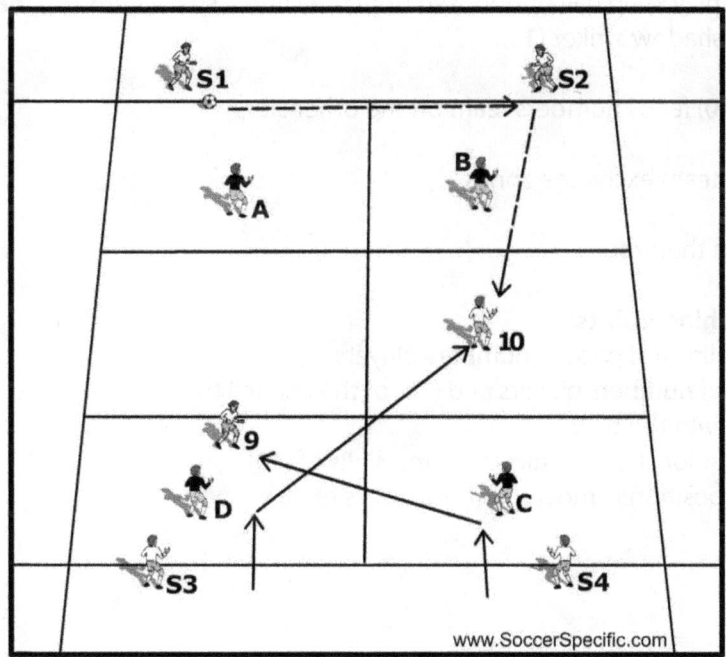

Or they could both come back in straight lines then switch late and fast to make their ultimate diagonal runs, to lose markers in a game situation for example.

SUPPORT STRIKER PRACTICE

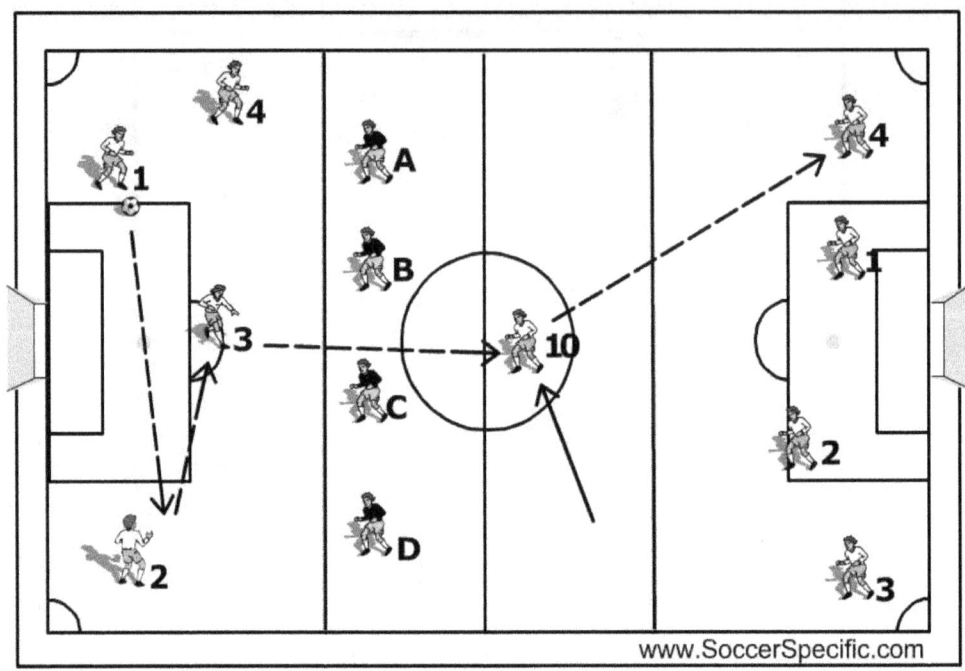

Numbers team play keep ball unopposed until they find a space between the letters players to feed shadow striker (10).

On receiving, (10) feeds numbers team on the other side.

(10) and letters team exchange zones.

All teams stay in their zones.

Technical Coaching points:
- Passing quality and pace of numbers players.
- Awareness of numbers players and (10) of the chance to combine to provide shadow striker (10) with the ball.
- Support position, body angle, receiving skills of (10)
- Defending positions / movements of letters team

COMPETITIVE PRACTICE

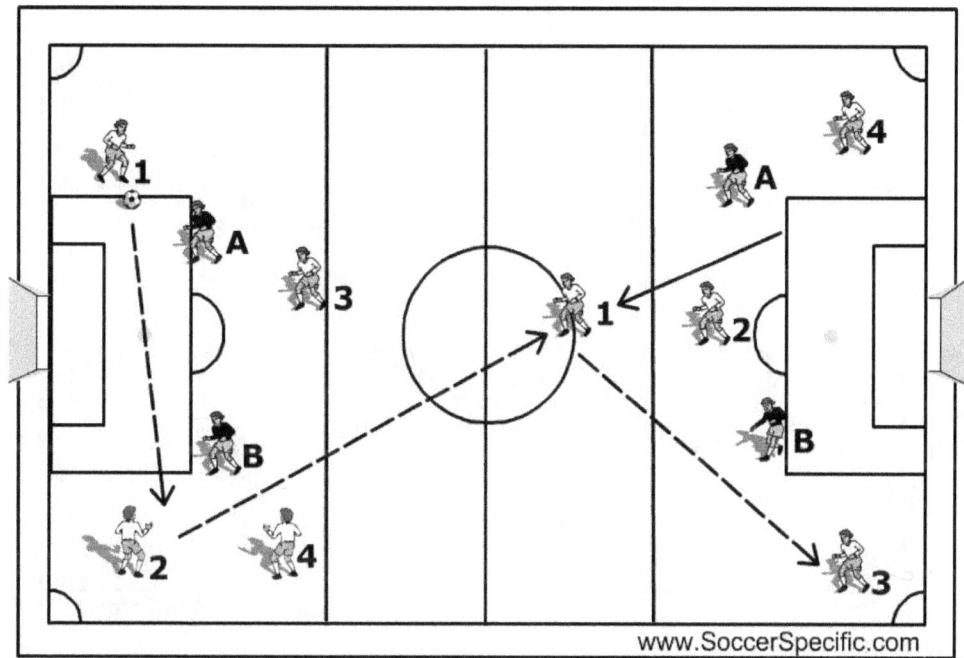

Developing quality passing and support play in a 4 v 2 overload.

Progression 1: Start with two 4 v 2's and a player in the middle all the time. Play through this player from one side to the other.

Progression 2: Keep ball in a 4 v 2 until the opportunity arises to play a pass into the middle zone. A player from the other group now drops into the middle zone to receive and transfer.

Player drops into the middle zone:
- Correct time
- Awareness
- Body angle / shape
- Good first touch
- Release of pass or run the ball into the end zone into the 4 v 2 again.

Play until an opportunity opens up in the other side.

Look for angled passes as well as straight passes, angled runs short into the middle zone to receive as well as straight runs.

SUPPORT STRIKER AND MIDFIELD

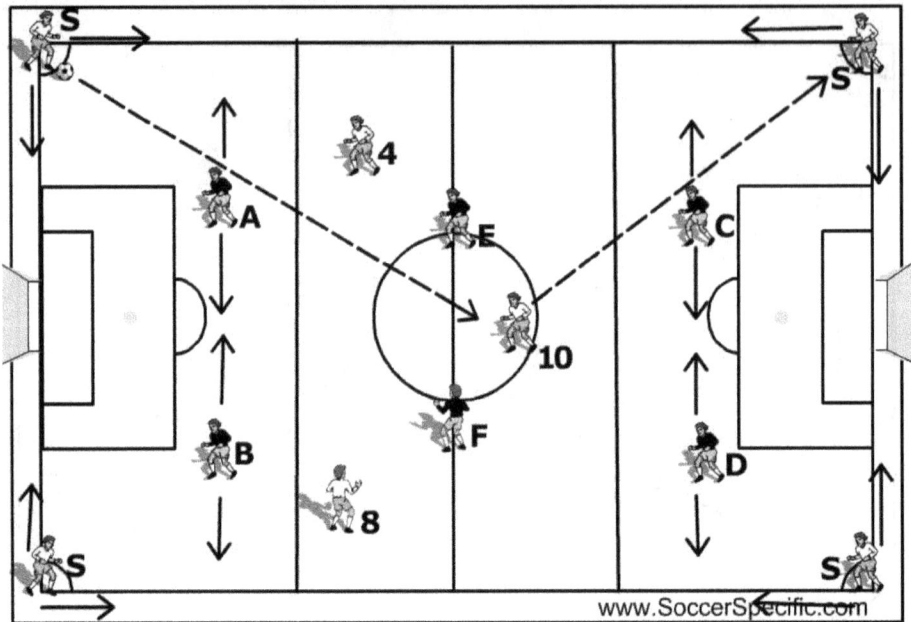

A 3 v 2 in the middle third (or a 2 v 1).

(A), (B), (C), (D) act as defenders along their lines. If it doesn't work easily, consider using only one defender at each end to begin.

S's receive and feed the ball into the middle third for (4), (8) and (10).

All players stay in their own thirds.

Technical Coaching Points:
- Movement and support positions of (4), (8) and (10).
- Awareness by (10) of the ball and the other players' positions
- Receiving skills and combination skills with other players
- Releasing and passing skills (timing and accuracy)
- Support and passing skills of end players.

Any player in the 3 v 2 overload can be the shadow striker. The passer has to find the free player who can then be classed as the (10).

The free player can become the shadow striker from the next pass as well, for example (4) may receive it and then (10) becomes available to receive and pass on.

Progression: You can ask the defending players in the middle to immediately man-mark two attacking players so the Server has to pick out the free player and pass to that player.

COMBINING THE TWO PREVIOUS IDEAS
4 v 2, 3 v 2 and 3 v 2

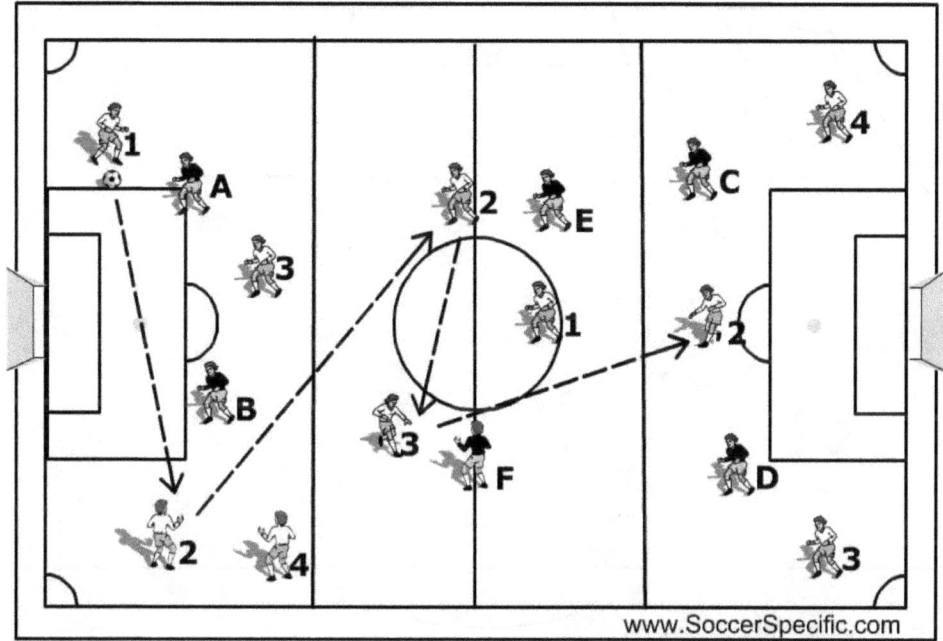

Here we now have competitive small sided games in three separate areas on the field.

Progression 1: Have players move between the thirds to support each other.

Progression 2: Have the players miss out the middle third players and pass from the back to the front. Players in the middle then support behind in a shadow striker capacity. Maybe have a coned area that the shadow striker can move into and not be marked to show this clearly.

A PHASE PLAY FOR THE SHADOW STRIKER POSITION IN THE 4-2-3-1

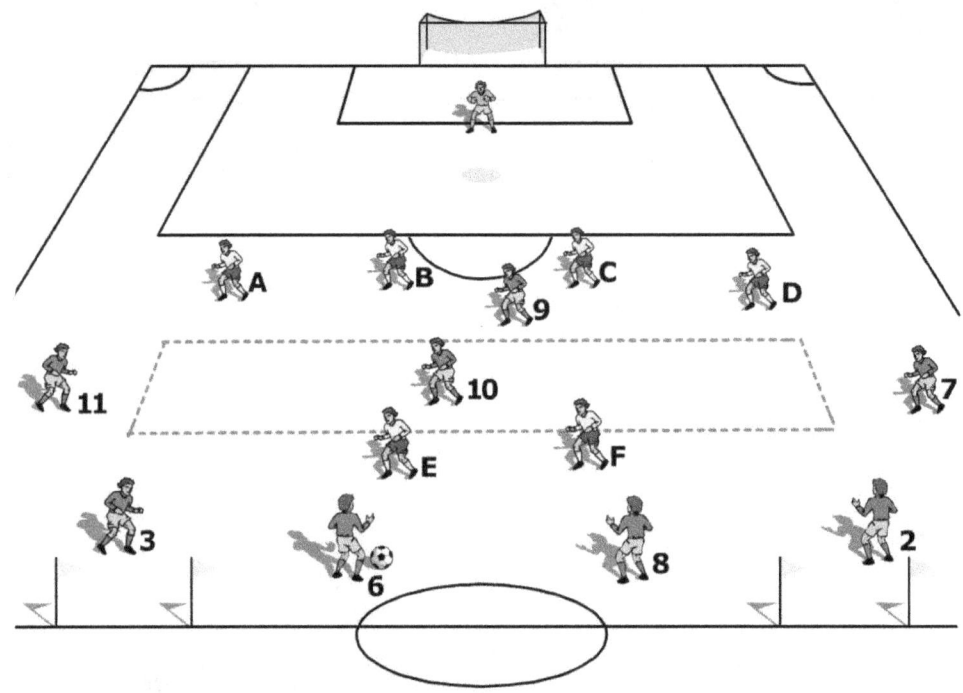

The set up is a 4-2-3-1. The only players not included in the attacking numbered team are the two center backs and the keeper.

The ball starts at the center midfielder here, but essentially it can start from anywhere.

Maintain the same start position for simplicity.

Dotted area is Zone 14 for the shadow striker to patrol or interchange with teammates.

As mentioned already the idea is to play a shadow striker (usually known as Number 10) who links up with players around him, but who also can interchange with various players to keep opponents guessing.

If the same player always drops into the free zone it becomes too predictable

Understanding between players as to where and when is essential here.

Try to receive and front up so facing forward on reception (Bergkamp / Baggio / Zola).

Here (10) enters the zone 14 area in anticipation of the pass.

If this player goes in too early in an actual game situation and takes a defender in, they need to get out and take the defender out to create space for a teammate to enter that vacated space.

This is unselfish play by the shadow striker.

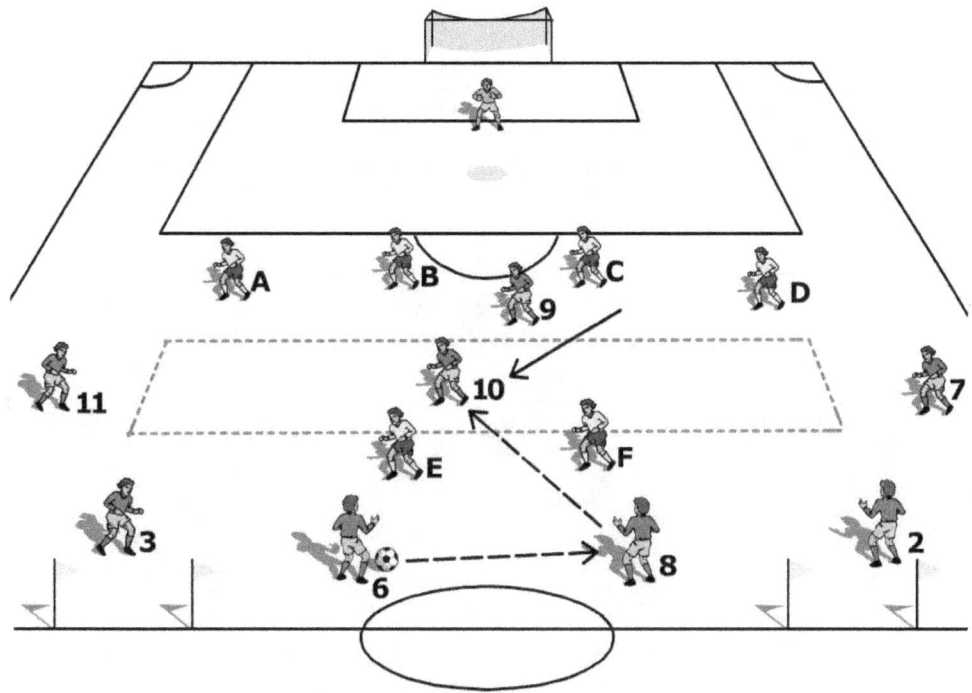

Here (10) arrives as the ball arrives and gets free to play, in this instance the first pass and run is free to get the play started successfully.

Once the shadow striker gets the ball the play is live.

Technical Coaching Points:
- Support angle / distance of (10)
- Receiving skills of (10)
- Passes into and from (10)
- Awareness of (10) of options BEFORE receiving the pass

Player (10) dropping into the middle zone:
- Correct timing of the pass / timing of the run
- With awareness of options in advance of the ball
- Body angle / shape; try to be open and facing forward if possible.
- Good first touch

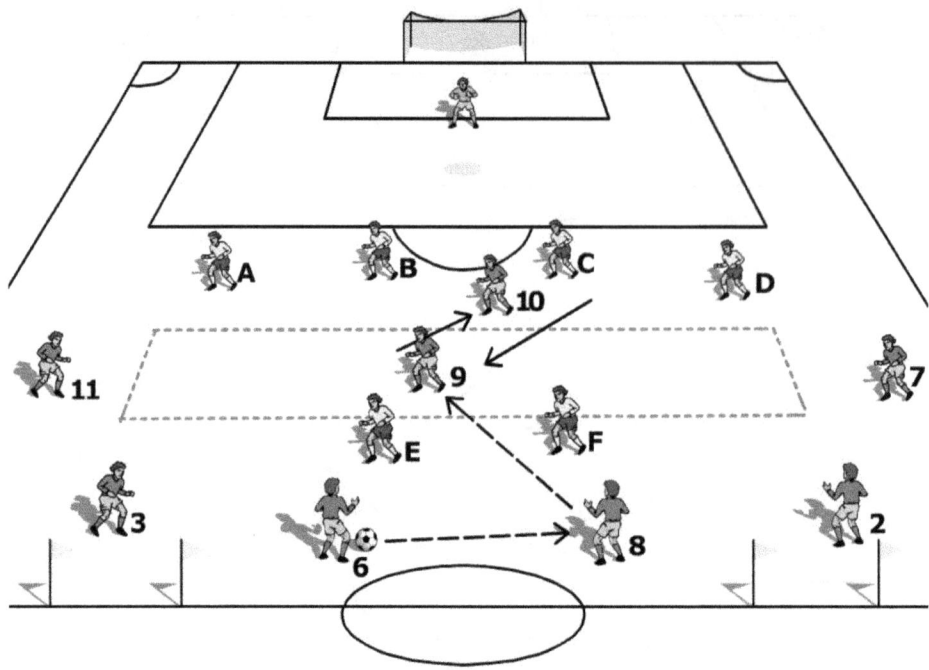

Here we have an interchange between (9) and (10); striker (9) now becoming the shadow striker.

This movement may disrupt the defenders enough to get one or both of the strikers free to receive.

(9) tries to receive at least facing side-on if not forward. His angle of approach to the ball can help determine this.

COACHING STRIKERS

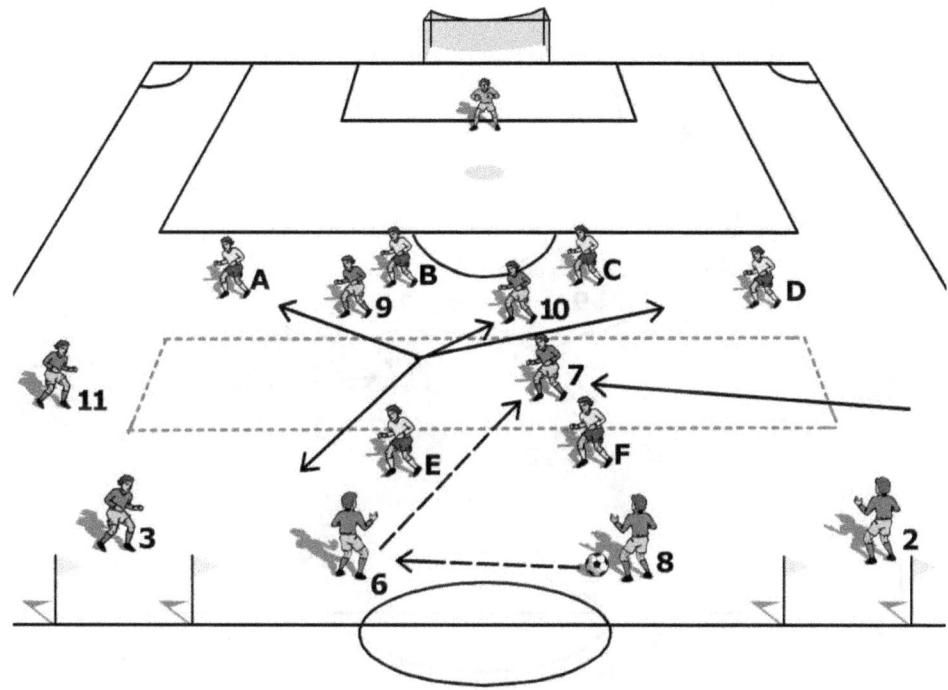

Here wide midfielder (7) cuts inside to make the run to receive in Zone 14. Shadow striker (10) has moved out of the zone to free up the space as before but this time for a different player.

This outside to inside run can prove very effective as it is harder to pick up.

Again showing various movements (10) may make based on where defenders are and where the best spaces are.

All the movement based around the shadow striker for it to be most effective means players must think unselfishly and work for each other.

COACHING STRIKERS

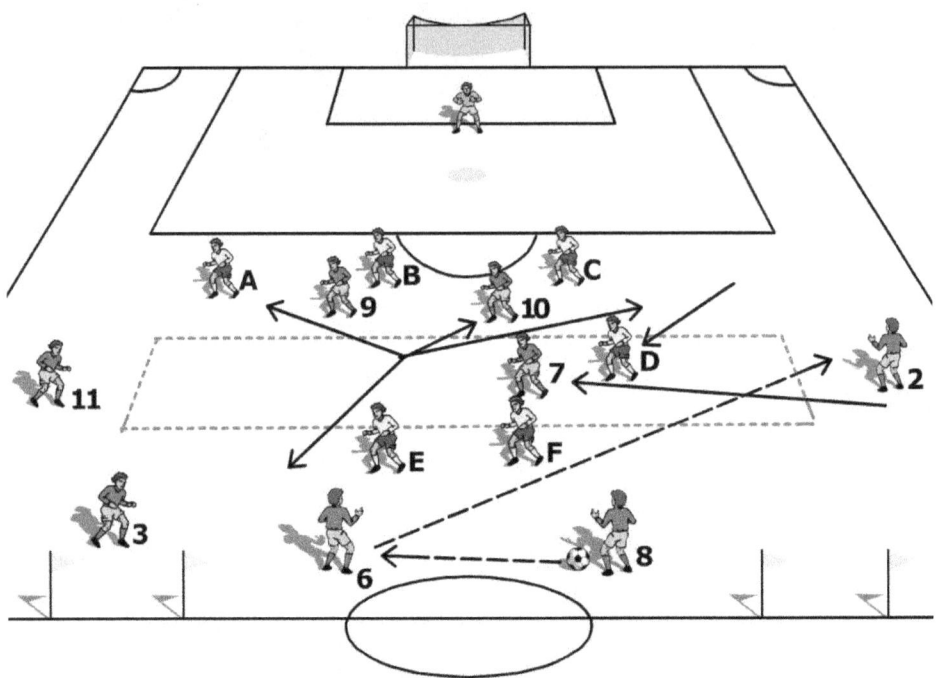

Here that unselfish run has created space in the wide area (7) has come from, especially if defender (D) tracks (7) inside and into Zone 14, leaving the outside area wide open for the attack.

This is the beauty of playing through Zone 14, defenders have to decide do I track the player into there or do I pass them on, and who do I pass them onto?

Hence fullback (2) gets a great chance to attack and get a cross into the box acting as an attacking and overlapping winger.

This interchange of positioning is what we are looking to create as much as we can within the team concept.

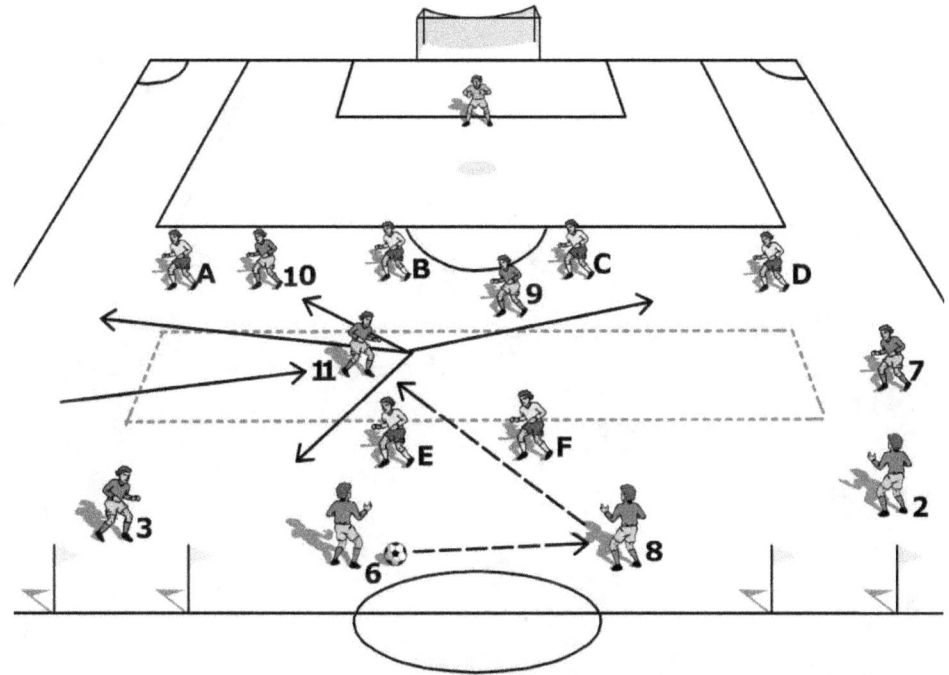

Opposite side now (11) gets into the action coming inside to receive the pass and attack the back four. Again depending on how defenders react we may get (3) free to receive instead of (11).

COACHING STRIKERS

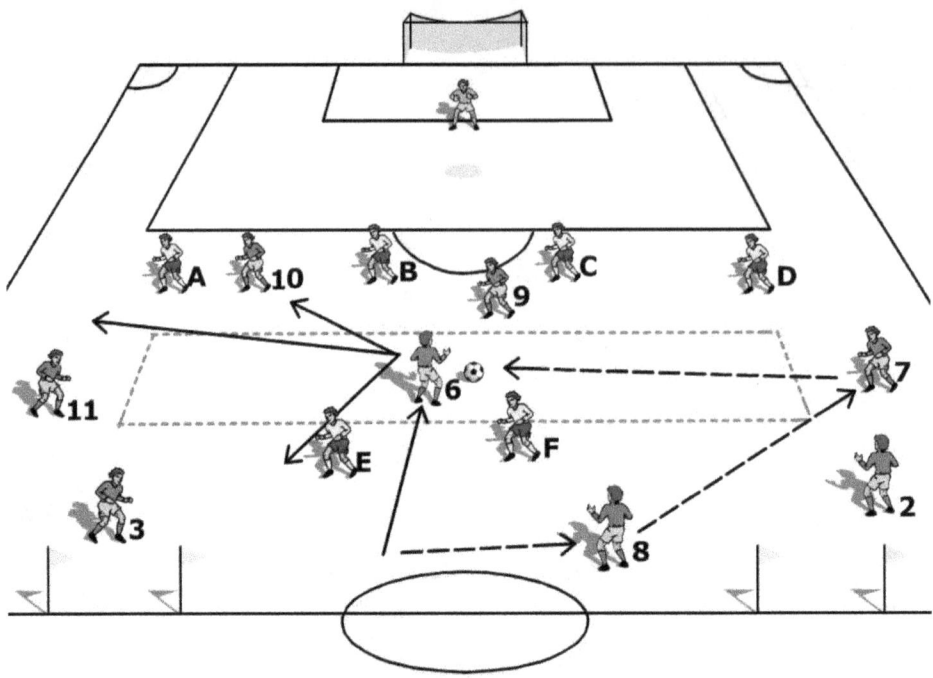

Here we get (10) clearing the space and showing various runs to make depending on where the best spaces are to go into.

This frees up central midfielder (6) who makes a forward run into the space to receive a pass from (7)

This is technically a 3rd man run from (6), hopefully on the blind side of his marker.

Making the run from behind and getting the timing of the run and the pass in sync means (6) can receive the ball facing forward and in a good position to run at the defense or work a combination with another player already in front of him such as (9) or (10).

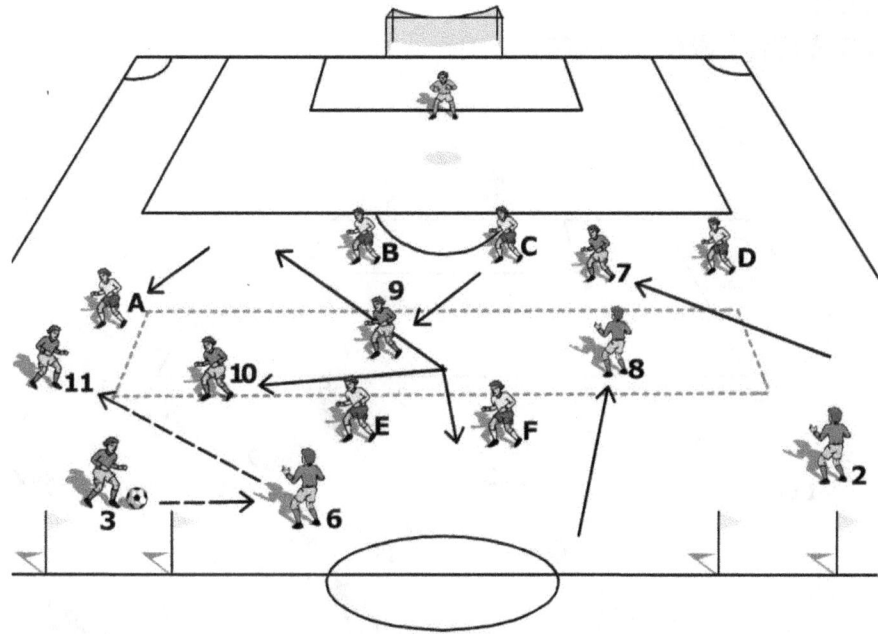

Here we have the CF/MF/ "Shadow" rotation mentioned in the introduction as one of the many interchanges players can make; this one being more sophisticated than previous ideas with a three or four player development, making movements off each other.

(10) clears the space for (9) to come into.

Here we get two players into Zone 14 and wide midfielder (7) makes a run in front of the furthest front player (9) who has effectively become the main shadow striker now by checking to the ball to possibly receive from (11) if that is the best option.

The best option will depend on what the defenders do.

Technical Coaching Points:
- Movement and support positions of (7), (8), (9) and (10).
- Awareness (by (9) in this case) of the ball and the other players' positions.
- Receiving skills and combination skills with other players
- Releasing and passing skills (timing and accuracy)
- Support and passing skills of players.

PHASE PLAY FOR THE SHADOW STRIKER POSITION WITHOUT THE FREE ZONE 14
PLAYING WITH TWO STRIKERS

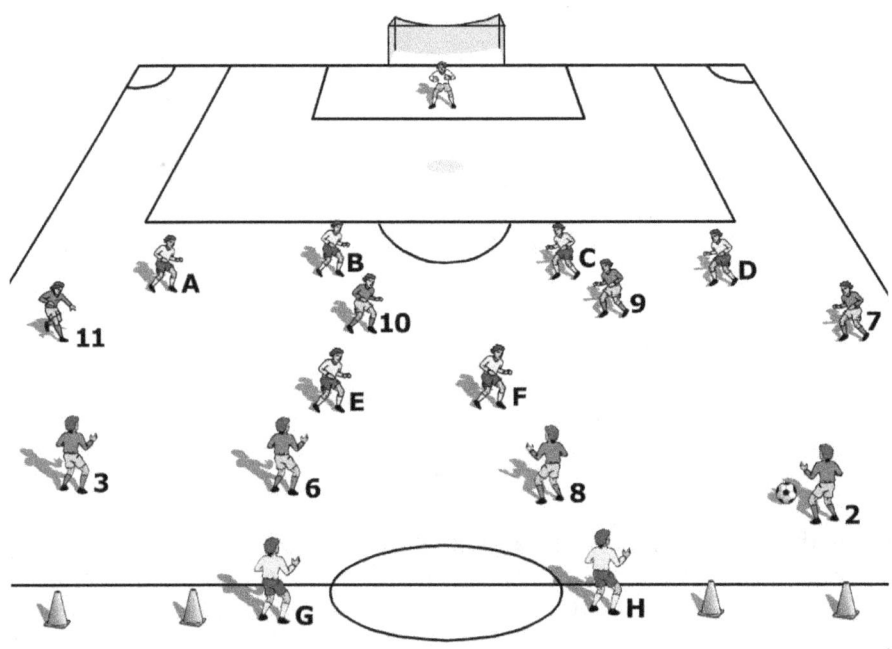

An 8 v 6 situation where the attacking team have greater numbers. We are focusing on attacking play. The attacking team has to try to score in the regular goal.

The defending team has two target players they have to get the ball to and play a 1-2 to score in the two small goals.

The first thought is to have one of the strikers drop into the shadow zone in front of the defenders and behind the midfield so they are not quite sure who should pick them up.

Develop: One player always dropping into the shadow area is too predictable, so have the players rotate as to who does it, either (9) or (10).

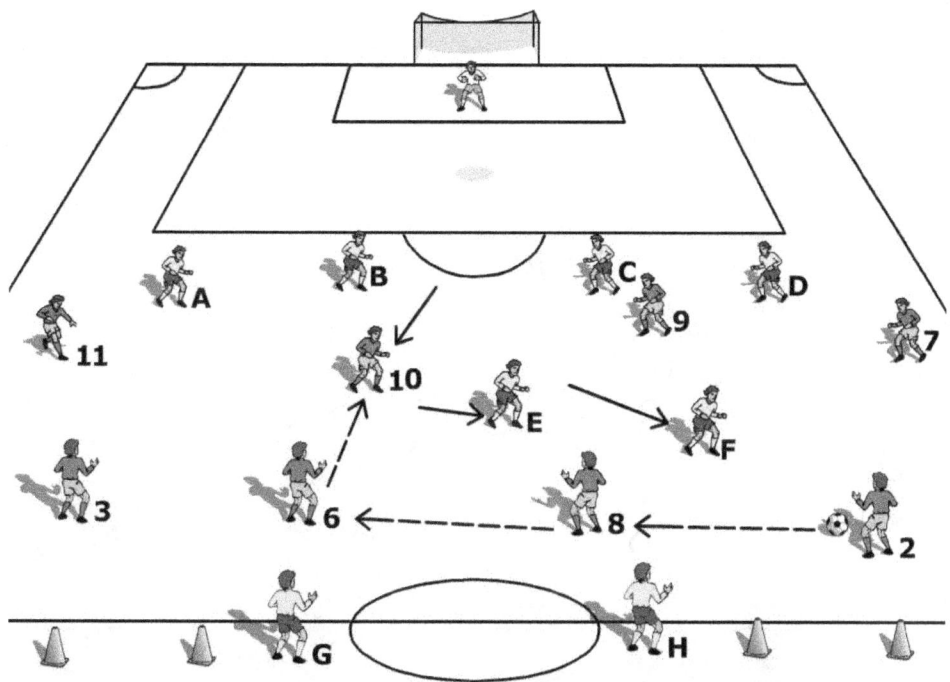

(10) drops into the shadow zone and gets free. You can condition the center back to let this happen to begin to gain success. Have (10) focus on receiving half turned and side-on so his first touch is forward.

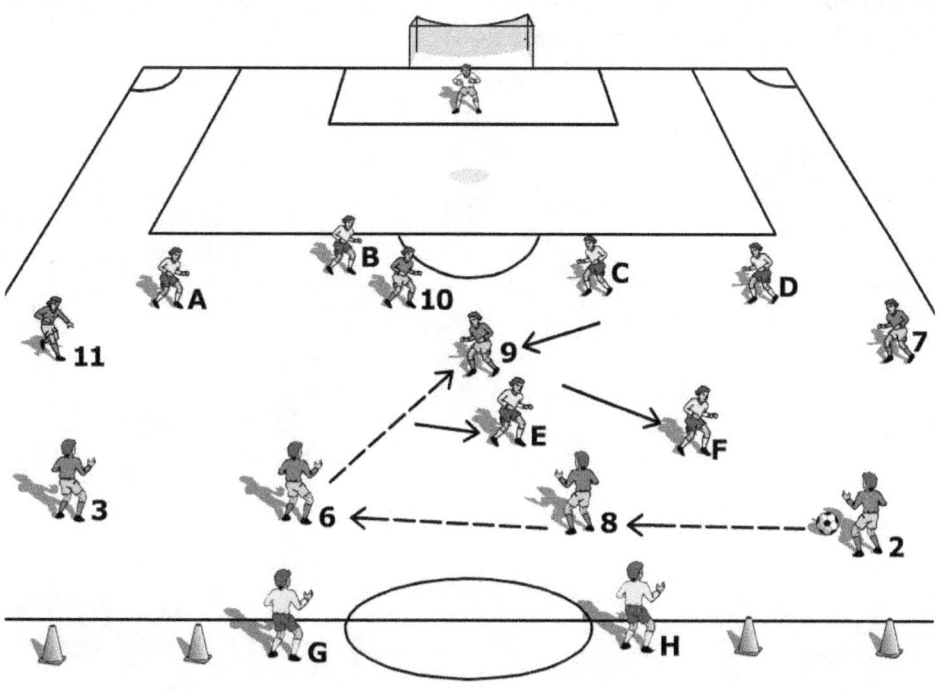

Here (9) drops into the shadow zone instead.

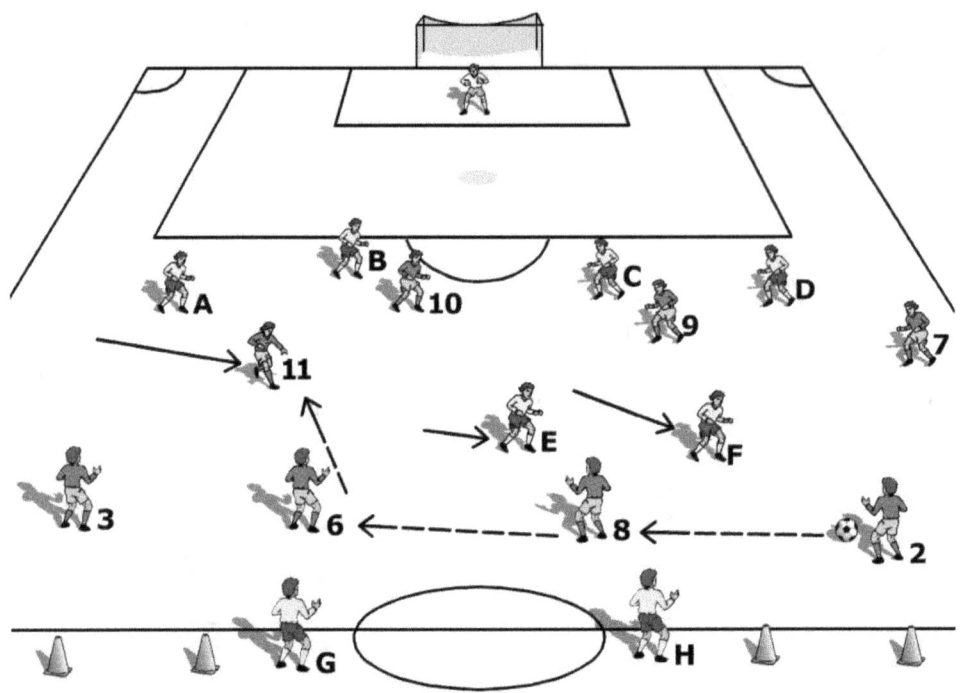

Instead of the central strikers making the same run now we have the wide midfielder (11) making an outside to inside run into the shadow zone.

(10) may even make an inside to outside run and switch positions with (11) which is especially effective against man marking teams for creating space if the timing of the movements and the timing of the pass are right.

THE 3-ZONE AWARENESS GAME

DROPPING OFF TO RECEIVE AND TURN IN POSSESSION

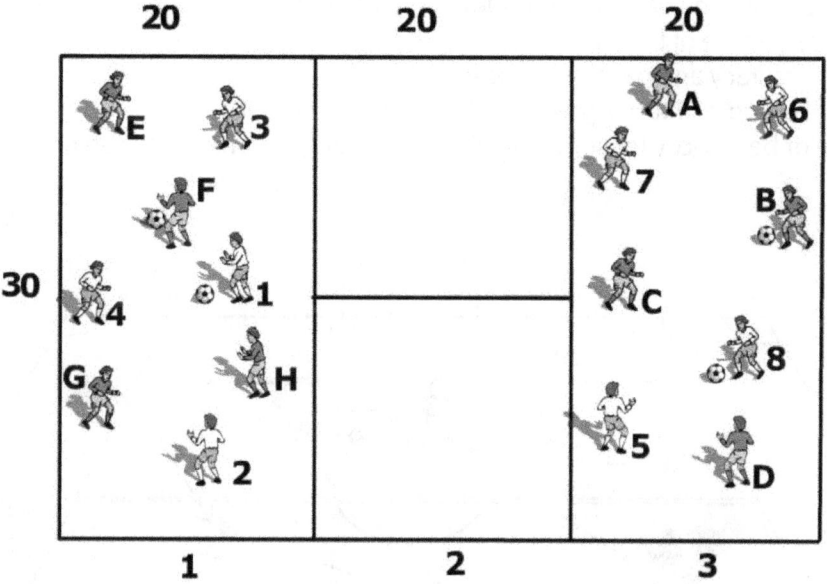

A three zone clinic focusing on zone 14 and emphasizing movement back towards the ball to receive and play forward and the consequent interchange of players between the three units.

You can bring in so many different ideas to the session and it all involves mental challenges to the players with regard to playing, moving and thinking quickly (and ahead of the ball).

Through trial and error we have found it best to have equal numbers in each third, so do the session with all the progressions with 3 v 3 or 4 v 4 or whatever number of players you have.

Also start with 4 balls going back and forth, one for each team of 3 or 4 players.

A 3 v 3 in each end zone (can be any number based on the number of players at training).

Teams are not playing against each other yet.

The central zone is the shadow striker zone known as zone 14 and usually where the number 10 plays, but 9, 7, 11, 8, 2 or 3 or even 6 can also enter this zone.

COACHING STRIKERS

Coaching Points:
- An awareness of the passing player of when and where the shadow striker drops into the free zone
- An awareness of the receiving player as to when the passer is ready to pass
- Good communication via visual cues through eye contact or aural cues through speaking makes this work
- Movement OFF the ball by the shadow striker to get free and into open space
- Timing and angle of the run
- Timing; accuracy and pace of the pass
- Good receiving and turning skills with an awareness of what is behind before receiving
- Receive or be a decoy for someone else; depending on where the defender is.

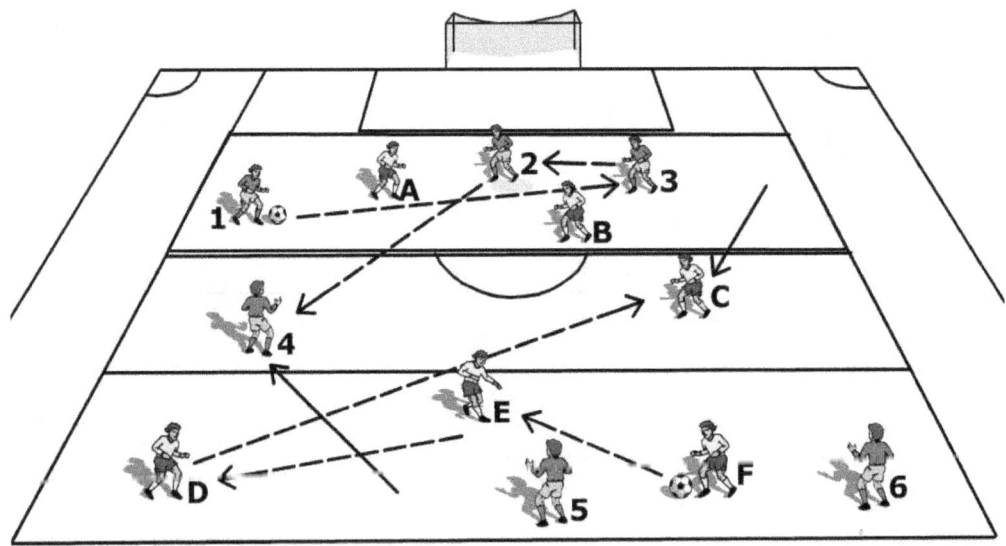

Passing and moving, (4) drops in to receive as does (C) going the other way.

Movement OFF THE BALL to receive in the middle zone (zone 14).

(4) takes the ball back into his own end zone, as does (C) in the other end zone and play continues. All players are moving to find space to receive the ball. The two teams pass between each other but cannot tackle each other.

Coaching Points:
- Timing of the pass
- Timing of the run
- Angle of the run
- Timing of each has to be exact for it to work.
- Have the receiving and dropping off player CALL THE NAME of the person he will pass to next BEFORE he receiving the ball.

3 ZONE GAME: DEVELOPING PERIPHERAL VISION

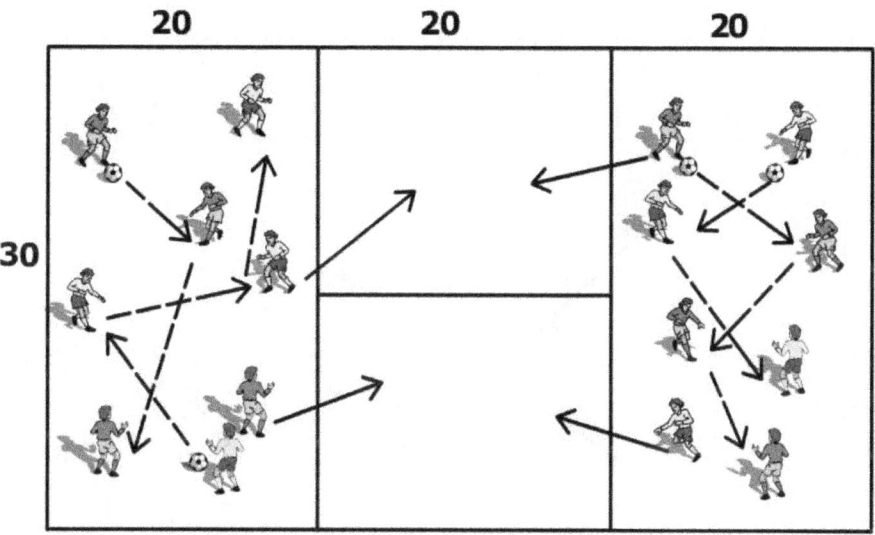

Coaching Points:
- Players are looking at the teammates in their own zone to pass to but also into the other zone for a player to drop into and support so they can switch the direction of play. No pressure to start and the defender must stay in the same zone so the receiving player is always free.
- Looking for good angles of support at all times; avoid straight line support as it limits vision behind the play.
- Players try to support in a sideways on stance to open up their field of vision.

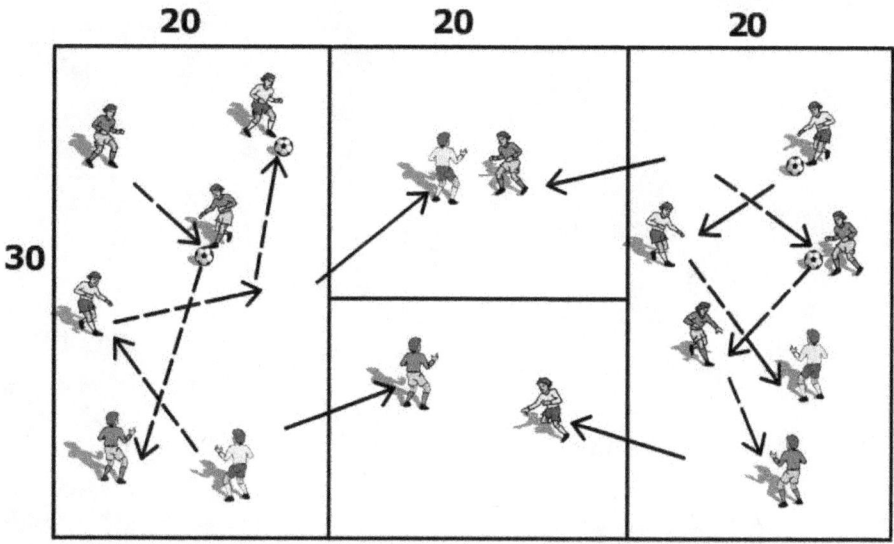

Movements have occurred now and players drop into the middle zone to receive and turn and pass back into their own zone. Soccer balls constantly being exchanged.
Players in each end zone must constantly scan the middle zone to see if players are

dropping into support positions so they are looking AWAY from the ball as they are doing this. Too many players just focus on their immediate surroundings and the ball itself and so don't see "peripheral movement" and miss the opportunity of the pass to change the point of attack.

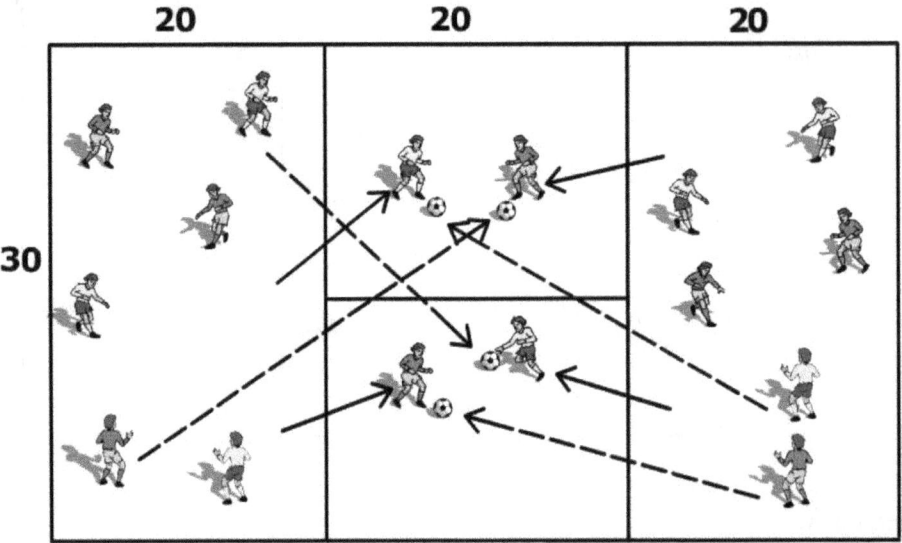

Trying to always have 2 balls in each end zone, one with each team.

Players might not all come in at the same time but they need to do it close to each other to maintain the balance.

As players drop in they are looking behind them to see where their next pass will go BEFORE they receive the ball.

PLAYERS SUPPORT AT WIDER ANGLES TO IMPROVE PERIPHERAL VISION AND BODY POSITION

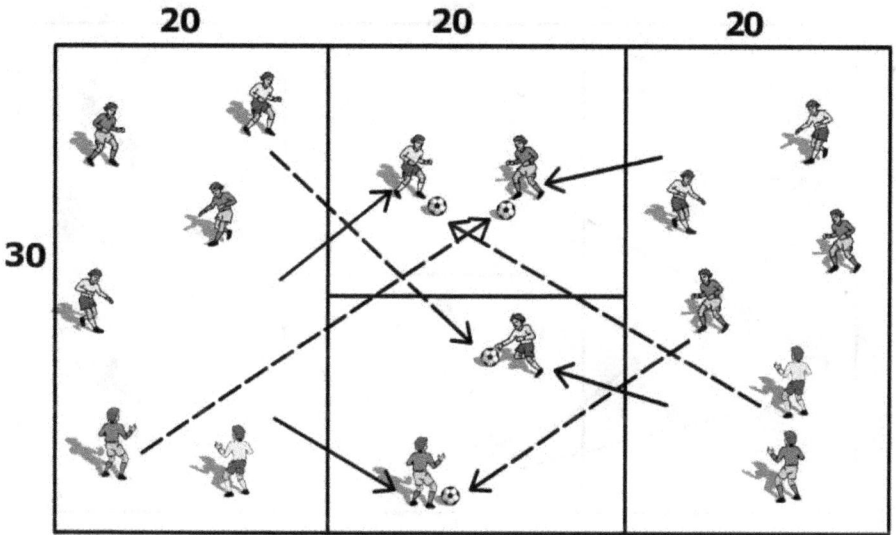

Greater angles of support to enable receiving players a larger peripheral vision of the field.

Each player should be positioned SIDE-ON, not with their back to the zone which they just came out of so they can see as many passing options as possible.

Passing can be at an angle, as can the support position of the receiver. So a player on the right tries to pass to a player on the left dropping into the middle and vice versa.

The cue is more specific now. If a player receives the ball on the right of the grid and has his head up looking to pass, this is the cue for a player on the left side of the opposite grid to drop into the middle to receive and turn.

DEVELOPING MORE DIMENSIONAL THINKING AND PLAYING

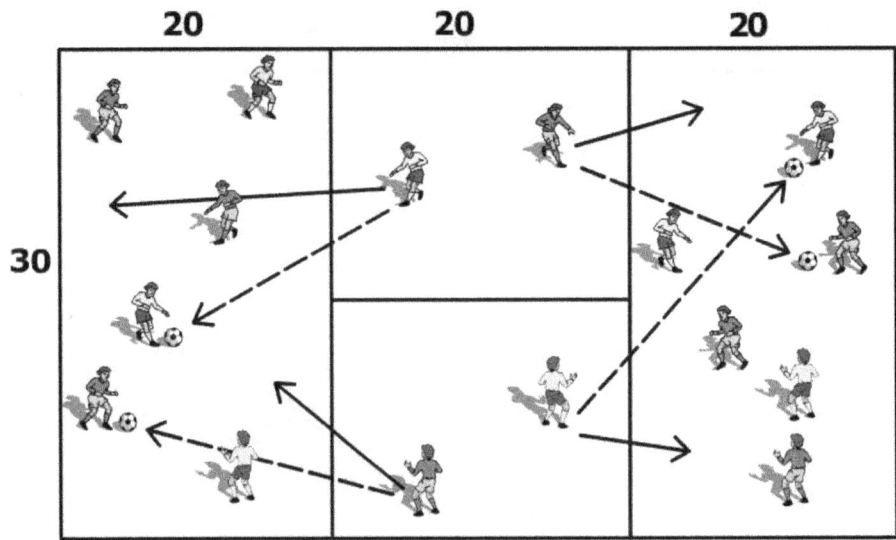

Now middle zone players drop back into their own zone and continue passing and moving with their teammates. Again, they are scanning what is happening in the other end zone watching to see when a player drops in to support and switch the play.

So a red player (for example) must in effect do 4 things at once:
1. Move to support his or her teammates on the ball.
2. Avoid the other team's players. So they must scan their positions too!
3. Scan the spaces to move into to receive a pass.
4. Look away from the immediate area of play and away from the ball to see if a support player is dropping into the middle zone.

COACHING STRIKERS

ONE BALL IN EACH SIDE AND 2 PLAYERS RECEIVING

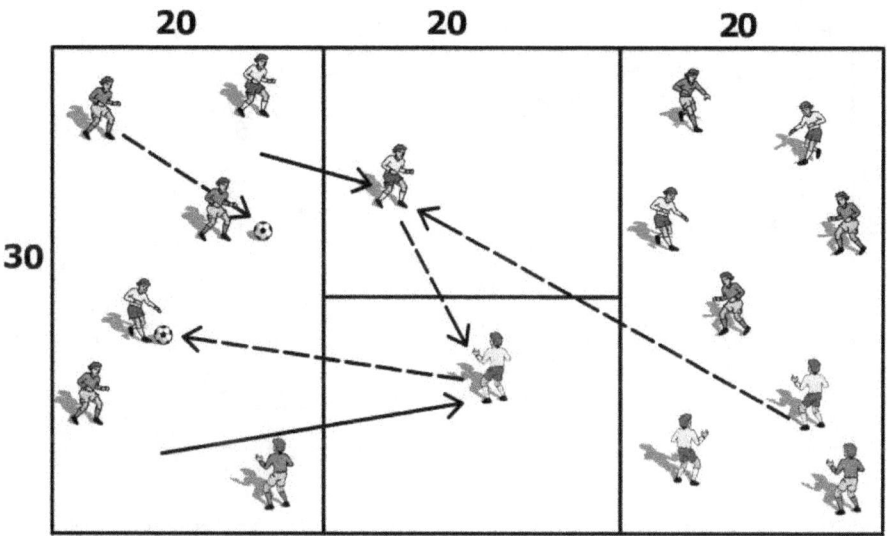

Still non competitive: Two players drop in to receive and combine and then play the ball back into their own zone.

Good communication is needed here for the two players to go at the same time and at angles to each other.

Showing just one team transferring the ball for clarity but both are watching to see when two players drop in to receive and combine.

COACHING STRIKERS

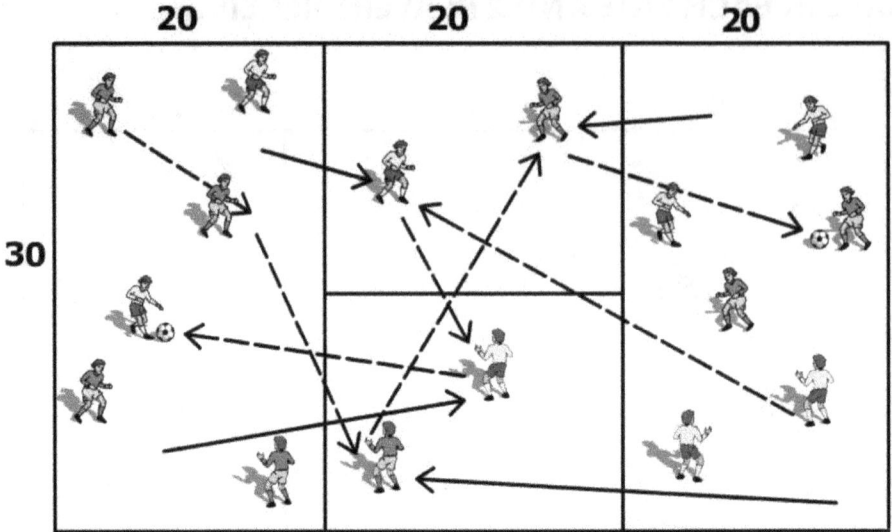

Now showing both teams passing and moving and receiving and turning. Still non competitive. Once the ball is passed back into their own zone they drop back and continue playing.

ONE BALL IN EACH SIDE AND 2 PLAYERS DROPPING BACK IN

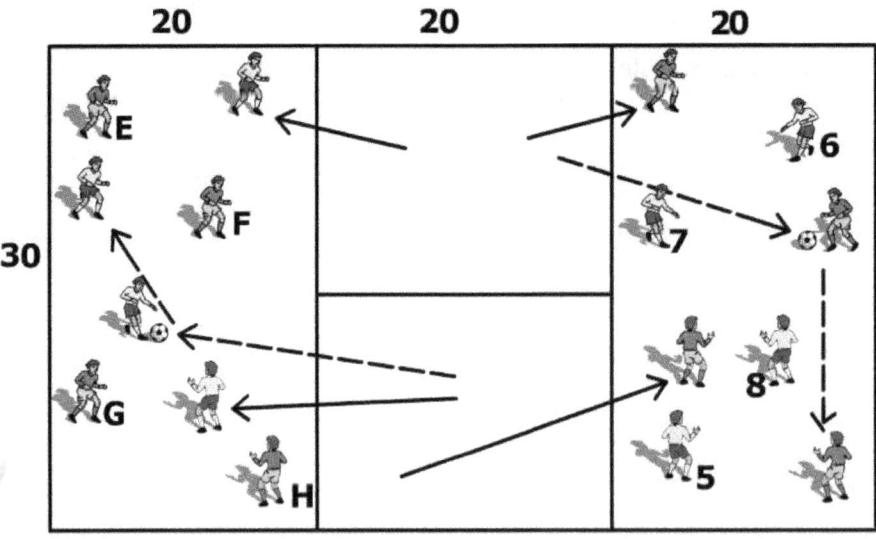

Passing sequence has occurred, the ball has been transferred and the middle players drop back into their own zones to join in the passing and moving again.

Now two of (5), (6), (7) or (8) get ready to drop back in as do two of (E), (F), (G) or (H).

MOVEMENT FROM THE BACK TO THE FRONT AND CHANGING ZONES

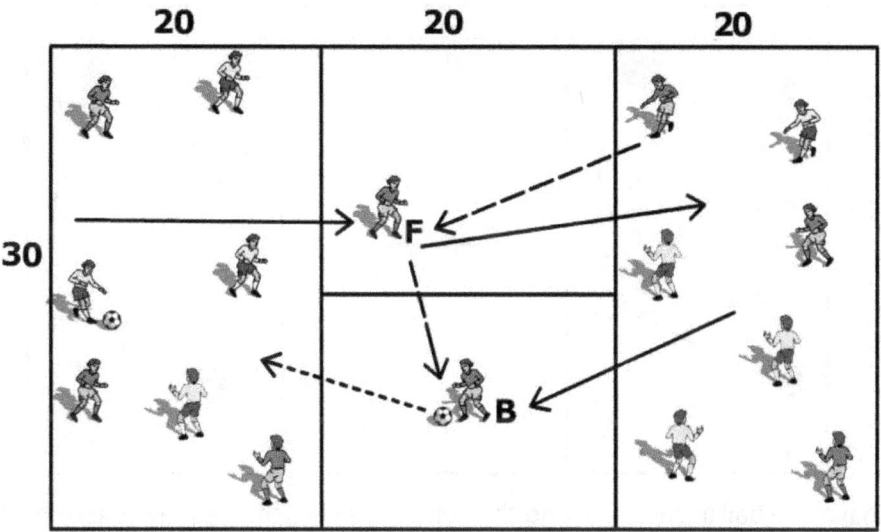

Players don't drop back into their own zones on this progression, they switch zones.

Just showing one team for clarity.

Now we get rotation across the zones with players switching, again a good exercise for testing the thinking processes of players to READ A SITUATION, work it out and execute it. (B) and (F) switch zones. Liken it to a player (B) attacking from the back and another player (F) dropping in as cover.

TWO COMPETITIVE GAMES PLAYING AT ONCE

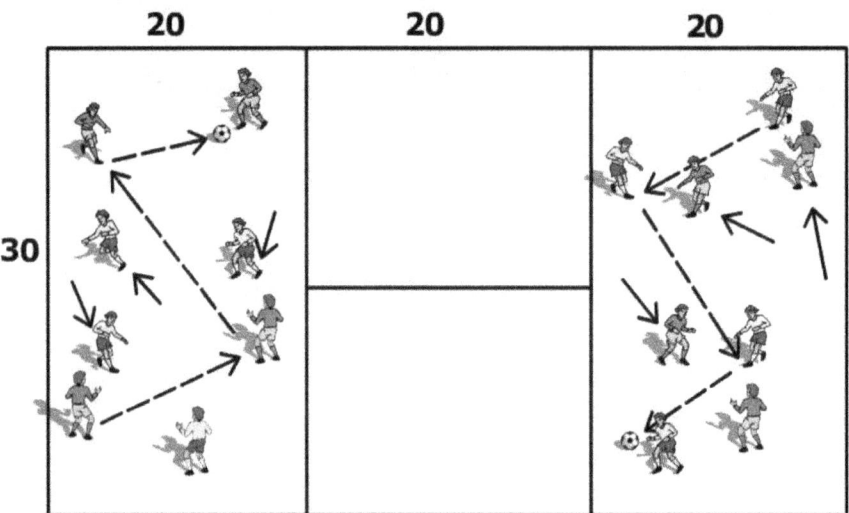

Now we have one ball in each side and the two teams in each side play against each other maintaining possession but also looking to transfer the ball into the middle zone for a player dropping off to receive.

It could be a red team with the ball on one side and a blue team with the ball in the other, so which player drops into the middle depends on which team has the ball in the other side.

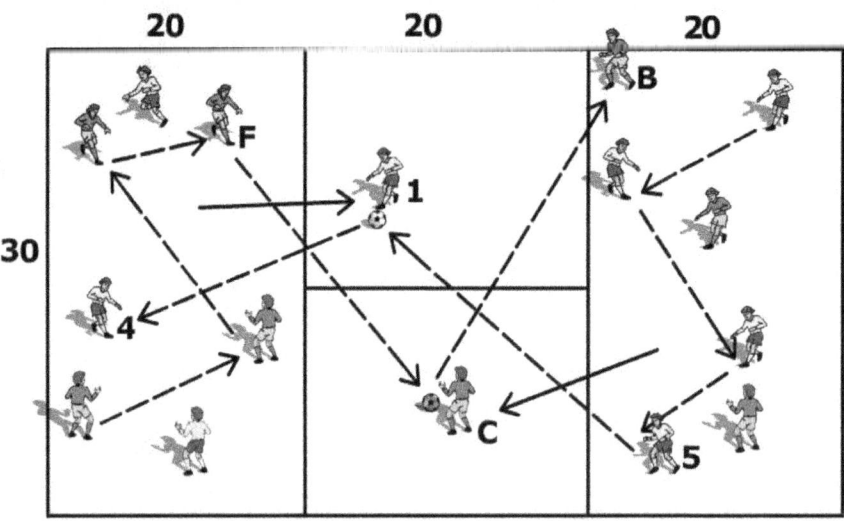

Here (1) drops off to receive the pass from (5) and (C) drops off to receive the pass from (F).

(C) is defending in Zone (3) but at the same time looking away to see his team in the other zone in possession and needing support. This helps the development of a mental transition from defending to attacking and vice versa.

(1) turns and passes to (4), (C) turns and passes to (B).

COACHING STRIKERS

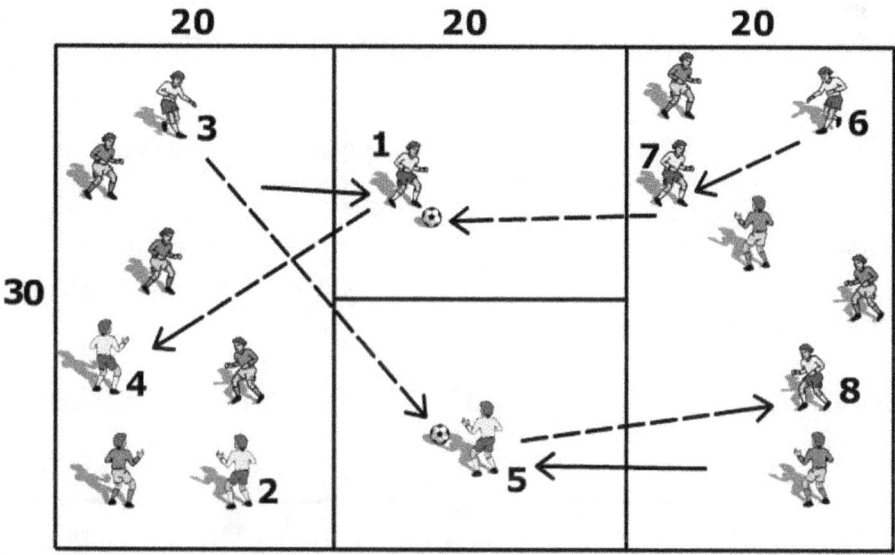

Both numbers teams may have possession of the ball in each side so now we have a numbers player from each zone dropping in to receive and transfer the ball.

DEFENDER CAN CLOSE THE ATTACKER DOWN ON THE FIRST TOUCH ONLY

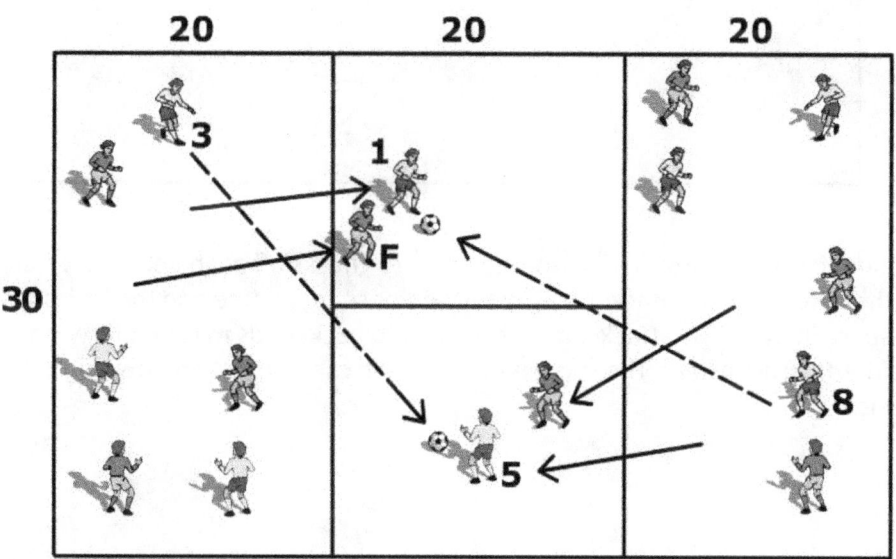

Development 1:
Now defenders can close down the attackers going short. Once the receiving player (1) who has checked to the middle receives the ball (on his first touch), that is the cue for the defender (F) to close him down and pressure.

This should still give the receiver (1) enough time to receive and turn and pass without losing the ball but we are building up the pressure on that player. It is almost a passive movement because the defender (F) has so much ground to make up to get close.

COACHING STRIKERS

Development Two:
The defender can now close the ball down as the passer moves, he does not need to wait for the first touch.

This changes the options considerably depending on how good the defender is. (1) and (5) both need to be imaginative now in their play if the defender is tight to them. Do they play 1 touch around the defender, allowing them to get tight and spin and pass? Do they keep possession then play back to a supporting player in their own zone? Do they try to turn and beat the defender 1 v 1? Do they drop off the defender's shoulder to face forward and receive facing forward? Many ideas to try.

RECEIVER MOVES OFF THE SHOULDER OF THE DEFENDER

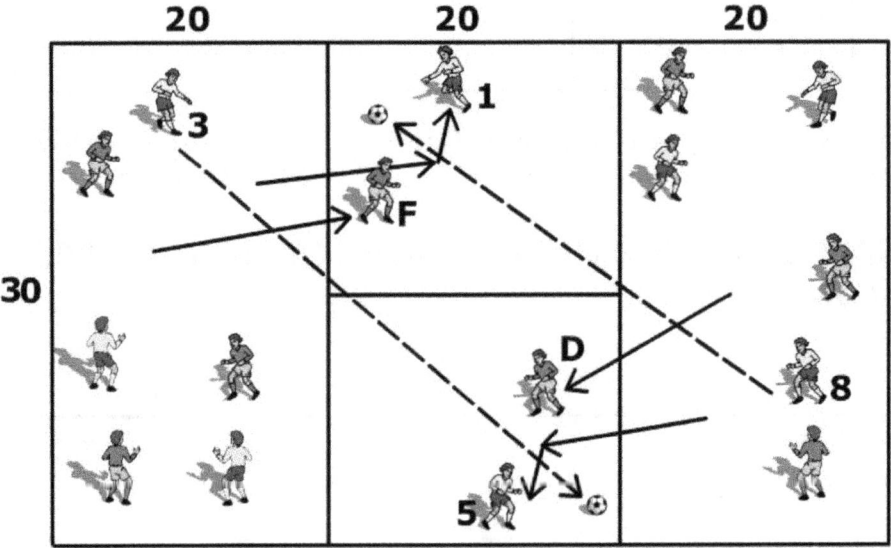

The defender closes the attacker down. The attacker checks off at an angle very quickly to deceive the defender. The attacker may get a yard or so to get free and the ball is played into the space in front. The attacker goes from facing backwards to facing forwards or at least side-on in an instant. The success of this move can depend on how bright the defender is.

RECEIVER MOVES OFF THE SHOULDER AND CHECKS BACK

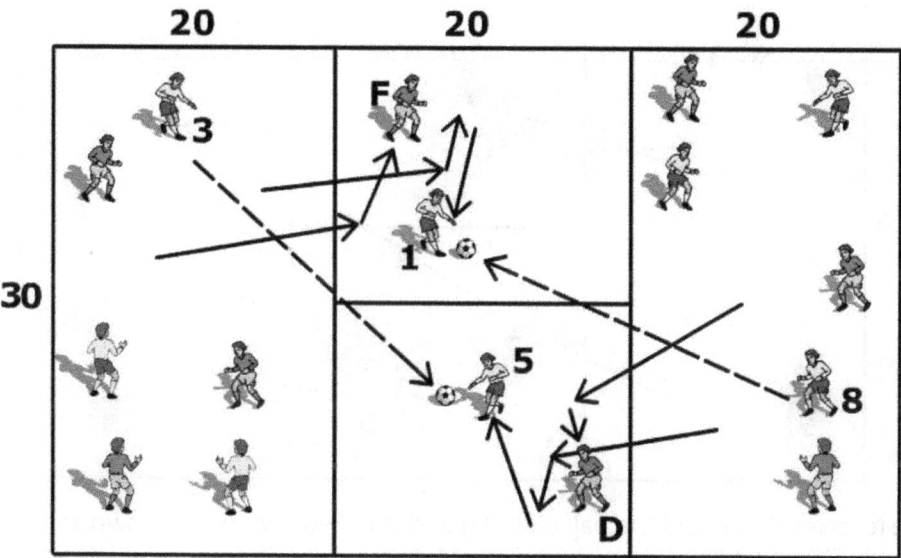

The defender sticks tight, so the attacker then checks back into the space he came from to receive the pass. Timing and angle of the pass and timing and angle of the run have to be totally in sync here.

DEFENDER CLOSES THE ATTACKER DOWN; ATTACKER CAN'T TURN

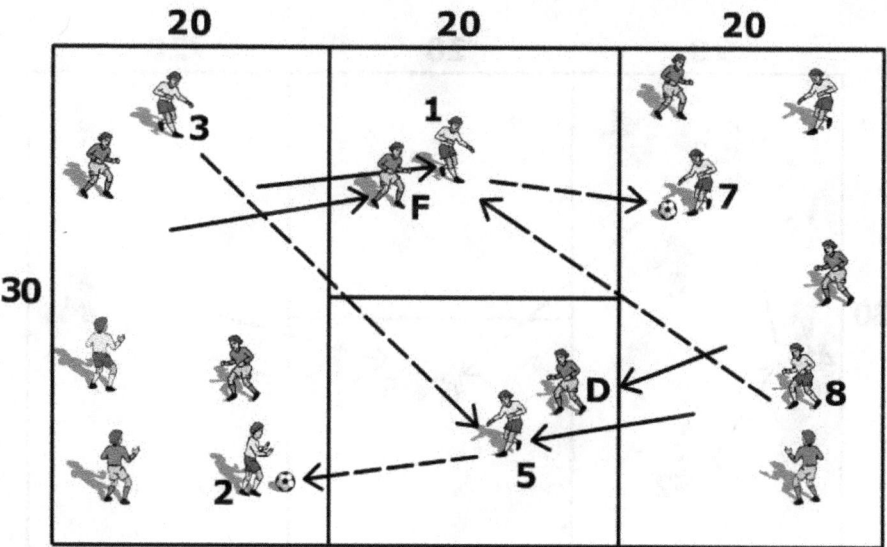

Here we show the receiver (1) still receiving the ball under pressure but he can't turn, so he lays the ball off into the same zone it came from to another player (7) in that zone.

COACHING STRIKERS

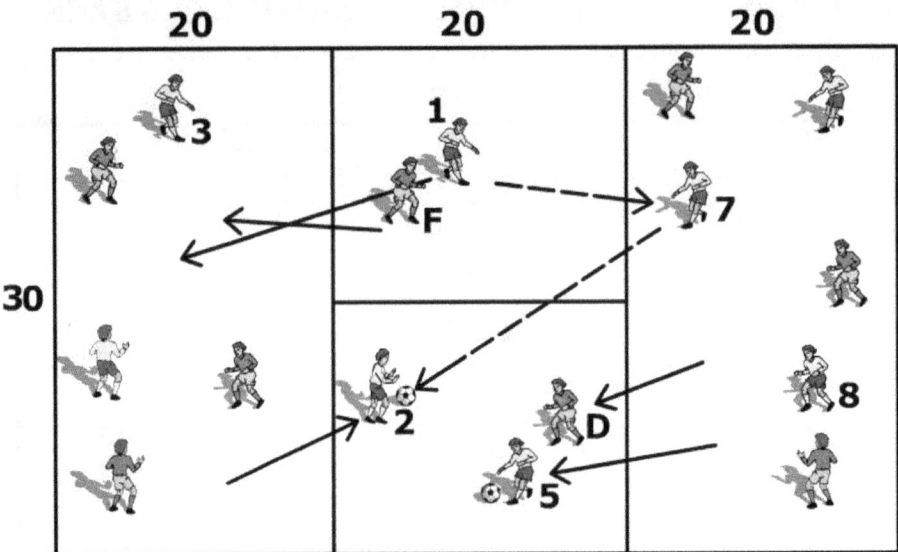

Here the receiver (1) has laid the ball off to (7) and checked back into his own zone, taking the defender (F) with him and another player (2) becomes the new receiver from a pass by (7) and gets it to feet in a free area to turn and pass. This can be like a striker dropping off between the defender and midfield of the opponents. You can also liken this situation to a midfield player dropping off the marker and receiving from the back four.

Rotate the defenders.

NOW ONE BALL ONLY

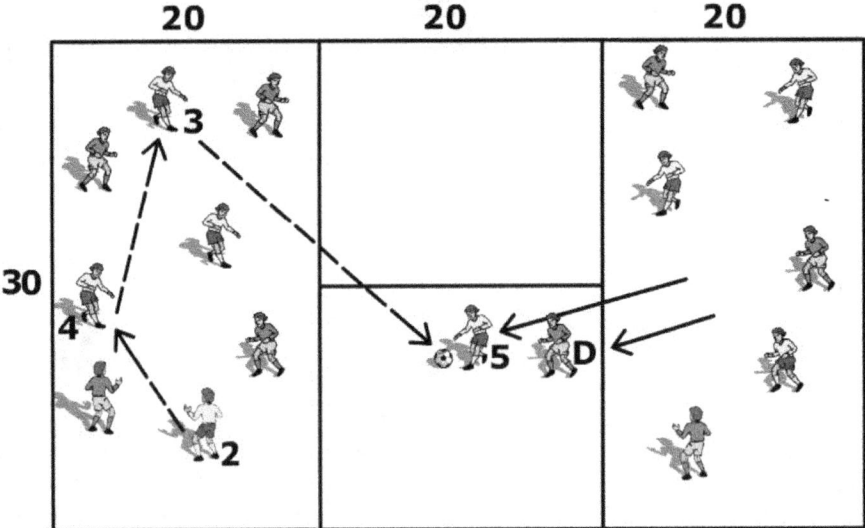

One ball game now. We are looking to play quickly, to transition quickly for both teams to work hard to win possession and change the point of attack as often as possible.

All players should be on their toes and active as we want all the players to be involved as much as possible.

COACHING STRIKERS

PLAYERS SWITCHING SIDES

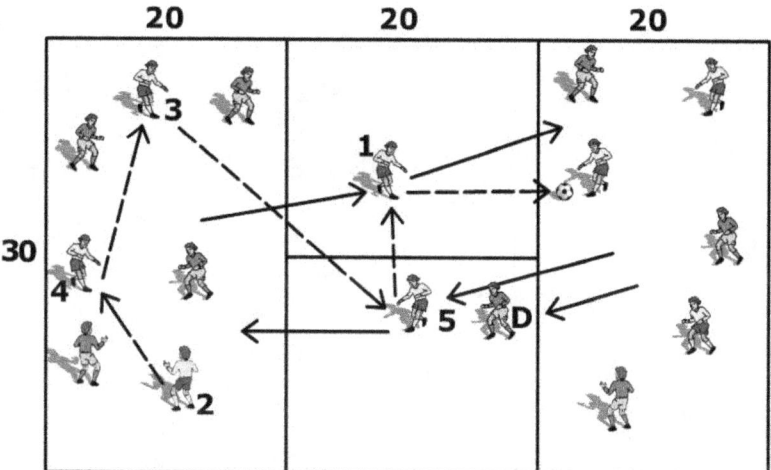

This really gets the brain cells working. As a player (5) drops into the middle zone to receive, another player (1) joins in to receive a lay off as shown. Now (1) passes FORWARD and follows the pass into the other end zone and (5) switches zones too in order to maintain the balance.

So now as the ball is being passed into (5) from (3), one of the numbers players must see this as a cue to attack forward to support (5). This keeps players thinking ahead of the ball and forces supporting runs to happen.

BYPASS THE MIDDLE AND GO FROM BACK TO FRONT

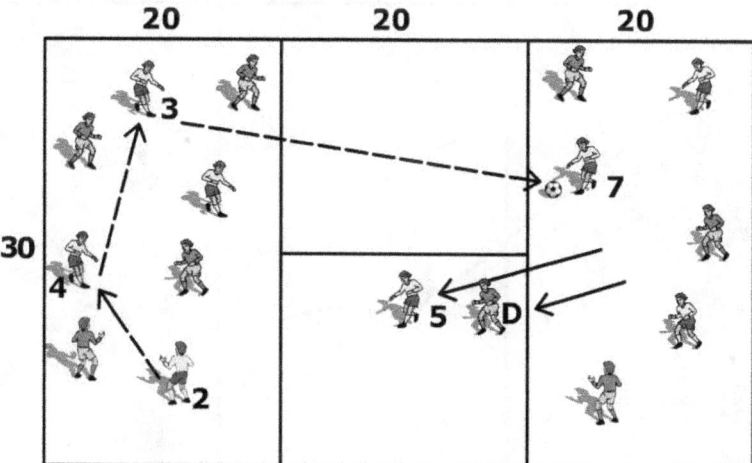

Another option for the passer (3) is to avoid the receiver (5) who is tightly marked and whose movement has changed the position of the defender (D). This has opened up a pass to a teammate in the other end zone.

Two players may go short at the same time. Don't worry about this as it may happen in a game anyway.

COACHING STRIKERS

PLAYING DIRECT: 4 V 4, 1 V 1 AND 3 V 3

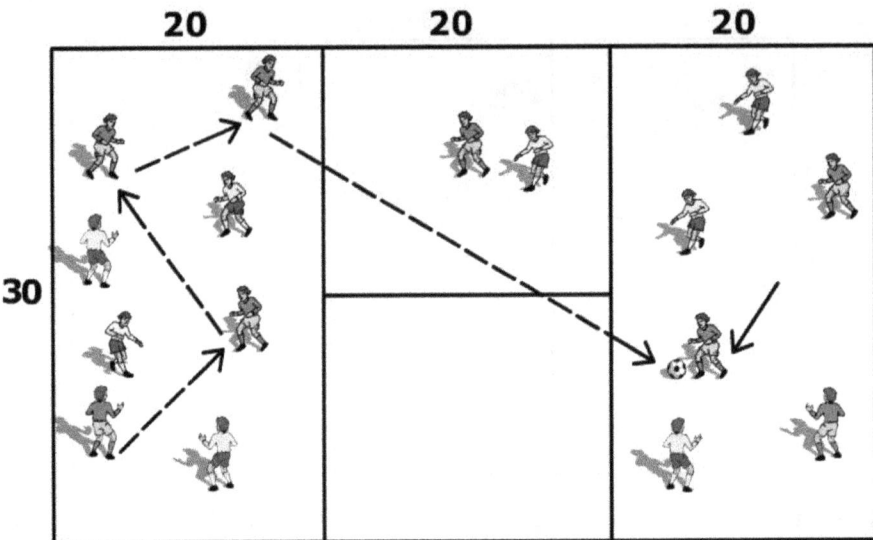

Progression: Have the players miss out the middle third players and pass from the back to the front. Players in the middle then support behind in a receiving capacity but now going the other way.

If the defender wins the ball in an outside third, he either passes to his own color in the middle who then pass to a teammate in the other outside third, or direct to the other end zone.

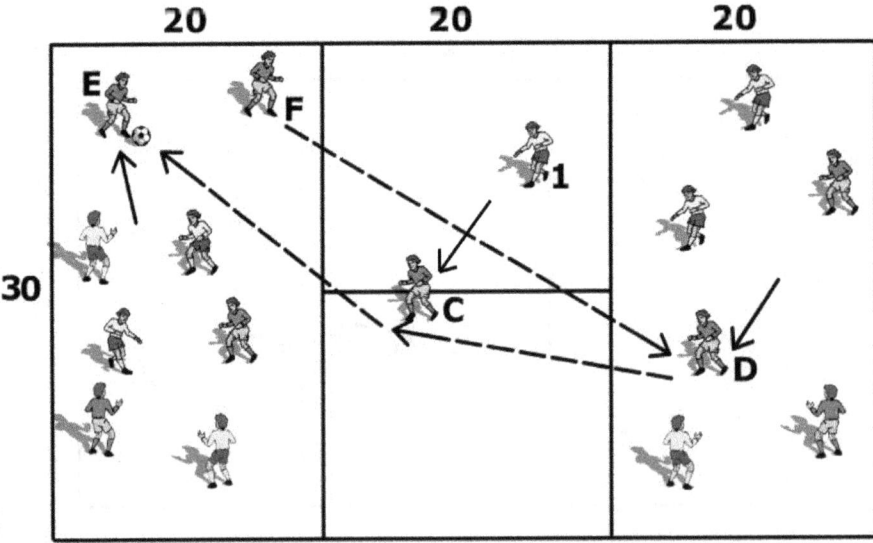

Progression: As the ball is played into (D), (C) in the middle moves away from (1) and finds space to receive and turn and pass to (E). Instant switching of the point of attack.

COACHING STRIKERS

NEUTRAL PLAYER ADDED: 3 V 3, 1 V 1 V 1 AND 3 V 3

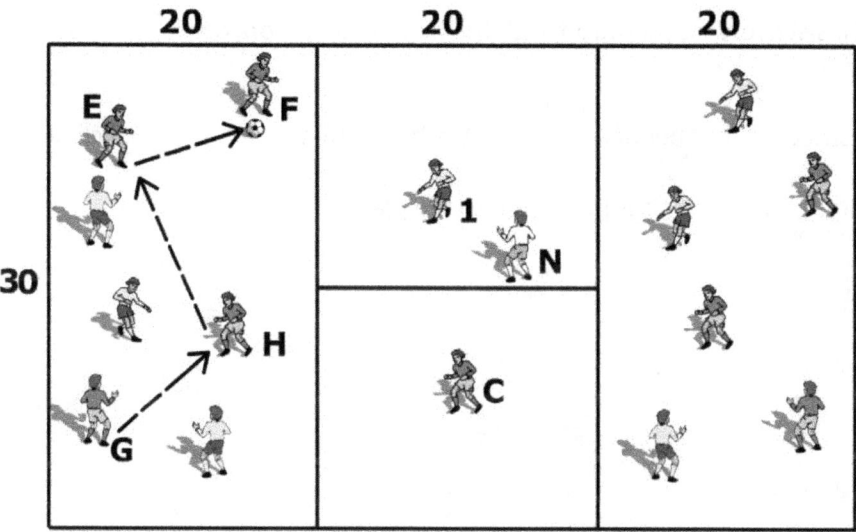

It is always a 2 v 1 in the middle now, with the neutral player always on the attacking team.

Again color coordination and recognition plays a role in the play. Players have to pass to a player of their same color or the neutral player in the middle and then these players actually pass to the players in the other side.

Here we now have competitive small sided games in three separate areas on the field.

3 V 3, 2 V 2, AND 3 V 3

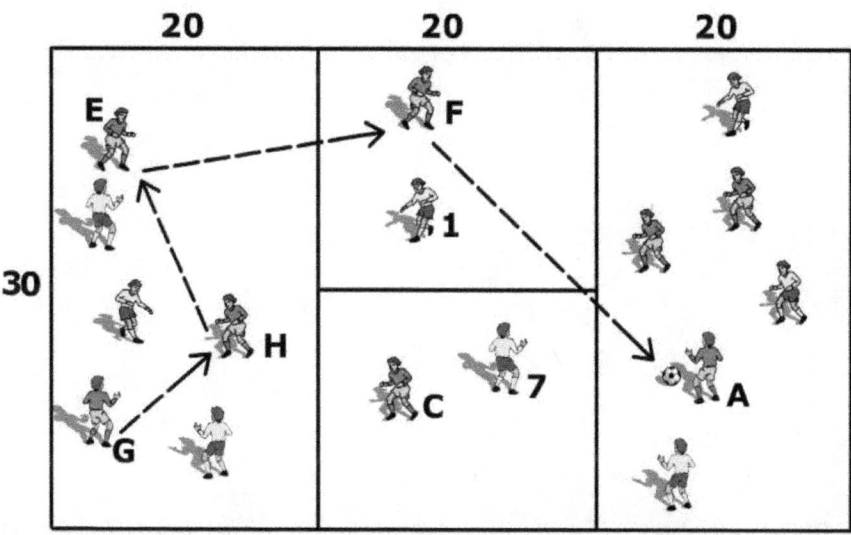

Now we play from the back thru the middle to the front and back again trying to maintain possession of the ball.

COACHING STRIKERS

You can try different ideas here, so many passes in each end zone before the ball goes to the middle one, for example.

You could insist every player must touch the ball to really work on the possession side of the game.

You can restrict the number of touches on the ball to up the pressure and challenge.

Keep changing the challenges presented to the players.

ABOUT WAYNE HARRISON

Wayne has spent years perfecting his Football Coaching and Training Methodology and is now Co-Owner of a developmental training company "Soccer Awareness Elite Academy" based in San Diego, California. Their aim is to teach the game to players in its "purest form", and avoid the pressure of wins and losses in the club scene. This ensures that players are taught in a way that prepares them for the game in a positive, relaxed and productive but also a very competitive training environment.

"A major aim for us is building the most confidence we can in every player we teach for them to play to the best of their abilities and without fear or negativity. We work on teaching the psychological side of the game primarily to develop Thinking Players."

Wayne has a wealth of knowledge at the highest levels of the game both as a professional player; having played for Blackpool and Sheffield Wednesday Football Clubs in England and Oulu Palloseura in the Finnish Premier league; and a professional coach, having been the Director of Coaching of Youth Development for Blackpool amongst other coaching positions. He has also represented Great Britain as a player in the World Student Games in Mexico.

A former Academy Director at Blackpool Football Club in the English Championship League, he is a "bestselling" author who currently has 12 Coaching books to his name as well as authoring many articles for "World Class Coaching" and "Soccer Journal" Magazines in the United States and "Insight" Magazine in England and he has many videos on soccer development.

He was also more recently the Director of Coaching for the Youth Academy of Al Ain Football Club in the United Arab Emirates, one of the most famous and prestigious professional football club in the Middle East and Asian Regions of the World and former Asian Cup Winners. During his 2 year spell, as their DOC in charge of Youth, Al Ain won 7 National Youth Championships and were the most successful professional academy in the country. They were also officially acclaimed as the most professionally developed academy by the renowned Marco Monte of Inter Milan, the Consultant for the Abu Dhabi Sports Council. Mr. Monte compared the academy Wayne developed as the closest to the best European academies he has experienced in his work. High praise indeed.

He holds the prestigious UEFA "A" License, and the NSCAA Premier Diploma, as well as an English Bachelors Degree in Applied Physiology and Sports Psychology. Having achieved the Premier Diploma he is now able to educate as a Staff Coach with the NSCAA.

He is also a successful football clinician for the education of coaches, presenting at coaching symposiums worldwide, including the NSCAA Convention, the World Class Coaching International Seminar, the Reedswain Soccer Coaches' Super Clinic and many State Symposiums throughout the United States.

This is his 13th Published book on coaching the beautiful game and it addresses an important part of player development, the tactical movement and the finishing techniques of strikers.

soccerawareness@outlook.com
www.soccerawareness.com

For inquiries regarding his Soccer Awareness Elite Academy:
wayne@soccerawarenesseliteacademy.com
www.soccerawarenesseliteacademy.com

SoccerSpecific.com

Your resource for...
  Sessions from soccer professionals around the world!

As well as...

FREE Soccer Drills, FREE Articles, News, Coaching Software, Fitness, Nutrition, Interviews, Sports Injury, Sports Psychology, Videos, AND MORE!

SoccerSpecific's exclusive Session Planner 2.0

See video demos at
www.SessionPlanner.com

The BEST soccer software available!

Create and print drills and sessions in minutes

Affordable, easy, and used by thousands of coaches and national soccer associations

www.ingramcontent.com/pod-product-compliance
Lightning Source LLC
Chambersburg PA
CBHW080534170426
43195CB00016B/2558